D0823459

STICK WITH IT

STICK WITH IT

A SCIENTIFICALLY PROVEN PROCESS FOR CHANGING YOUR LIFE—FOR GOOD

SEAN D. YOUNG

HARPER

NEW YORK · LONDON · TORONTO · SYDNEY

HARPER

FIRST HARPER PAPERBACKS EDITION PUBLISHED 2018.

Designed by William Ruoto

Library of Congress Cataloging-in-Publication Data has been applied for.

ISBN 978-0-06-269288-7 (pbk.)

18 19 20 21 22   LSC   10 9 8 7 6 5 4 3 2 1

For Melody Isabelle Shira

To forever remember your Dadda-O

CONTENTS

CONTENTS

stead . . . Lasting change starts with action . . . Use these mental shortcuts to reset your brain

INTRODUCTION

People have trouble making lasting changes. They quit nutrition plans, don't adhere to medication regimens, and can't keep New Year's resolutions to lose weight or stop procrastinating.

The advice offered up by recent bestsellers?

Charles Duhigg's *The Power of Habit* and Gretchen Rubin's *Better Than Before* insist that the secret to success in both your personal and business lives is to develop good habits. Yet they base this on just one study suggesting that habits account for 40 percent of behaviors in life and work. So what are we supposed to do about the other 60 percent of our behaviors?

Conventional wisdom also fails to solve the problem. It tells you the answer is to change who you are. If you want to stick with your fitness goals, learn to love exercising like Richard Simmons. To be a successful entrepreneur, become a creative genius like Steve Jobs. If you want to be a good salesperson, morph into a social butterfly like Mary Kay Ash. And the list goes on of people we're told to become like.

Changing your character is easier said than done: every individual has a core personality that doesn't change much throughout life. Fortunately, you don't need to change who you are as a *person* to make change last. You just need to understand the science behind lasting change and how to create a *process* that fits who you are. That's what this book delivers.

INTRODUCTION

Over the past fifteen years, working with some of the top minds in science, I have identified the seven psychological forces that undergird lasting behavior change in any context.

I'm a medical school professor at UCLA, and the executive director of the UCLA Center for Digital Behavior and the University of California Institute for Prediction Technology (UCIPT). My research has received more than ten million dollars of funding from organizations such as the National Institutes of Health (NIH), corporations like Facebook and Intel, as well as leading hospitals and foundations. Participants in our research studies have made lasting changes in how they eat, sleep, exercise, and manage medication and chronic pain. As a result of our behavior-change work, participants have been able to avoid contracting diseases like HIV, or have sought out medical treatment to save their lives. I've developed interventions to help thousands of people change their health behaviors. I've also helped dozens of startups and companies change behaviors related to their businesses.

My approach is similar to what social psychologist Robert Cialdini did in *Influence: Science and Practice,* one of the most successful business books of all time. Cialdini reviewed three decades of research, integrated it with his own fieldwork, and distilled it into a set of universal principles. Like Cialdini's principles, my forces are additive: using one may be effective, but using two, three, or more will be even more effective.

By using the methods I describe in this book, I have repeatedly achieved almost a 200 percent increase in lasting change for both individuals and groups. This means that people who used these methods were nearly three times as likely to change their behavior as people who did not.

You can harness the forces I present here in your personal life or your business. They transformed the life of Josh Nava, who hated never being able to follow through on projects, whether a daily assignment

INTRODUCTION

for school or a book he wanted to complete for pleasure, and who is now a successful business owner who sticks with his work and hobbies. They transformed the life of Rishi Desai, so anxious and shy that he couldn't talk to a stranger, now a successful doctor and creator of the world-renowned Khan Academy medical school curriculum. And they were used by Joseph Coulombe to help Trader Joe's go down in history as a company that effectively made lasting changes in consumer grocery buying behavior.

Stick with It offers scientifically proven ideas that will help you achieve your goals—no matter how big or how small—by applying them to your life and work as they fit your needs.

STICK WITH IT

CHAPTER 1

THE SCIENCE OF LASTING CHANGE

Hellhole Bend is a deep gorge in the Grand Canyon, smack in the middle of Navajo country. Despite its name, it's ravishingly beautiful, with majestic pink, brown, white, and gold-colored rock formations rising above the Little Colorado River. But Nik Wallenda isn't enjoying the view. He's holding his breath as he balances on top of a wire as wide as one of his toes. The wire is held taut between two rocky promontories and is the only thing between Nik and the hard ground 1,500 feet below. The wind is gusting at thirty miles an hour. That's enough to snap tree limbs and cause telephone lines to whistle. It's certainly enough to make Nik's legs shake.

Nik is attempting to walk more than a quarter of a mile across the Grand Canyon under these less than ideal conditions. He concentrates on breathing. In. Out. In. Out. Nik refused to wear a safety harness, or to spread a safety net below him. His only prop is a thirty-foot-long, forty-three-pound balancing pole that he holds at a precise 90-degree angle to his body.

Nik knows that the stakes are as high as they can get. Numerous family members have died or been paralyzed attempting stunts similar to this. Born into a family of circus performers brought to the United States from Germany in 1936 by the Ringling Bros. and Barnum & Bailey Circus, Nik can look back on generations of acclaimed tightrope walkers, including his father and grandfather.[1] In 1978, Nik's great-grandfather Karl Wallenda, arguably the most talented high-wire artist in the family, fell and died during a tightrope performance much like Nik's current one.

With extraordinary concentration, Nik picks up his right foot and edges it forward until it is positioned directly in front of his left foot. Step thirteen. Done. One thousand three hundred eighty-four more to go. He tries to block the background noise, and to ignore the reminders from the loudspeaker below that 13 million viewers are tuned into the Discovery Channel from around the globe to view this stunt live. They can hear him praying out loud through the headset and microphone he's wearing. "Dear Jesus," Nik whispers.

He knows a certain number of observers—it's inevitable—are hoping he'll fail. For the drama. For the spectacle. *I was there when* . . . Nik pushes that thought from his head. He tries not to remember that his wife and his three kids, Yanni, Amadaos, and Evita, are watching below. He does remember being twelve years old and emphatically telling a reporter that he would not follow in the footsteps of his family. Never, ever would he become a high-wire artist. "It's just not worth it," he'd said.[2]

What made Nik change his mind? And, more incredibly, how had he managed to stick with his training over the years despite daily reminders that his chosen vocation could kill him at any moment? Although Nik might not have the answer to that question, scientists do. And although Nik's story might not seem to have much relevance for you personally, stay tuned. You'll soon see that you have more in common with him than you thought.

According to current science, Nik Wallenda's path through life was actually quite *predictable*. Although not aware of it, Nik had intuitively done everything right to "stick with it" and succeed with a plan of action. (By the way, Nik's walk across the Grand Canyon was successful. Next on his list: walking across the twelve-hundred-foot wide Tallulah Gorge, Georgia, while making time for three headstands on the wire.)

Recent research shows that seven psychological forces support the ability of people to stick with their plans—in both life and work. The more of these forces people incorporate in their behaviors, the more likely they are to stick with something until they reach a goal. Nik harnessed all seven during his training.

This new science is also capable of helping millions around the world. Forty percent of dieters quit within one week[3] and more than 50 percent end up weighing more than they did before they started their diets.[4] Businesses shut down because they can't get customers to keep buying their products or services. Health departments and health insurance companies fail because they can't get people to take their meds or change their lifestyles or otherwise competently manage their health. These failures cost society hundreds of billions of dollars a year.[5][6]

On the surface, these may seem like completely different problems with completely different causes. After all, don't people have very different motivations for failing to achieve personal goals like daily exercise than for ceasing to buy a particular brand of cereal or to stop using a certain mobile app? Yes . . . but no. Personal resolutions might fail and product sales may flounder for different reasons, but the problem at their core is the same: *People have stopped doing something*. If we know the psychology behind how to get people to stick with things, we can address all of these challenges.

So how do you get people to keep doing things?

Conventional wisdom comes down to: change your personality. Become like those people with extraordinary willpower, develop your presence, or fire yourself up to want something so passionately that you will overcome all difficulties in your path. This kind of advice attempts to change the *person*, not their *process*. But different people are, well, different. Every person has a core personality.* This personality doesn't change much throughout life.

Fortunately, you don't need to change who you are to make lasting changes. You just need to understand the science behind change and create a process that fits who you are. That's what this book delivers: the seven forces behind lasting change, and how to use my framework—called SCIENCE, which stands for Stepladders, Community, Important, Easy, Neurohacks, Captivating, Engrained—to adapt them to meet your particular needs.

Nik Wallenda harnessed all seven of these forces to keep himself disciplined and on track with his training year after year so he could perform death-defying tightrope acts. But most people have more modest goals. While Nik's story is thrilling, most people have more mundane things they're trying to stick with. Most of us aren't trying to stay motivated to walk across skyscrapers like a superhero. For most of us, just remembering to floss our teeth or rubber-tip our gums every day next week is a big feat. So let's step back and recalibrate from Nik's story to a more typical story, like that of suburban dad Josh Nava.

---

* I use the word *personality* because it's easy to understand, but it's not the correct term, scientifically. The more precise idea is that people have a specific psychology. The way they act is affected by their culture, race, religion, genetics, and even the current moment. Collectively these things make people who they are, and it's really hard to change this collective "personality."

Josh Nava hated the fact that he never followed through. As a student he couldn't get himself to do his homework even when he liked the topic. In later years, he collected shelves full of books but would drop one book midway to start reading a new one. Married with two children, he now found it harder than ever to stick with things. He had gone through a string of jobs and struggled to find balance between his wife, kids, and work. Having attention deficit hyperactivity disorder (ADHD) didn't help. He was easily distracted, and even small tasks like sending an email would take more than an hour. Josh would set his mind to do something—and inevitably fail to follow through. He asked himself, "How do I get myself to keep doing things I want to do, when I keep getting in my own way?"[7] Was there anything that could help him change?

How about a wooden spoon?

Josh had an idea. What if he started simply, focusing on something small? What if he tried doing this small thing every day, no matter what else was going on in his life? Josh had always enjoyed crafting things like chairs and cutlery, so in 2014 he created an Instagram account called @365spoons (Instagram is an online platform where people share photos and videos with friends). His plan: to craft a different wooden spoon every day and share it online with whoever wanted to "follow" him. His goal was to do it for a full year—365 days—and to stick to it, even if he only ended up with a handful of followers. He knew from bitter experience that he'd tried things before and would quit as soon as the novelty wore off. But this time he planned to do it differently.

Each day, Josh crafted a wooden spoon from recycled or unwanted materials and posted the image with a caption to Instagram. He also shared that with this project he was trying to solve the problem of always being "a quitter." Within weeks, Josh gained hundreds of followers wanting to hear about his struggle to stick with a hobby, to see images of the beautiful spoons he had created, and to encourage him to keep going.

All that was good for Josh, but as he had anticipated, after a month the excitement of the project wore off. It became a chore. The last thing he wanted to do after a long day at work and spending time with his family was to complete a new spoon design. Josh was in a familiar head space—and ready to quit. But his Instagram followers wouldn't let him. After he expressed his fatigue and discouragement, he was barraged with encouragement.

"I would not be able to maintain this project for a month and I am single with no kids. I have HUGE respect for your commitment. You are an inspiration!" wrote one fan. "You're speaking my language brother! Your persistence in this knowing we have similar struggles is so impressive. So proud of you!" wrote another. And another commented, "You have inspired me! One collage a week for this year I'm going to do!"

Their words of encouragement kept Josh going. He not only completed his goal of creating a new spoon every day for the year, but also accumulated an active Instagram following, too. Josh said he had come to an important realization for the first time in his life. "I learned that I was capable. It had just been buried. Like putting a stake in the ground, I realized I could follow through. . . . It wasn't about creating spoons. It was about confronting myself on an important issue. . . . To look back and see that pile of spoons growing was meaningful." Along the way, Josh tapped five of the seven forces of lasting change. Not incidentally, he now has a successful custom woodworking business called Suburban Pallet, where he sells spoons and other crafts to people who follow him or have heard his story.

You can harness these same forces to impact the behavior of others, as Tom Sosnoff did. In 2011, after a successful career, first as a market maker on the floor of the Chicago Stock Exchange and then as an entrepreneur, Tom used some of the techniques outlined in this book to create a new approach to delivering financial education online. Today tastytrade has nearly twenty thousand viewers watching at any point in time, with almost one hundred thousand total daily viewers.[8] The average user watches the show for two and a half hours a day. Tom has disrupted traditional financial media outlets—and achieved all of this by creating a process based on the science of how to get people to stick with things.

My path to study lasting change started from a personal need. While I was completing my doctoral degree at Stanford, my cousin came to visit. We had been playing in a band together, and he drove up from Los Angeles with our bandmates so we could play a show on campus. But the next day, at the point when our bandmates were ready to drive back home, my cousin was in too much pain to go with them. He had long suffered from a chronic intestinal malady called Crohn's disease, and he thought it was merely acting up again. But he was in so much pain we decided to go to the emergency room. It turned out that his intestines had burst. Minutes away from dying, he was rushed into emergency surgery. Happily, the surgery saved him. After taking a couple of weeks to recover, he was released, prescribed daily medication and a new exercise and eating regimen, and returned home.

Try to put yourself in my cousin's situation (as I did). You've narrowly escaped death. You've been instructed to change your lifestyle if you want to remain healthy in the future. How likely would you be to do that? If you're like my cousin—indeed, if you're like most people—you'd confidently respond that you would change for good. You'd start eating differently, exercising differently, and taking your prescribed daily medication. Well, my cousin is a really smart man. He's health conscious and he's motivated, so I of course thought that he would change his lifestyle after this dramatic incident. But he didn't. And I now realize that most of us wouldn't, either.[9] He kept on eating what he always ate, exercised only sporadically, and didn't take medication as advised.

Why on earth not? I was scared for him. I was also confused—and frustrated. I had been by his side in the hospital when he almost died. What was I missing? To try to understand I turned to people who were experts in education, medicine, and business. And I kept getting the same response. "Your cousin's case is the same as all the other patients who don't follow what they should be doing for their health. He needs to be better educated on why he should be taking his medication." And they would hand over brochures, recommend websites, and point me to associations that provided material for people like my cousin. In other words, education and good marketing should get people to do what's good for them.

This explanation didn't satisfy me. I could see that it didn't explain my cousin's behavior. And as I did more research, I realized it didn't explain the behavior of the rest of the world. Moreover, other aspects of my life started converging on this issue.

We wanted our band to succeed—but needed fans to keep coming back to our shows and buying our albums for that to happen. How could we change people's behavior to get them to become regular "consumers" of our music?

I wanted to make new friends at Stanford, but also to maintain strong relationships with my old friends from Southern California. I was finding it difficult to juggle both of these things. How could I do it?

I saw this through my academic work. Mobile apps for smartphones were in their infancy. Some of the kids around me were becoming millionaires; others were desperate to get users to download and use the apps they'd developed. Entrepreneurs were reaching out to the psychology department at Stanford for help answering these questions. I volunteered to coteach a class with my friend Jonah at the Graduate School of Business, to try to provide some solutions to the challenges businesspeople were facing. What I found was that contemporary psychology theories could explain how to change people's behavior—but just once. The studies weren't designed to answer questions about how to get people to make lasting changes in their behavior—to keep doing things.

Everyone, it seemed, had problems with making lasting change in their lives. More than 50 percent of people don't take their medication as prescribed.[10] People know that exercise is good for them, but most don't exercise consistently. Companies spend a lot of money on advertising and marketing, but this doesn't lead to loyal customers. I thought: there has to be a better way.

Fast-forward fifteen years. After completing my master's in health services research/health economics and PhD in psychology, I devoted much of my research energy and resources to discovering some answers. I worked as a psychologist at NASA's Ames Research Center, helped found and advise various start-ups, and am now the executive director of the University of California Institute for Prediction Technology and the UCLA Center for Digital Behavior, and a UCLA medical school professor. For more than a decade, I've worked with some of the brightest minds in the fields of psychology, technology, health/medicine, and business to develop interventions for behavior change. We've applied this work to general health and well-being, sexual health, substance abuse, and mental health behaviors. We've successfully changed people's behavior in the United States and internationally. We've gotten funding from government agencies (national institutes of mental health, drug abuse, human genome research, alcohol abuse and alcoholism, and allergy and infectious diseases); the University of California president Janet Napolitano and others; health care organizations (UCLA Health System); and businesses (Facebook and Intel). We've helped build technologies incorporating the science we learned. And we've come up with some answers on how to change behavior—and make the changes last.

But despite our successes, I always struggled when students, clients, and health professionals asked me what they could read to learn about the science of lasting change. Important research studies are too dense and theoretical for casual readers. There are clinical books on behavior change, but most people can't digest those—it takes a doctor to know how to act on their advice. Even Robert Cialdini's *Influence*, a classic book on changing other people's behavior, tells us little about how to change our own. It's also more than thirty years old, and a lot of new research and discoveries have been made since its publication. Many books have been written by journalists or businesspeople who are great storytellers, but the authors don't have direct scientific experience with what actually gets people to change. Charles Duhigg's *The Power of Habit* and Gretchen Rubin's *Better Than Before* both share interesting stories about habits—the unconscious things we do repeatedly, like biting our nails or automatically locking the door when we get out of a car. But they write that unconscious habits are only 40 percent of human behavior. These books don't tell us about the other 60 percent. And very few of the many books on motivation are based on proven science.

To truly change behavior, people need to understand why they do things. They need to know the science behind the full 100 percent of human behavior. To that end, my book brings together both classic and cutting-edge research to demonstrate exactly how change happens in all of human behavior.

But more than just informing you how change occurs, this book also provides a blueprint for achieving change in your life. It teaches you how to use the seven SCIENCE forces behind lasting change to alter the three types of behaviors—Automatic, Burning, and Common (or what I call the A, B, and C's of behavior). Bringing these pieces together, the book offers a simple two-step model for creating lasting change: First, identify whether the behavior you're trying to change is an A, B, or C behavior. Second, use the forces needed to change that type of behavior. The end result is a road map for change that's tailored to the problem behaviors you want to change.

Lately, people have been frustrated hearing that they've gotten incorrect information about news and science. Incorrect information has led to failures in politics, personal health, and business. We need news from reputable journalists, and science from people who understand and can correctly articulate research. As a scientist, I thought I needed to write this book to teach people what does and doesn't work in changing behavior. Most of the research I present in this book was either conducted by my mentors and colleagues, or by other researchers within one degree of separation from us, or personally, in my own research. By using the methods I describe in this book, I have repeatedly achieved almost a 200 percent increase in lasting change for individuals and groups.[11] By this I mean, when compared to a "control" group, people in my research studies who used these methods were almost three times as likely to change their behavior.

I deliberately use the word *forces* instead of *principles* because psychological forces are constantly pushing and pulling people to make different choices. These forces determine what people do and how they feel. They create emotional, chemical, and neurological changes. One set of forces might push you to sit on the couch, pour a glass of wine, and turn on the television. Another set of forces pushes you to put on a pair of running shoes and get some exercise. Which action will you take? Whichever one is pushed harder by these forces. But you can get these forces to work *for* you.

You can think of these psychological forces as akin to the physical forces that affect inanimate objects. To fly a plane safely, engineers, pilots, and flight crews need to be aware of all the forces—such as wind and gravity—that push the plane down, lift it up, and shift it from side to side. The more that they can harness these forces to work in their favor, the more likely it is the plane will fly the way they want.

Getting people to keep doing things in the face of opposing

forces is just as complicated. Yet, when it comes to behavior change, most people seek simple solutions. They think it's a matter of will-power, or motivation. But people are more complicated, so we need a more nuanced model for how to change behavior. The purpose of this book is to give you the science and tools to propel you to do what you want with your life and work. You can use these forces to get yourself to stick with things you want to do, and you can use them to help others stick with things, too.†

Some of the forces I present may, at first glance, seem like common sense. They may already feel familiar. But I will show that what you know about these forces is either inaccurate or incomplete.

I describe the seven forces of lasting change, one in each chapter, using a framework I call SCIENCE. I call this SCIENCE, not because you need to be a scientist or doctor to understand and apply it, but so that you'll remember that these forces are based on thousands of validated, peer-reviewed, scientific studies.

1. STEPLADDERS

Science shows that people have a better chance of success by focusing on small steps. Yet even when they know this, people repeatedly fail to make changes last. That's because they don't understand just how small those steps need to be and don't have a model to guide them. As Chapter 2 will explain, small means tiny.

2. COMMUNITY

We like to think that we're unique, that we don't follow the crowd. Chapter 3 will give you a new understanding of the power of com-

---

† My research is focused on changing others in order to do social good, like helping to prevent and address public health issues, educate people, and reduce poverty. The science I present is a powerful tool that can be used to change others, so please use it only for social good.

munity, and how to harness it to achieve lasting change in yourself and others.

3. IMPORTANT

If you want people to stick to a fitness routine or continue to buy your product, that action or behavior has to be *important* to them. Everyone knows this, right? Just as Chapter 2 redefines "small," Chapter 4 will teach you ways to redefine important.

4. EASY

People often think they understand *easy*, but they actually don't. This chapter will explain how to make things *really* easy and therefore more likely to stick.

5. NEUROHACKS

Have you heard the expression "If there's a will there's a way"? Or "Change your thoughts and your actions will follow"? That the mind controls behavior is the basis for many top-selling self-help and popular-psychology books. They teach that people can change their behavior by imagining and willing themselves to change. But this is wrong. Most smokers can't quit just by imagining themselves quitting. People don't stick to their New Year's resolutions by telling themselves that this year will be different than other years. Managers can't get their salespeople to close a deal just by telling them to visualize closing it.

Social psychologists know now that the truth lies in the opposite direction. People need to change their *actions* and their minds will follow. What you're doing is "tricking" the brain into realizing that change is possible. In this chapter, I'll teach you about neurohacks—a set of mental shortcuts to reset your brain so you can make positive lasting changes.

6. CAPTIVATING

How do you *make* something so captivating that people will keep doing it? One popular approach is to "gamify" it. The notion is that giving people rewards like points, badges, and money will make certain activities—or products—captivating, and get people to keep doing or using them. But gamification doesn't always work. When it does, it's because it makes use of psychological science. This chapter will show you how to make behaviors captivating enough to convince yourself—and others—to keep doing them.

7. ENGRAINED

A lot of successful people will tell you their success is not due to intelligence or talent, but because they know how to use their time efficiently. Barack Obama was known for routinizing food and dress so that he could save his time and energy for making important decisions about the country. Mark Zuckerberg said he owns about twenty versions of the same gray shirt to avoid having to decide what to wear every day. Ernest Hemingway was known for having a strict routine of writing only in the morning.[12] He'd use the rest of the day to think about and build excitement for the writing he would do the following morning. These individuals created an efficient process to keep them doing what they needed to do. They understood the power of the human brain and applied that science to their lives.

The human brain yearns to be efficient. It is designed so that people use the smallest amount of effort or thought to do things.

If you see, hear, or smell something repeatedly (even if you aren't aware of it), your brain stores this information so you can recognize it quickly and retrieve it again without having to think.[13][14] If you *do* something repeatedly, like taking the same route to work, your brain stores this information so you can go to work each day without having to remember how to get there. It does the same thing with people. If you interact with the same people repeatedly, your brain stores this information so that you'll automatically feel more comfortable with them.

This process of engraining patterns into the brain explains a large amount of human psychology. It explains why people prefer certain products over others; why they discriminate against people of other races, religions, or with other political views; and why people develop habits. This chapter will teach you how making something routine—so that it becomes engrained in your brain—will make it easier for you to keep doing it.

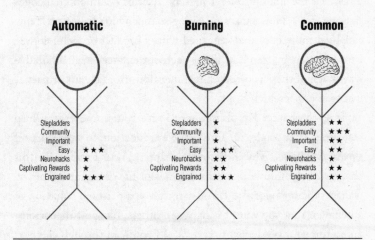

Figure 1. The SCIENCE Model of Lasting Change. This model will help you get yourself and others to stick with changes in life and work.

Although my research has primarily focused on how to change *other* people's behaviors in areas like health care, business, and entrepreneurship, it is based on social psychology—or why people act the way they do—and you can therefore apply this science to also change your *own* behaviors, like getting yourself to exercise more or to learn a new instrument. In fact, the seven forces for lasting change explained in this book will give you the ingredients you need for change in *any* context. To make it easier for you to understand the wide-reaching power of the seven forces, I've done three things. I begin each chapter with a story about lasting change on a personal scale. I use the bulk of the chapter to explain one of the seven forces. I end each chapter with an example of a business use of the force we discuss.

I've also provided specific recommendations for how people can apply the seven forces to address different problems within their lives and work. This book is therefore a mixture of science, business, and broad self-help information on how to apply the seven forces. In the final chapter I present a set of common challenges ranging from "How can I stop eating so much junk food?" to "How can I get more customers engaged with a product or technology?" I explain step-by-step how to use each of the forces in a cumulative way. Each of these is based on real questions from clients or participants in our research.

In each chapter I'm also going to give you an exercise to help you apply what you learn. This is the introduction, so we'll start off slowly (you'll see why in the next chapter). Your exercise for this chapter is to think about a behavior in your life or business that you want to change—for good. You can choose a personal behavior, or a behavior that you want to change in others, like getting customers to use your products or services. As you read through the next chapter, keep that behavior in mind and think of how you can apply what you learn to change it.

EXERCISE

1. Scan your life (or business) and ask yourself: Where would a lasting change benefit me most?
2. Choose a behavior that you want to change permanently—it can be a personal behavior, or a behavior in others.
3. Write it down on a piece of paper, and keep it by you as you read through this book.

NORTHWEST
HEALTHCARE PROPERTIES

- exercise/strengthen
- self care
- (+) thinking

CANADA'S HEALTHCARE LANDLORD
www.nwhp.ca

CHAPTER 2

STEPLADDERS

Brad Delson grew up just outside Los Angeles. Like many of his friends in suburban Agoura Hills, his dream from an early age was to be a rock star. He started playing trumpet while in primary school, but soon decided it wasn't "rock and roll" enough. In junior high, Brad switched to the guitar—an instrument with more grit. In high school, Brad got a band together with a seventh-grade friend, a vocalist/rapper named Mike; and Rob, a buddy who played drums.

Brad left Agoura Hills to go to the University of California, Los Angeles, but that didn't stop him from continuing to play music with Mike and Rob. He brought his college roommate Dave, a bass player, into the group and together they formed the band Xero. As a local band, they were considered pretty good. But they hadn't broken out by the time Brad graduated. Having attained summa cum laude status from one of the top universities in the world, law school was a safe career bet.[1] But Brad's heart was in his music.

He studied everything he could about "making it." Almost every successful musician said the same thing: dream your vision. Anyone could succeed if they stayed focused on their dreams.

Brad heard this story again and again. Not just from musicians, but from comedians, writers, and politicians. He heard it from professional athletes in commercials for athletic shoes. He saw quotes about it on billboards of students who got into their dream schools. And it was all over television—from people who had made heaps of money by following their dreams to be megarich. All said to focus on the endgame—keep your mind on your dream. But Brad had a feeling that the road map to success being pitched was wrong.

He reflected on his own life. He'd succeeded at school. But he thought about that differently than he thought about music. Whereas he had big—and rather vague—dreams for his music, in school he had methodically focused on short-term accomplishments. The full ten weeks of the semester was too long and the end of it too far away to worry about his final grades. There were too many day-to-day hurdles to pass. In his political science courses, for example, he had to complete three analytical papers and take a final exam. Although his ultimate goal for his class on the "Politics of the Cold War to the Present" was to get an A, he didn't focus on that. He focused on each small step forward. First, get the textbook. Next, read ten pages before band practice. Then, go over his notes from class before writing an outline for his essay on the Gulf of Tonkin Resolution. And that's what he did. Even though a long and difficult final exam awaited at the end of the course, he focused on the unglamorous little steps. That approach got him through UCLA at the top of his class. And that approach got him into a leading law school.

The only problem was, he didn't want to go to law school. He wanted—still—to be a rock star. That goal hadn't changed since fourth grade. But could he succeed at it?

I'll return to Brad later. First, let me tell you about my friend Olivier.

THE RIGHT FIRST STEP

In the summer of 2012, I visited Olivier in France, where his family has a beautiful chalet in the Alps. Olivier is an outdoor guy. I thought I was, too, but quickly found out we had different definitions of what that entailed. Our first-day hike was an all-day trek up the mountains. We picked ten different types of mushrooms and a few types of berries. As we ate them over a fancy, home-cooked French dinner that included an assortment of cheeses from around the world, he told me the next day's hike would be even better. It would be a two-day hike to an even prettier spot. I was game. He asked me if I'd ever been climbing. I told him I'm slightly afraid of heights but I'd gone to the rock wall at the gym once or twice and gotten to the top without anyone laughing too hard at me. He said I'd be fine.

Olivier, his seventy-two-year-old father, and I started off the next morning. It was a glorious day accompanied by some of the most beautiful scenery I'd ever encountered—filled with multi-colored rocks, snowcapped mountains, and glimpses of wildlife. But the previous day's hike, combined with walking for more than ten hours on this, the second day, was more difficult than I had anticipated. My energy was fading fast. But when I asked where we were setting up camp for the night, Olivier shook his head and said that we had quite a ways to go.

We were working our way around a mountain pass when I looked to the left and was amazed to see a group of people scaling a vertical wall that reached to the very top of the mountain. When I pointed this out, Olivier exclaimed, "That's a great idea! It will save us much time getting to the campsite!" I wasn't sure if he was serious, so I told him, "Olivier, I don't want to die yet. Let's take the longer route." Still, Olivier's father wasn't interested in hearing American-style complaints and hustled us to the base of the mountain. I looked up at the almost vertical slope. A series of ladders had been installed that led up the mountain face. But the ladders weren't connected. To get from one ladder to the next, you had to either sidestep along a narrow strip of rocks—if you were lucky—or grab a chain and swing like a monkey while hanging thousands of feet in the air.

Olivier's advice was sound. Forget about the mountain, he said. "Forget about the ladders, and stop thinking about getting to the top," he said. "Don't try and plan ahead. Just focus on the next step of the ladder."

He reassured me that he would be right ahead of me if I needed anything, but given that Olivier is deaf, I wasn't sure how I was supposed to get his attention when I was about to plummet to my death.

Still, I took Olivier's advice and focused on the first step. That wasn't bad. Then the second step. Good job, Sean. Then the third.

Now, you might be thinking that the lesson here is to stop dreaming or worrying. But that's not it. There is nothing wrong with having a vision, or with dreaming to change or better yourself. But dreaming *alone* is not enough. Dreaming won't get you through the day-to-day trials that life puts in your path.

Just as dreaming of reaching the top of the mountain wouldn't have been enough to keep me moving up those ladders, people need more than dreams to make lasting change. And the lesson isn't to give up on dreaming and *just do it*. That won't work, either—not for the long run.

The lesson is to focus on finding the *right first step*. Put all of your energy into achieving that first little step. Take the time to reflect on your progress. And then repeat.

With Olivier's advice, I made it up the first ladder. And with his father hurrying me from behind, there was no turning back. My body was weak, but by this point I had the force of *stepladders* behind me. I had the energy to push toward the finish. After getting to the top, I made it to our designated campsite, had a bowl of soup, and passed out—but not before loudly articulating every obscenity I knew into the landscape of mountains as a sigh of relief.

Figure 2. Olivier and I, at the completion of our journey climbing up mountains in the French Alps. Photo taken by Olivier's father.

DREAMS, GOALS, AND STEPS

Remember the first time you climbed a ladder or rock wall. It might have been scary. But as you put your foot on the first rung, then moved your hand up, then your next foot, then your other hand, you found a rhythm that made it easier. You probably were less frightened as long as you focused on the next rung and didn't look down.

With each step that you took, your confidence grew, making it more likely that you'd keep climbing. That's the force behind *stepladders*.

You may think that you already knew this, and that the stepladders concept is nothing new. But although the *concept* is easy to grasp, it's not so easy to do in practice. People might know intellectually that they should take small steps toward their goal, but they still plan steps that are too big.

There's a reason for this. It's hard to get excited about planning little steps. It's much more exciting to dream big.

For example, you could either make a resolution to lose ten pounds before a wedding next month, or you could plan to go to the gym *today*. How exciting is it to make a resolution to go to the gym today? Not very. If you're trying to shed a bunch of weight, then going to the gym one day doesn't sound impressive. It's not like you'll look any different afterward. It's more exciting to dream of losing every hated pound and making everyone's jaw drop as you walk into the reception hall.

This is why people like to read books or hear speakers promising they can lose 100 pounds, make a million dollars, or get a hundred million people downloading their mobile app. It's exciting. And yes, dreams like these have their place for motivating people to take action. But focusing *entirely* on achieving big, long-term dreams can actually have the reverse effect—people can become discouraged and quit because the dreams are *too* big and too far in the future.

You might wonder why it's not possible for people to focus their energy on a dream and still plan small steps to get there. The answer is rooted in how the mind works, and understanding the difference between dreams, goals, and steps. I'll explain the difference a little later in this chapter. First, let's concentrate on the idea of *small*.

HOW SMALL IS SMALL?

Most people think they are taking small steps, but in fact their steps aren't small enough. After all, the concept of *small* is subjective. If you ask five people to list all the small steps needed to accomplish a particular task, each person will come up with differently sized steps to accomplish the same thing.

Telling people to plan *really* small steps doesn't solve this problem, either. How, then, can we get people to use stepladders correctly? What I've learned is that instead of *telling* people to plan small steps, it's better to *teach* people how the mind works. Once they understand *why* people plan steps that are too big, they can use the stepladders force correctly.

Let's start by learning about a phenomenon that psychologists call "anchoring." It was discovered by Nobel Prize–winning psychologists Daniel Kahneman and Amos Tversky.

If I asked you to state the population of Chicago, you'd probably (unless you actually knew) take a guess and give me a number you thought was plausible. Depending on how much you knew about Chicago, you might say 300,000, 600,000, or three million. If I asked you that question while you were at the beach, or during a game of bingo, or while people were yelling random numbers in the background, your answer wouldn't be any different, would it? After all, it would be based upon your internal knowledge and intuition. Well, research on anchoring says that situations *do* change people's answers. Different situations cause people to focus on things that should be irrelevant but that actually affect people's decisions.

In one example of anchoring, people were divided into two groups and asked that exact question, to estimate the population of Chicago. But first, both groups were asked a question that shouldn't have affected their response. One of the groups was asked whether the population of Chicago was greater or less than five million, while the other group was asked whether the population was greater or less than 200,000. Both groups were then asked to estimate the population of Chicago. The group asked whether Chicago had greater or less than five million people thought more people lived in Chicago than the group asked whether it was greater or less than 200,000.[2] Why did the groups give different responses? Because hearing a number (five million versus 200,000) before responding caused them to use that number as an "anchor," or reference point.

In other words, a person will not always give the same answer to a question. Their answer will be relative to other information they are focusing on.

More broadly, this is an example of how people's plans to say or do something depend on their environment. Take Keith, sitting on the couch at a party. His host asks whether he would like some potato chips. Keith imagines being given a bowl of chips and says that he would indeed like some potato chips. Because he's trying to keep slim, Keith decides he'll allow himself five or six chips from the bowl. When the chips arrive, Keith finds that they don't come in the small bowl he had envisioned. Instead, he gets handed a giant bag of potato chips. Having access to a lot more chips than he planned, Keith readjusts his thinking and decides he'll just eat a few more—ten chips in total, instead of the five or six he planned to eat. Thirty minutes later he looks down and half the bag is gone.

Keith's plan to eat five or six chips shouldn't have increased to ten chips just because he was given more chips. He had a plan, and being given a bowl or a bag shouldn't have influenced that plan. But by being given more chips, his mind had to refocus. It adjusted to this change in focus by planning to eat more chips.

Plans to get yourself—or others—to do things work in a similar way. When people plan their steps to keep exercising or eat healthier foods, the size of their steps will change depending on what they're trying to accomplish.

Most people, when asked to write a list of steps to accomplish something, would come up with three to ten steps. This is regardless of the size of the goal.

Think about the implications: if someone were entirely focused on his long-term dream, his ten steps would need to be bigger and harder to accomplish than ten steps to achieve a smaller goal. And because people get frustrated when they don't see results quickly, focusing entirely on big dreams leads to fairly big steps, and can cause people to quit before they achieve their goal.

Take trading in the stock market. There are a number of techniques that have been proven to make money trading in the market. Many people who begin are aware of these strategies. Yet 60 percent to 95 percent of people who trade lose money and end up quitting.[3] Why is that?

Part of the answer lies in what they're focusing on. Most people begin investing in the market because they have a dream of quickly getting rich. When asked about their plans for how they will get rich, traders often give reasonable-sounding answers like "I'll buy low and sell high," or "I'll follow my rules." But most of these people still end up losing money and quitting.

Taking a deeper look, you can see warning signs. Just like seeing a big bag of chips makes a person plan to eat more chips, imagining a big pot of money makes these traders plan to quickly make a lot of money. Interviews with successful traders who have had long-lasting careers consistently show these traders have a different mindset.[4] Instead of spending their time focusing on dreams of getting rich, they focus on specific short-term goals, like not losing money *this week*.

THE STEPLADDERS MODEL: STEPS, GOALS, AND DREAMS

People often think they are planning small steps to reach their goals when they are actually creating really big steps. How do you get people to think small? I created the stepladders model of steps, goals, and dreams to solve this problem.

The size of the steps you plan depends on whether you are focused on *dreams* or *goals*. Dreams are bigger than goals. They are plans that typically take more than three months to achieve and which you haven't ever achieved previously—like the first time an app developer crosses the coveted one-million-downloads mark. People need to be reminded of their dreams to keep them motivated, but focusing entirely on dreams can lead people to give up. Instead, people should focus most of their energy trying to complete *steps* and *goals*.

Goals are the intermediate plans people make. There are short- and long-term goals. Long-term goals typically take one month to three months to achieve, like learning the basics of a new language. A long-term goal could take more than three months to achieve, but only if it's something you've already done before; otherwise it's a dream. For example, getting one million downloads would be a dream for most developers, but it's just a long-term goal for an entrepreneur who has successfully built other apps that have been downloaded more than one million times. If you already have experience doing something, then it's more realistic that you can achieve it and it becomes a goal rather than a dream. While long-term goals take one to three months, short-term goals typically take one week to one month.

Goals are also more easily quantifiable than dreams. "I want to be a famous rock star" (the dream) is infinitely less quantifiable, for example, than, "I want to sell 1,000 copies of a song" (the goal).

Finally, there are steps. Steps typically take less than one week to accomplish. Steps are the little tasks to check off on the way toward a goal. Getting a Spanish book is a first step toward achieving the goal of correctly pronouncing a menu at a tapas restaurant in Madrid. It takes less than a week to get the book. Blocking off your calendar tomorrow to make time for writing is the first step toward the goal of writing the first chapter of a novel.

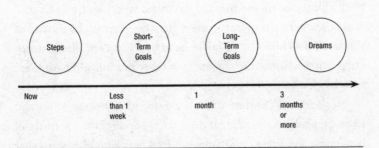

Figure 3. The Stepladders Model of Steps, Goals, and Dreams. Too often, people think they have planned a step but they have actually planned a goal or dream. This model will help you create steps, goals, and dreams that are the right size.

I typically find that the sweet spot is to have goals that take about one week to accomplish and to plan steps that take fewer than two days.˙ For example, in our research lab, my students and staff keep an updated end-of-week chart that describes the goals they set to achieve for the following week. The chart allows us to meet at the end of the week to discuss the steps they need to take to accomplish those things on time, and allows them to be excited when we meet each week because they followed their plan, accomplished their goals, and are sticking on the path toward their longer-term goals or dreams.

Here's an example of how the stepladders model can help people stick to their plans. A musician's dream might be to become a successful rock star. Her short-term goal might be to learn to play

---

˙ This is based on my personal experience. I don't know of any research showing the ideal length of time people should have for their goals. It will depend on the person or people working together.

her favorite song by the end of this week. Her steps could be to pick the song, get the sheet music, block off time in a calendar to learn it, and block off another time in the calendar this Friday to be ready to play the song. A teacher's dream might be to change the world by teaching students to become successful world leaders. His goal could be to get a struggling student interested in math by the end of this week. His initial steps might be to find a student who is struggling at math, invite the student to meet with him, and have them both block off times to get together.

Stepladders is the theory that brings together dreams, goals, and steps. Stepladders teaches that dreams are important for motivation, but focusing entirely on dreams can lead people to plan steps that are so big that they quit doing things early. Instead, *goals* are key. You need to focus on completing small, concrete goals to calibrate the mind and apply stepladders correctly. That will make change more likely to last.

You may find stepladders challenging at first. After all, the step-ladders model relies on you being able to accurately estimate how long it will take to achieve something. But people aren't always good at estimating. That's why I recommend finding three people whom you trust to help. You should map out your goals, and get their opinions on whether the things you think are goals are actually goals. If this group says it will take you more than three months to accomplish something, then you may have a dream. Keep the dream filed in the back of your mind to keep you motivated—but then pick a real goal that will take about one week to one month to achieve, and start planning the little steps to get you there.

It's important to understand that *stepladders isn't a formula for accomplishing dreams. It's a formula for keeping you on a path.* People who use stepladders are less likely to quit and more likely to keep trying to reach their goals—which should in turn help them reach their dreams.

But even though stepladders might be easy to understand in principle, it's tough to apply the theory to life and work.

But we need to because the science shows that it works.

THE SCIENCE BEHIND STEPLADDERS

Stepladders work for a number of reasons. The simplest explanation (you'll hear others in later chapters) is the power of the incremental. Take running a marathon. You could imagine the importance of training for a marathon in small steps. People typically train for months before they run a marathon. But a friend of mine didn't. He tackled the marathon head-on, thinking that even though he'd never run one before, his strong will would allow him to run a marathon without much training. In other words, it was a dream. On the day of the race he did well at first, but when he got to mile 19, his body gave up and he collapsed. He now says he's done with marathons for the rest of his life.

Like my friend, if you tried to compete in a marathon without training, you'd either succeed or fail. Great if you succeed—but if you failed, you probably wouldn't be excited to keep running. Alternatively, if you start small, by setting a short-term goal to run two miles more each time until you're comfortable, along with the short-term steps to get there, like learning breathing techniques, then you could gradually increase your abilities. You'd get to where you could consistently run five to eight miles, then ten to fifteen miles.

In one research study showing this effect, 126 overweight women tried to lose weight over a six-week period. During each week, the women filled out surveys asking how much they thought about the day-to-day stepladder process of eating healthy versus focusing on the dream of losing a lot of weight. The questions on stepladders asked them things like "During the last week, how much did you

think about what you have to do to eat low-caloric and low-fat food?"
The questions on their dream were similar to "During the last week,
how much did you think about what weighing less would be like?"
The researchers measured which group stuck to its diet plan. Well,
what happened? The women who focused on stepladders were more
likely to keep eating healthier throughout the six-week study. They
also lost more weight than the women in the other group. In fact,
those who had focused on dreams actually gained weight.[5] Many
studies confirm this principle: to change behavior, focus on the day-
to-day process, rather than the outcome.[6] [7] [8]

Scientists studying behavioral economics have a different explanation for why stepladders work. They call it *intertemporal choice* or
delay discounting: people assign greater value to smaller, quick rewards over larger, more delayed rewards.[9] In other words, people are
impatient to get results quickly. How does this apply to stepladders?
Focusing on small steps allows people to achieve their goals faster
than if they focused on dreams. Focusing on small steps also keeps
people happier and more motivated to keep trying because they get
rewarded more frequently. If you're opening a new business as a
consultant, ease yourself into it by scheduling to meet with two potential clients tomorrow (a step) rather than focusing on the longer-
term reward of achieving the dream of picking the office space and
new car you plan to lease after your first big paycheck. Research on
delay discounting says you'll be happier doing it and that that will
keep you sticking to your plan.

Neuroscience research also shows how stepladders create lasting
change, based on how the brain reacts to rewards. Each time the
brain gets a reward, a powerful chemical runs through it that makes
people feel good, leading them to want to repeat that behavior to
feel the chemical again. Eating chocolate, earning money, or having
great sex releases this pleasure-inducing chemical dopamine and

makes people want to do it again. The interesting thing is, brains understand rewards in *relative*, not absolute, values.

Here's a neuroscience study that tested that concept: researchers found that the brain releases dopamine if a person is expecting either a small or medium reward and gets the medium reward. But dopamine doesn't get released if someone's expecting a medium or large reward and gets the medium reward. Take Robert. If he's expecting to get $1 or $5 and he gets $5, then dopamine is released in his brain because he gets the larger amount of money. But if he's expecting $5 or $25 and he gets $5, then dopamine isn't released because he got the smaller amount. In both cases, Robert got $5, but his expectations were different. When he gets more than he expected, the brain releases dopamine, and when he gets less than expected, the brain doesn't release dopamine.[10]

How does this apply to stepladders? People don't feel good based on what they *actually* accomplish; they feel good based on what they *expect* to accomplish. A new gym salesperson might have a dream of selling 100 memberships next month, but if she has the goal of selling 10 by the end of the week (and ends up achieving it) then she could feel almost as good as if she had sold 100 by next month. Then she could set another small goal, like selling 20 memberships by next week. If she accomplished that goal, she'd get dopamine. It would make her feel good and want to keep selling. Ultimately, she'd feel better getting daily and weekly doses of dopamine rather than waiting for the dream of selling 1,000 memberships by the end of the year. And she'd be more likely to sell the 1,000 memberships.

At this point, you probably understand why stepladders are important but might question where and how to properly apply them in life. In the next few sections, I'll give some examples of how people have applied stepladders to their lives and businesses.

USING STEPLADDERS IN LIFE

A smart kid who was raised in a conservative Indian family in California's Orange County, Rishi Desai was so academically advanced that he graduated from high school at age fourteen. But he was socially isolated: anxious, awkward, and extraordinarily shy. He was also naturally very lonely. Like other teenagers, he dreamt of making friends, meeting girls, and having a normal social life. He was accepted to UCLA and ready to begin as a fourteen-year-old freshman in September, but he knew he needed to make some big changes so he didn't go through college without friends. But what could he do?

During his senior year in high school, Rishi decided to apply his smarts to gain friends and happiness by designing a program for himself. The program was structured with exercises of small steps and goals designed to gradually teach himself to be more social. His plan was to force himself to approach and talk to strangers for a short, fixed amount of time. He would start by finding people to talk to for one minute. Once that was successful, he would increase it to three, then five, and eventually he would be able to have long conversations with strangers. To make it more challenging, he would seek out a variety of people: men and women, young and old, and people of different races and backgrounds. But this seemed like a daunting task. He had no friends or experience making friends. How could he walk up to strangers and practice talking with them? He realized that he could start even smaller.

This was back in 1997, when instant texting programs like ICQ and AOL Instant Messenger were all the rage. Rishi decided he would execute his plan starting with ICQ so that he didn't have to approach people and worry about talking to them face-to-face. Rishi made use of the ICQ "chat with a stranger" feature, which was a pre-2000 version of chat roulette. ICQ (say it out loud and you'll realize it means "I seek you") would randomly pair two people to chat together. Rishi set weekly goals to begin chatting with strangers—men, women, older people, younger people—for short periods of time. He quickly gained comfort and the ability to talk to strangers for an increased number of minutes.

When Rishi got to UCLA, he upped the ante on this plan. After graduating from being able to meet strangers in chat rooms, he felt ready to apply his process to the real world of in-person conversations. But real-world conversations would add a level of difficulty he wasn't used to, so his plan was to return to the simple step of talking to a stranger for one minute. He walked the halls of his dormitory and found an opportunity when he saw a girl with whom he'd been wanting to talk. He reflected on his confidence in talking to people online and began chatting with her. He found the conversation went well and he reached his minute successfully.

Rishi continued this process of setting small steps and achieving goals and quickly made a large number of friends at UCLA and abroad who know Rishi only as a highly social individual—many of them remain close to this day. Not a hint of the shy, awkward fourteen-year-old boy is visible. Sticking with his process to overcome shyness has helped him become enormously successful. In his work life, he leveraged his expertise with online technologies and used it to connect with and influence the entire world. Rishi is now a successful doctor and creator of the world-renowned Khan Academy medical school curriculum, which teaches kids about medicine through short, engrossing online videos. His process has kept him sticking to being social. Today at house parties and social events, he purposefully makes his way around the room, meeting as many people as possible and asking them questions about their lives. By continuing to follow his process to change, Rishi has earned the respect and friendship of thousands of people, both online and offline. And it started with his first little chat on ICQ.

But what if you're not trying to become more social? What if you want to stick with a simple hobby, like learning a new instrument?

The oldest known reference to the North Indian classical percussion instrument the tabla dates back to 200 BC in the Maharashtra state in India.[11] The tabla is composed of two drums. One is the smaller, higher-pitched drum played by the dominant (typically right) hand. The other is the larger and lower-pitched (bass) drum played by the nondominant hand. Because the tabla has been around for so long, there are centuries of rules and techniques that new players need to learn. For example, in most Western music, we have a common time pattern for playing most music (called 4/4, for those of you who remember your piano or clarinet lessons from elementary school). Indian music has hundreds of these patterns. There are also more than nine ways to make sounds on a tabla and more than nine different names for these sounds. If you've been to an Indian restaurant, you probably have heard the tabla playing in the background music. And like most beginning tabla players, you probably didn't notice all the complicated patterns and styles. It just sounded like drumming that was accompanying a sitar (an Indian guitar). That's why a lot of tabla students quit learning before they can play. Students think it will be immediately easy but it's not. And that's what makes it tough for Indian music teachers. They have to figure out how to get students to stick with it long enough to learn.

So listen to Abhiman Kaushal, a tabla master and instructor. He teaches his students to start learning tabla by playing a simple pattern, called a bol. He tells them to practice repeating that simple pattern. But most of his students (eighteen- to twenty-five-year-old Americans in Los Angeles) didn't ask him for lessons so they could play the same five-second pattern for a month straight. They wanted to learn tabla because their dream was to jam with other musicians. Because they focus entirely on reaching this dream, Abhiman's students often complain that they're bored playing the basic repetitive patterns that a beginning tabla player needs to learn. "When will I be ready to get onstage and rock out with other musicians?" they ask.

But Abhiman teaches students to not focus on this question. Instead, he tells them to focus their expectation on the goal of playing the right sounds and patterns. Reaching this goal can take a couple of months and requires the students to take a series of steps, like learning how to position their fingers correctly. Abhiman assures them that after focusing on the goals of learning to correctly play the drumming patterns, the rest will come with time. Through decades of experience, he has found that the students who focus on the dream of playing with other students quit at much higher rates. The students who learn more incrementally by focusing on the shorter-term goals keep playing for years or throughout their lives.

Just as Abhiman teaches his students, parents and teachers need to start teaching kids at a young age to focus on stepladders, especially in the classroom. In a study on this topic in New York, researchers tracked the grades of 373 seventh graders over a two-year period. Students took tests to measure whether they focused more on dreams or incremental stepladders. Two years later, the kids who focused on the incremental stepladders approach had gained progressively better grades than those focused on the long-term "dream" of getting good grades by the end of the class.[12] In follow-up studies, kids were taught to think more incrementally. These kids showed long-lasting improvements in school as a result.[13] Studies continue to show that people should focus more on their shorter-term goals rather than longer-term dreams.

Technologies can be really helpful in getting people to take their first little steps. Take Susan Brown, who suffered a devastating stroke eight years ago and was told she would never walk again. Or Roberto Salvatierra, who had a tremendous fear of wide-open spaces—agoraphobia—leaving him trapped in his house afraid to step outside. Or John Dawley, who has a form of autism that made it difficult for him to interpret social cues or have relationships with others. Each of them has been able to overcome these challenges with lasting success. They've done it by using a virtual-world technology that helped them to focus on their steps and goals rather than their long-term dreams.

In the same way Rishi Desai used Internet chat rooms, virtual worlds like Second Life and Oculus Rift software are being used by therapists and doctors to rehabilitate patients with physical and mental health issues by teaching patients to focus on the short-term goal of rehabilitation in a virtual environment. Patients choose an online avatar, or representation of themselves, to present online. It can be humanlike, or an object like a watermelon. They then use that avatar to participate in a virtual world. In Second Life, which has an active community of about one million people, people can walk around virtual rooms in virtual buildings, talk to each other's avatars, and even gamble, score drugs, or go skinny-dipping.[14] Second Life users say that they like it because they can dress, talk, and move exactly the way they would want to in real life, without having the stress or fear they would have in the real world.

Mental health patients, such as agoraphobics, anxiety/depression patients, and military veterans with post-traumatic stress disorder (PTSD), have used virtual worlds as a first step in addressing fears. An agoraphobic who is scared to step outside doesn't have to. Through a virtual world, the person can focus on what it would feel like to go outside, without entering the real world. The agoraphobic person can temporarily ignore the dream of interacting with strangers in the real world by focusing on the small steps and goals. Taking that first step, of something as small as creating an online virtual world profile, creates a powerful force that leads a person down a path toward connecting with the real world.

Virtual worlds aren't only used for stepladders in mental health therapy. They rehabilitate stroke victims, can improve public speaking, improve sales performance, and even make people comfortable on nude beaches.[15] [16] [17] [18]

And the model of stepladders isn't limited to helping people stick to personal plans. The model can also be applied to business to get other people to keep doing things, like using a mobile app.

Now that you've seen how other people use stepladders, you might be asking how you can incorporate stepladders in your own life. What are the ingredients needed to apply stepladders in areas like personal health and business?

WHAT MAKES AN EFFECTIVE STEPLADDER?

There are two important ingredients needed to use stepladders correctly. The first is to use the model to plan the right incremental steps, goals, and dreams. Let's take a business example this time, using wearable technologies like Fitbits, Apple Watches, Intel bands, and Jawbones. Device manufacturers are making big bets that these wearable technologies will create lasting change in health behaviors. They are trying to do things like take people who never exercise and get them to walk every day (a dream) by showing them how much they are walking. The devices are giving people quantifiable goals to achieve, such as walking ten thousand steps a day. And after users walk ten thousand steps a day they are given another goal. This might sound like a stepladders approach, but it's not. Yes, giving people an initial daily goal of ten thousand steps involves taking incremental steps, but ten thousand steps a day is too much for most people as a starting point. Although the device manufacturer thinks this is a goal, it's actually a dream. Most people walk fewer than five thousand steps a day.[19] Asking them to consistently walk ten thousand is a big jump. It would require people to not only increase their fitness level to be able to walk twice as many steps every day, but also to find the time in their day to do this. That could mean they would need to change their schedule or reprioritize walking over other activities. This process could take months. And by having such a faraway dream of ten thousand steps, people are missing out on the dopamine rush they could get by having a goal that is easier to achieve. So let's make it easier for them so they can accomplish their goals and feel better about it, too.

Instead of having people focus on the dream of ten thousand steps, an easy way to incorporate stepladders into these devices (or into your own fitness routine) would be to find out how much each user typically walks and give the person a starting goal of walking every day for a week with only slightly more steps than that. That way, the person can plan the steps needed to achieve the goal. Once people achieve this goal—say six thousand steps—they then increase the step-count goal for the following week. That's the stepladders way.

The other essential ingredient of stepladders is reflection. Reflection is the act of looking back on a successfully completed behavior and having a small celebration. People don't have to invite their cousins from Atlanta to party with them when they reach their six thousand steps. They just need to quietly celebrate internally for a few seconds. The point is for people to realize they did well and accomplished their goal.

Reflection is important not only to keep up personal behaviors, but also to keep up business behaviors. It's more obvious how people could reflect on their personal behaviors. They could celebrate that they went to the gym today by eating a favorite food or spending a minute to congratulate themselves. But how do you incorporate reflection into business behaviors? For example, how do you get your customers to reflect on the steps they have accomplished by using your product or service?

Therapy provides a good example of how to do this. For each

weekly session, therapists can ask their clients to talk about something good that they did this past week (like whether patients followed the therapist's advice to remember to breathe during an anxious situation). Getting patients to express this progress and congratulating them for doing it leads them to reflect on progress and makes them more likely to keep using that technique.

Product designers could use reflection, too. They could build elements into products to get users to reflect on how the product is improving their lives. For example, our Center for Digital Behavior is building an app that helps people stick to their New Year's resolutions. It incorporates reflection through a calendar page that users visit each day after they have completed their daily steps. This calendar page has them put their finger on the date and wait while they reflect on their progress. This allows people to reflect on the success of sticking to their resolution, and helps create lasting change in behavior.

This process of reflection helps to build something that psychologists call self-efficacy.[20] Self-efficacy is the idea that change is attainable. Reflecting on past progress helps people to realize that they were able to complete the last step, and the step before, so they should be able to complete the next step. Just giving people information about *how* they have changed isn't enough to increase self-efficacy. It's important to prompt people with a question, reward, or conversation that gets them to *realize* what they accomplished.

One thing worth mentioning is that people should only reflect on their past step if they think they accomplished the step. Otherwise this process can backfire. Take a person trying to lose weight by changing the way he eats. If he steps on the scale and finds he gained weight, then asking him to reflect might backfire and make him more likely to quit his nutrition plan.

A nd now back to our opening story, about the guitar player with a dream of being a rock star.

I was a nineteen-year-old UCLA ethnomusicology student and a bass player in a band with my brother and two other buddies. We loved playing local parties and festivals but dreamt of being rock stars, where we could share our music with the world. I knew my brother and I would be playing music together over the long haul so I kept my heart with our band but played with other outside musicians for fun.

One of those musicians was my friend Ashkan, a singer/rapper from nearby Glendale. He told me to meet some of his buddies in a band called Xero. Xero was looking for a bass player and he thought I'd be a good fit. I met with the drummer and had a great time. We planned to get together again the next week with the rest of the band.

The day came. Ashkan honked the horn of his Toyota outside my college dorm room at UCLA. I grabbed my bass, ran downstairs, and jumped into his car. Two other bandmates from Xero were in the car. Mike was in the front passenger seat. He was wearing a beanie and had the Limp Bizkit look of a rock-rap singer from the late 1990s. In the back with me was Joe, the band's DJ. Two members of the band weren't in the car. The drummer I had met before was waiting for us at the studio. The other, the guitar player, was a UCLA student trying to make a career out of music instead of going to law school. His name was Brad Delson.

We went over to their studio and I was immediately impressed. During rehearsals for my band, Genohm, we crammed into a small space in my brother's garage in West Hollywood. Each practice, we'd try to quickly get through a set before his eleven-year-old Russian punk neighbor would interrupt us by opening the garage and attempting to steal our set list and instruments, or by asking us to buy lemonade he made from lemons he stole from my brother's refrigerator. But Xero's setup was very different. It was focused and professional. No sign of little Alex, and they had a line of seats set up to interview bass players they were auditioning. They told me that before we played, they needed to go over band business.

They had a whiteboard with the band's name, Xero, at the top (very impressive for a garage band to have a business whiteboard). On the board there was a list of short-term goals they were trying to accomplish along with the daily steps they were taking to achieve them. They had scheduled some parties and festivals and blocked them off on the calendar. They had become friendly with a guy in the film music industry who could help them score a soundtrack deal. They celebrated for a minute over this connection with some fist-bumps and went back to strategizing about next steps. Unlike our pie-in-the-sky conversations at Genohm, not one conversation was focused on the long-term dream of becoming big stars with a huge fan base. Xero was 100 percent focused on the next small goals, and the steps to reach those goals.

They finished band business and we jammed. I had a great time and was delighted that they invited me to play in their band. The one caveat was that I'd have to quit Genohm. Since I wasn't going to quit playing with my brother, I tried to convince them that I could play in both. They wouldn't allow that. They were focused enough to know that they needed someone entirely devoted to Xero.

I lost contact with Xero, but a few years after I met them, they changed their name to Linkin Park and had a great run of success. I was at one of their shows in Prague a few years later. I caught up with them afterward and we talked about their path to attain their dream. It was clear they had stayed focused on the short-term steps and goals. We only chatted for a bit that night because they were shooting a video on the Charles Bridge the next morning. Other musicians might have spent their time partying all night without regard for future commitments, but they were different. Linkin Park had a force behind them that was keeping them playing music and being successful. In a time when bands disappear within a year, Linkin Park had already established themselves as a lasting success. They were at the top of the charts for more than ten years, reached multiplatinum status, and sold more than 60 million records.[21] But that wasn't enough for them to abandon stepladders. They were still focused on the little steps to being lasting musicians. And that has made all the difference.

APPLYING STEPLADDERS IN BUSINESS

Think of a time when you went to a website or downloaded a new mobile app. How did you feel during the onboarding/registration process? If you've signed up for more than a few websites or apps in your life, you've probably had an experience where they ask for too much of your time on that first screen. What's your username, password, birth date, gender, phone number? Maybe they throw in some other questions like a best time to call you, your first-grade teacher's name, and whether you prefer green or red salsa on your burrito. You probably weren't too excited to fill in this info or keep using the application. Asking all that private information feels invasive. It also feels pushy for the app creators to jump right in requesting so much data without even showing what they have to offer.

When building a technology application, incorporating stepladders—by getting people to gradually give information—dramatically increases user engagement and retention. There are two reasons why this happens. First, it gets users to give information slowly so they don't feel overwhelmed. Answering only a small number of questions makes users feel more comfortable.

Second, it allows people to agree to use the product. They can give their buy-in through small steps. Developers are excited about the final product they built. They can't wait for people to see how this new technology will allow them to keep track of their daily tasks, do their taxes, and even give their dog treats. But users need time to appreciate all of those features. The developers need to wait for users to be ready to see everything the app can do. For example, showing users too many buttons the first time they use your product is like trying to get people to focus entirely on the long-term dream of what the app could provide down the line. People aren't ready for this and it could lead to high quit/bounce rates before they see the product's potential.

So instead of showing first-time customers every feature of a new technology product, give them little steps to walk them on board. Developers will know when they are getting buy-in from users because the users will click on buttons. A simple step like clicking on the "next" button teaches developers that the user is ready to learn more about the app. And this can lead developers to accomplish goals like getting users to log in and use the product every day for a week. Getting user buy-in on simple features before they see more complicated features or are asked to provide their personal information will lead to higher engagement and retention.

In my research, I looked at more than one thousand different mobile applications, with all different levels of user engagement. My intent was to determine what made the successful apps successful. We found that most of the successful apps incorporated stepladders, especially in the "onboarding" process.

Take MyFitnessPal, an app that attempts to motivate people to exercise and eat healthy. This app does a great job of onboarding users. How do they do this? The first screen in MyFitnessPal has just two buttons. These buttons ask users to sign up using either their email address or Facebook, and to choose a password. After users have read the terms and conditions, the next screen asks them one question, and gives them three choices to answer. "What is your goal?" To lose weight, maintain weight, or gain weight? After responding to this question, users see the next page. This page asks people one question but with four response choices. "How active are you?" Not very active, lightly active, active, or very active. Users then finish registration and go to the home screen.

Is it a coincidence that the first screen of the app asks users a question with two buttons to answer? That the second screen gives them a question to answer with three choices? That the third screen gives them a question to answer with four buttons? I don't think so. By gradually increasing the number of buttons that users see, MyFitnessPal is using stepladders to get users to just focus on the initial small steps. Research has proven that people don't like to have to make a decision when there are a lot of choices.[22] MyFitnessPal gets past this psychological barrier by making it easy for people to make a choice. This incremental process of getting users to slowly give their buy-in helps explain why MyFitnessPal has more than 60 million registered users and more than 90 percent of users completing some of their workout programs.[23]

Figure 4. Gradual increase in commitment (or difficulty) gets people to keep using products. On the first two screens of MyFitnessPal, notice the frequently used registration screen that presents two buttons to sign up with email or with Facebook. As users move to the third screen, they are shown three buttons instead of two. This increase in buttons from two to three is a gradual increase in commitment for users. This user has to use slightly more energy to make a decision compared to the last screen because there is an additional choice. This increases the likelihood that users will keep using it. On the next screen, the user sees four options. This gradual increase from two to three to four choices leads to a gradual increase in commitment and makes users more likely to keep using the application.

STEPLADDERS

People are tired and emotionally drained from failing to change. If, every year, you make a New Year's resolution to be more active, and, every year, fail to keep it, it's only natural that you'll start to get frustrated and think lasting behavior change is impossible. If you're an entrepreneur and every product you create fails to get customers to keep coming back, you might start to question whether you're a failure. But you're not. And, more important, you can be successful. Behavior change isn't easy, and it won't happen magically, but it is *doable*. You don't have to be superhuman. You don't even have to become like someone else. You just need to use the right process. You need to have an honest answer to this question: "Have I been trying to achieve a (realistic) first step or goal, or was it actually a far-off dream?" Stepladders will help you find the answer and will help you learn how to truly think small. It will keep you on the path to accomplish your steps and goals, and might even lead you to achieve your dreams.

EXERCISE

1. Take out the piece of paper on which you wrote the behavior you wanted to change at the end of the last chapter. You might have picked exercising more frequently, holding back from eating that late-night snack, or going to bed earlier. Or you might have wanted to change a behavior in your business. Maybe it's getting your employees to be more open to a new process, accelerating your management team's ability to make decisions, or getting your customers to keep using your product.
2. Regardless of what behavior you picked, stepladders can be applied to it. Start by using the stepladders model. Ask three people you know well and who will give you an honest opinion to tell you whether your plan is a dream or a realistic goal.

3. Use the table below to write down your dream, a short-term goal, and a list of immediate steps you will take to reach your goal.

4. Now that you've created your list of steps, goals, and dreams, take a moment to congratulate yourself on having finished it.

5. Do the first step on the list you made, and congratulate yourself again after you did it. You've started the process for change and are on your way.

Worksheet for How to Use the Stepladders Model of Steps, Goals, and Dreams

Use this table to enter your dream, the goals leading up to the dream, and the steps leading up to the goals. This table is for illustration only, as you might have a different number of goals or steps than the chart allows.									
What is your dream?	1.								
What are your goals?	1.			2.			3.		
What are your steps?	1.	2.	3.	1.	2.	3.	1.	2.	3.

CHAPTER 3

COMMUNITY

When Janja Lalich first heard about the 1978 Jonestown massacre—where nine hundred cult members committed mass murder and suicide in Jonestown, Guyana—she sided with the cult. Although she felt badly for those who died, she supported the group's socialist mission and steadfast ideals. In fact, the "People's Temple Agricultural Project" (the real name for the Jonestown group) shared a lot in common with the group Janja had been working for during the previous few years, where she and others had pooled their financial resources, adopted new names, burned all their previous belongings, and embraced the ideals of the paramilitary-style group.

But Janja wasn't the "type of person" who would belong to a cult. She was smart, educated, and from a good Wisconsin family. Just a few years earlier she had been a Fulbright scholar living in Spain, then relocated to San Francisco with the dream of making the world a better place.[1] So if Janja wasn't the type of person who would join a cult, how did she find herself holding a leadership role in an organization that required her to sit for days around a fire burning new members' clothes, diaries, and marriage licenses, punishing people by calling them their given birth names when they violated organizational rules, and overseeing the group's publishing business to raise money for these activities?

When Janja arrived in San Francisco in 1975, the city was still fresh with social and political passion from the Vietnam War. She had recently come out as a lesbian, and loved being a member of a strong, vibrant gay and lesbian community. She was also excited to meet new friends who shared her socialist ideology and desire to create positive social change in the world. While she was working part-time in a leftist bookstore, a colleague invited her to a study group. At the study group, Janja met other like-minded socialist females who wanted to help make the world a better place and was invited to live with them. She also listened to the teachings of the study group leader, Marlene Dixon.

Dixon, a former sociology professor at McGill University with strong Marxist-Leninist and Maoist leanings, had quickly amassed a following of students during her teaching career. When relations between Dixon and the McGill administration grew tense, she decided to stop teaching and form the Democratic Workers Party, the host of Janja's study group.[2]

Janja was impassioned by what she witnessed within the group. She was impressed by Dixon's antiracist and gay liberation viewpoints, and intrigued at the possibility of belonging to a commune composed of female socialists.

She decided to join. She quickly felt welcomed by new friends and guided by a clear life purpose. She bonded with the group members by creating a new name for herself, shared every penny of her earnings to serve the group cause, and was honored when they asked her to run the group's publishing business and promote it at national trade shows. Janja felt like she was working for a larger purpose and was excited that they needed her just as she needed them. Of course, there were times when Janja questioned her commitment, such as when her mother died and they refused to let Janja attend the funeral. She was reprimanded for being selfish by putting her own needs in front of the group's. During these days of doubt she was given emotional support from other group members, who advised her to dig deeper into the teachings of Marlene Dixon—who was now known as General Secretary Dixon—until her discomfort passed.

Janja Lalich stayed with the Democratic Workers Party for twelve years. She only left when the group disbanded. Marlene Dixon had started to lose faith in her dream for a Marxist revolution in the United States. Seeing that the United States working class wouldn't be able to create revolutionary change, she called Marxism-Leninism a failure in advanced capitalist nations and began adopting beliefs of the petite bourgeoisie, like acquiring possessions. Dixon's erratic behavior alienated many group members, and that, combined with Dixon's alcoholism and her expressed desire to leave the party, caused the group to vote to disband the party and liquidate and return assets to members. Still, many members of the group—including Janja—would have happily stayed members if the group had not disbanded. The forces keeping the group together were so strong, it took the erratic and self-destructive behavior of its leader to end it.

Janja Lalich is now a sociology professor at California State University, Chico, where she teaches students about the psychology and sociology behind cults. She looks back at her time with the Democratic Workers Party with mystification. Although she understands the power behind cults, she still has trouble understanding how she succumbed to it. How radically it took her over and changed her.

Janja's mission is to help people prevent being pulled into cults. Her academic research and work revolves around analyzing how cults can convince people who are educated and well-intentioned—

seemingly not cult personalities—to join and become committed cult members.

I would consider it safe to bet that most of you have no interest in starting or joining a paramilitary cult like the Democratic Workers Party or People's Temple. You might be questioning how Janja Lalich's story applies to getting you to stick with things.

The forces behind cults actually have a lot of relevance. By studying the psychology of how cults get people to do extraordinary things—like burning their personal possessions or even committing murder or suicide—we can apply that science to areas where people actually *want* to change of their own free will—like practicing piano every day or calling their mother once a week. By understanding the science behind cults we can empower people to make *positive* lasting changes in their lives and work.

So what is the secret psychology behind how cults get people to do things?

THE FORCE OF COMMUNITY

Cults have mastered the science behind how to build successful communities. A community is a group of people with shared characteristics. They might have the same beliefs or cultural or religious backgrounds. They might share a financial status. Or they might have similar hobbies. There are communities of people who use Androids instead of iPhones, prefer dogs to cats, and listen to Pandora rather than Spotify.

Communities can also be based on things you *didn't* choose, like where you were born, the religion of your parents, and whether your parents sent you to a public or private school.

Some communities have a designated meeting spot, like a certain church for religious people of different denominations, the Santa Cruz boardwalk for yoga fans, or the upstairs/departures level at the airport for people waiting for pickups from Lyft and Uber drivers.

Because a community creates a social bond, it needs at least two people. An extended family, a group of Republicans or Democrats, and a country of citizens are all examples of communities.

Even though people might understand that communities facilitate lasting change, *creating* these engaging communities is still difficult. A community will only lead to lasting change if its members are engaged. How, then, do we create an engaging community for change? That's what this chapter is about.

THE SOCIAL MAGNET

The strongest communities have what I call a "social magnet." The new types of scavenger hunts are a good example of social magnets. Scavenger hunts aren't just for children anymore. Adult versions have become really popular recently. They're popping up in every major city.

Here's how they work. You join the scavenger hunt usually by registering online with a group of three or more people. At the hunt, one person from the group gets a list of activities the group needs to complete. Unlike traditional scavenger hunts from fifteen or more years ago, new age scavengers use their smartphones to take pictures of things, upload pictures to social media, or research the answers to questions. And the hunts don't end in an hour or two. They can last for up to forty-eight hours.

Why would people give up forty-eight hours, or a full weekend of their time, to do a scavenger hunt? Because of the social magnet. Group scavenger hunts aren't just fun, they also have a magnetic force that keeps people participating. The scavengers are a team on a joint mission, pulling each other together to keep working like a magnet pulls metal toward it. The team members might have moments where they get bored, lose motivation, or get tired, but they can't stop what they're doing because of the magnetic force from the team. That's a social magnet, and that's how it creates lasting change.

Take social media. How many of you were reluctant to join Facebook, Twitter, LinkedIn, or any other social network? Remember the first time you got an email from Facebook asking you to join? You might have been unimpressed. Maybe you thought that social media was only for people with too much free time. They could post what they ate for breakfast and who they bumped into during the day. But then you realized that the invite from Facebook was sent by a good friend. Maybe that wasn't enough to motivate you to sign up, but it was enough to get you thinking about it and to remember the site. Soon enough, your other friends and coworkers started inviting you, too. Some of them began using Facebook instead of email. Now you had to join to keep in touch. By that point, you realized there was a community of your peers on it. Even though you were reluctant to join at first, you joined so that you weren't left out of this growing community. And you kept using it once people started commenting on things you wrote. That made the community even stronger.

This is how the force of community compels people to keep doing things.

But it's not as easy as it sounds to build or leverage a community for lasting change. Even if a community is designed for the right purpose, communities also need to have a social magnet. People often attempt to build or join communities that don't have this social magnet. And they usually won't work.

Take gym buddies. For many people, it's easier to keep going to the gym if you have a gym buddy to go with you each time. But what happens when you or your gym buddy gets sick or goes on vacation for a week? The routine typically ends and it's tough to get started again. That's because it's missing the social magnet.

It's not enough to find a buddy who will go with you to the gym.

Building a community from the ground up requires giving to the community to form the social magnet. People do this by setting expectations of other group members, like texting a gym buddy, sending a link to an article on a new type of workout, and expecting her to show interest and reciprocate by responding to it. Calling out a specific person or group of people, for example by sharing a video and tagging a person or group of people, is one way to build that social magnet. But not everyone has the time or energy to build their own community to keep them doing things. If that's the case for you, then join an existing community. Just make sure it already has a social magnet. You'll just need to know what to look for, and we'll explain that soon. But remember this important fact: for the community to continue to have a lasting impact on people, there needs to be enough people in the community who are nurturing it to create a social magnet. I've found that for very small communities (fewer than five people) to create lasting change, everyone in the community needs to work on building the social magnet. For larger communities, about 15 percent of the people involved in the community need to be building the social magnet. More about these details later when I describe an example of how to build a community.

Communities push people to keep doing things that are good for them, like exercising regularly.[3] They also push people to keep doing things that are bad for them, like smoking cigarettes.[4]

But do we choose our communities, or do our communities choose *us*?

There are few better examples of how communities influence the highs and lows of people's lives than the story of the actor Robert Downey Jr. Maybe you heard some of his stories about his life when on drugs and alcohol, like when he was found half-naked on an eleven-year-old's bed after breaking into a house and passing out. Or maybe you've heard the success story of how he turned around, cleaned himself up, and has become Ironman 1, 2, and 3. What most people don't know about him is the story of how communities influenced his journey.

From his early childhood, RDJ was surrounded by people using drugs.[5] He didn't have to search for this community; it was brought to him by his father, a long-term drug user. When RDJ was eight, his father offered him marijuana at a party so they could socialize together.[6] He said, "When my dad and I would do drugs together, it was like him trying to express his love for me in the only way he knew how." This lifestyle quickly created an addiction. As RDJ got older, he searched for friends who could help him satisfy his addiction. Every night he started by drinking alcohol and making "a thousand phone calls in pursuit of drugs."

When RDJ moved to Hollywood as an actor, he found himself surrounded by another group of drug addicts. Famous actors known for their binge drinking and drug use like Kiefer Sutherland, Mel Gibson, and Rob Lowe became part of RDJ's close circle of friends. As his alcoholism and drug use continued, he was arrested numerous times for things like cocaine and heroin use, carrying a .357 Magnum, and for that story of trespassing and falling asleep on a stranger's bed while under the influence. After going through court-ordered rehab a bunch of times, he finally hit a low enough point where he felt he had no choice but to get clean. That's when he found a new community to keep himself free from drugs. He believes that the social communities of his family, Alcoholics Anonymous (AA), and therapy have led him to kick his addiction.

Social communities like AA, Narcotics Anonymous (NA), or psychotherapy have helped RDJ and a large number of other people change their lives. But they're not just for alcoholism or drugs. Communities also help people make changes in diet behaviors (Weight Watchers), fitness behaviors (gyms like CrossFit), and relaxation (yoga and meditation groups). While these groups work for a large number of people, there's also a large group of people who don't get help from them. Why is that?

There are a number of reasons. One is that attending group meetings can be time-consuming. Not everyone has the ability to attend frequent meetings. Many people who go to community meetings spend hours of time each day traveling to meetings, attending them, and communicating with people at them. This can be especially tough if people have full-time jobs or have to take care of their families.

Another reason communities like AA or therapy aren't for everyone is that there is still a stigma of going to face-to-face meetings for help. Even though therapy is supposed to be secret and anonymous, many people still fear the possibility that others will see them seeking help. People might learn about their low points in life and judge them. This stigma makes people reluctant to go. It also makes them reluctant to actively participate in the community in the way they need to achieve lasting change.

Take HIV prevention communities, like local HIV clinics. These organizations have a tough time finding and keeping customers because going to an HIV clinic can stigmatize people.[7] Other people might see them and think they're infected with HIV. They could lose their jobs, families, and friends.[8] People go to great lengths to avoid stigma. They're willing to seek help to quit smoking because smoking is less stigmatizing, but they avoid getting help for stigmatized diseases like HIV and STDs.

So how do you get someone to join a community to help them if they don't want to be part of the community?

APPLYING COMMUNITIES IN LIFE

Our research team studied that problem. We looked at how to create communities to increase HIV testing among the groups at the highest risk for HIV: African-American and Latino men who have sex with other men. Men who have sex with other men (or MSM, as it's called in the public health world) are a highly stigmatized group. Although the term *MSM* includes people who identify as gay, it also includes men who have sex with other men but don't self-identify as being gay. In fact, many MSM have girlfriends or wives. They might have antigay views and wish to keep it a secret that they are having sex with other men because of the stigma associated with being gay. African-American and Latino MSM are especially stigmatized because these groups have particularly strong antigay views.[9] The stigma around being MSM, particularly an African-American or Latino MSM, explains why MSM are often reluctant to test for HIV and have higher rates of HIV than non-MSM. It also explains why public health professionals have focused so much time and money over the past few decades, in what sometimes seems like an uphill battle, on increasing rates of HIV testing and treatment among African-American and Latino MSM. This was the problem we sought to address, because, well, why tackle a problem unless it's a tough and important one?

To build a successful HIV prevention community that African-American and Latino MSMs would be willing to join and stick with, we needed to address stigma. We also needed a community that was fun, supportive, and didn't take much time. Social media was growing in popularity and had the potential to do all of these things, so we decided to create an online community. We thought HIV prevention online communities might work because they're accessible to people around the world and would eliminate the stigma of face-to-face HIV prevention community settings. People could ask questions and share their thoughts without having to go anywhere or feel judged.

The problem was, how could we design an HIV community engaging enough to keep people involved? People have a lot of things they could be doing other than talking online to strangers about HIV.

Also, although the men we were targeting were at high risk and needed help, how could we change them if they weren't interested in changing? And how could we do this in only twelve weeks?

Jordan Salazar was a weekend meth user. On a typical Saturday night, he'd go to a dance club, meet a guy, and sleep with him. He never thought about wearing condoms or getting an HIV test. When he saw an online advertisement for a research study on men's health called HOPE—it said he could meet other men there—he decided to give it a try. All he had to do was sign up to join an online community about men's health, take a thirty-minute survey, and he'd get paid thirty dollars. He could even drop out of the group and close his online community account right after that. It seemed like an easy way to make thirty dollars, so why not do it and then drop out of the group? What he didn't realize was that the HOPE community was based on the science behind how to create lasting behavior change.[10]

After Jordan went to healthcheckins.com and joined the group, he looked around the site and saw people were talking to each other, but he didn't know what to do. He hadn't been in a research study before, especially not one centered on an online community. Perhaps he shouldn't drop out yet. It was interesting that these strangers were talking to each other. He was told they were all gay men. Some of them had cute pictures, so maybe he'd even get to meet someone? He skimmed through the chain of conversations and found something surprising. The other men in the group were sharing really personal information, like when they first came out to their wives that they also liked men, or really vivid experiences about having sex in prison. It freaked him out a little because he wasn't used to talking about this stuff. He decided to give it a try and responded to some messages from people. After a few weeks, he got more used to it, and after one of the group members shared his fear of getting HIV and asked Jordan what he thought, Jordan decided to share. He said he'd never really thought about getting an HIV test, and that using condoms seemed like a waste of time and not fun. Plus, he didn't trust the doctors who were telling him he should get tested.

After being a wallflower for the first few weeks and then gradually sharing things about himself, Jordan was ready to respond to a chain of conversations on what it was like coming out.

I never sat down with my parents and said, hey I am gay. My mom overheard a phone conversation with my first boyfriend in college. Her response was shock initially and then silence. My dad didn't seem to care or say anything. We never discussed it and no one talks about it to this day. I used to bring home a long-term partner every year to visit. No one ever asked anything even though we sleep in the same bed. I'm from the South. I still believe what I do in bed and with whom is my business. I am me. And, I make apologies to no one including my parents and family. My grandmother was a God-fearing, Bible-beating southern Baptist woman who said all gays would go to hell. My mom was more supportive. She said he's still my baby and that's all that matters. Her fear was the fact that I would be alone with no one to love me and grow old with. So, imagine a parent's fear for their child. I totally get it now.

Once he'd taken the leap by telling his story, Jordan started to connect more with other group members. They shared videos about their lives and personal stories, and so did Jordan. They shared how they felt people treated them for being MSM, and so did Jordan.

They shared their fears about contracting HIV and the need to get an HIV test, and Jordan even started talking about this, too. He started having sex with fewer people, having more long-term relationships.

Eventually, he got an HIV test. And his test came out positive.

Before joining the group, Jordan wouldn't have gotten an HIV test and would have thought it would have been the end of his life—literally—if he had tested positive. But because of his involvement in the HOPE community, he was able to psychologically deal with it when he tested positive, and has stayed involved in the community as they help him stay healthy. To date, Jordan has been keeping on his medication. He has what is called "an undetectable viral load," meaning that his HIV is managed so well that tests cannot detect that he has it.

HOPE is scientific proof that community can create lasting behavior change. We managed to bring together a group of men who were at high risk for HIV but didn't want to talk about HIV or test for it. Even though almost none of them wanted to be part of a community focused on HIV testing, the force of communities—especially the social magnet aspect—got them to actively participate and get tested. People who joined HOPE were more than two times as likely to get tested for HIV compared with people who didn't join HOPE. And we created lasting change. At the end of the twelve weeks, 94 percent of group members were still actively involved.[11]

When we followed up with them after fifteen months, more than 82 percent were still active in the community.[12] At the time I'm writing, it's been more than five years since we created that community, and people are still involved. Since then, we've repeated HOPE in other countries—to change not just HIV risk, but other behaviors related to other diseases. We've proven that community can create positive lasting changes throughout the world.

THE NEW SCIENCE OF COMMUNITIES

Now that you know the power of community, let's talk about how to create a successful behavior change community.

The Six Ingredients for a Successful Community

Every successful community has six ingredients that address people's psychological needs. I'm going to list and define those ingredients below and then we can put those ingredients to practice by walking through an example of how to create a community.

THE NEED TO TRUST: When people trust other community members—whether family, friends, coworkers, or strangers—they become more willing to learn, more open-minded, and more willing to change. This trust is formed when people share thoughts, experiences, and difficulties with others. In our studies, we found that communities can create trust (and ultimately, lasting change) by getting people to share personal information by doing something as small as getting people to talk about what they did today.

THE NEED TO FIT IN: Most people strive to fit in. They might not need to fit in everywhere, but they need to have some community where they fit in, whether it be their family, friends, or a social club. For people to know how to fit in, they need to understand the social norms of that community. For example, a community formed to get people to vote for Democratic candidates would make that social norm clear. It would praise Democratic candidates and the people who vote for them. Communities that have a clear social norm will be more successful in creating lasting change. Most people are willing to change their attitudes and/or behavior to fit in these group norms and with the community.

THE NEED FOR SELF-WORTH: People keep doing things that make them feel good about themselves. Communities that get people to feel good about themselves can increase self-esteem and keep community members motivated.

THE NEED FOR A SOCIAL MAGNET: We explained the concept of the social magnet earlier in the chapter. The social magnet is essential for a strong community to promote lasting change. If you join a community and you don't feel the social magnet, then it probably won't help you to change. Find another community. The same is true if you are building a community. If your community members don't feel the social magnet, you need to change the psychological elements of the community.

THE NEED TO BE REWARDED: Anyone who has seen an episode of Cesar Millan, "the dog whisperer," has seen him change dogs by rewarding them for good behavior. People are similar to dogs in a lot of ways (this is no secret to dog lovers). People, just like dogs, will keep doing things if they get rewarded for good behavior. Eventually, these behaviors can become habits. We'll go into a lot more detail about this need to be rewarded in Chapter 7 (Captivating).

THE NEED TO FEEL EMPOWERED: Just as people have to feel good about themselves to satisfy their need for self-worth, they need to feel like they are in control of their lives to satisfy this need. Empowerment (or self-efficacy, as you might remember from the last chapter) is one of the strongest predictors of change. People who belong to a community that empowers them, by leading by example with mentors or role models, are more likely than those who don't to achieve lasting changes in their lives.

You now understand the psychological ingredients needed in communities to promote lasting change, but you might be asking at a more practical level, how can you build or identify communities that address these needs? We've found the answer lies in having *peer role models*. Below, I describe the detailed science behind our HOPE communities. You can use this science to help you learn how to build your own community or identify whether a community you're joining or getting someone else to join is built for lasting change. We use the process I describe below to build online communities, but this same process can be used to build any type of community.

How We Build HOPE Communities

To create a HOPE intervention, we recruit peer role models to start the community. We've found it's important to have approximately 15 percent of the community as peer role models, so if you were to create a community of one hundred people, you should have about fifteen peer role models. We pay these peer leaders a small incentive each week (an online gift card in most cases, but we'll describe in a later chapter how you don't have to use money for incentives) for twelve weeks for their involvement. After the twelve weeks, their official role is over and the community is usually up and running by itself. Just like hiring a new employee, there's a lot of up-front work to be done with these peer leaders when creating communities, but after a few weeks the communities organically grow by themselves.

We start by identifying the right peer role models. If we're building a health community, say for reducing stress, we partner with organizations that focus on health and reducing stress, like a health clinic or meditation center. We ask them to refer people they think would be good peer role models for this community. We also search online to invite peer role models. Our criterion for role models is that they share the same demographic and psychological characteristics with the other people who will be in the community. For example, if we're trying to create a community of high school students to get them to do their homework, we need to know that the peer role models will also be high school students. It's also important that the peer role models have achieved a level of success in the area of lasting change (for example, students who consistently do their homework). They also need to be interested in helping others, be sociable, and either appear like they would be well respected by their peers or be referred to us because they are already. We invite these peer leaders to participate in training where we tell them about the purpose of the community and how they can empower change in people.

We then open up the community for people to join. If it's a community for helping to reduce addiction, for example, we invite people who are at risk for addiction and overdoses. Just like Jordan Salazar, it doesn't matter if they aren't interested in joining the community. We pay them to take a quick survey and join the community but they can then drop out at any point.

Here's a quote from one participant, Susan Baer, in one of our pain and opioid management communities expressing her apprehension on the public wall after just being added to one of our online groups: "Hi group, I could not feel more uncomfortable posting here, I guess for the same reasons as others. I've spent much of life in doctor's offices and hospitals, and at the same time (since about 10) taking care of my mom, and then dad, who both died of cancer."[13]

Susan's quote shows what a lot of participants in our studies feel when we first add them to a support community. After years of hardship and failure, they're uncertain about the purpose of the group, whether they'll get anything out of it, and they're reluctant to contribute. That's why people drop out of so many other groups designed to help people. And that's where we use the science behind communities to make our participants feel differently this time.

Although we automatically add participants like Susan to the online group as part of their participation in the study, they are able to leave anytime. That's why it's up to us to make it an engaging enough experience for them to stick with us, and where our trained peer role models help. The peer role models begin talking with the new community members. They publicly (over the online community forum wall) post thoughts, videos, and other content we've given them in the training to help engage the new community members. Peer role models reach out directly with a private message to community members who aren't responding with their own thoughts, "likes," or other ways of engaging with the peer leader content. This is how we create the social magnet. Every community member must feel the healthy pressure of a peer role model reaching out to them and wanting them to participate. It's important that this is a healthy pressure, that it makes the community member feel trusted and supported for participating, rather than punished for not participating.

For example, a peer role model named Albert Berke responded to Susan saying, "Welcome, I know it can be hard at first, and believe me when I tell you I understand what it's like to have a family that does not talk about anything. I was born in Ukraine, and my father-in-law is an Armenian married to a Brit. It's like the perfect storm of 'don't talk about anything with anyone, ever.' Over the last decade, I've spent more and more time contributing to online support groups ranging in everything from marriage and psychology to information technology, medication, and substance use disorder treatment. If you stick with it, not only will you find that it gets easier to communicate about your issues with other like-minded individuals like us, but you'll also have a clearer internal dialogue with yourself, which can help you sort stuff out, and many other things."[14]

After a few weeks, community members no longer need the peer role models to guide them. Many community members begin acting as peer role models themselves, encouraging other community members to take on the social norm.

Here's a quote from a participant, Kellene Colson, in one of our health communities, "I know it is hard to share [@participant Tristell Roberts] but believe me, after you start to share it really does help. I never wanted to talk when my epilepsy started but groups like this truly have helped with being brave enough to say something that you're going through." Kellene sounds like a peer role model in this quote because she's using the public online community to tell other participants like Tristell how this group has already improved her life. But Kellene isn't one of our trained peer role models; she is a participant who was helped by our intervention and naturally became a peer role model to spread the word about how we've helped her.

We teach our peer leaders to initially focus on building trust within the communities, but after a few weeks, once trust has been built and the community is following the social norms, the peer role models begin shifting the community social norms toward the purpose of the community, such as getting people to exercise, to stop using drugs, or to show up to work on time. After twelve weeks of this process, the peer role models have finished their formal role. We stop giving them weekly incentives to help and let the communities run on their own.

We find that this recipe for creating communities consistently leads to lasting change. Compared to those who haven't, people who have joined our HOPE communities are almost three times as likely to change their behavior. This change lasts and the communities remain active and strong. After three months, we typically find that more than 90 percent of people in the communities continue to stay engaged. After eighteen months, it's typically more than 80 percent. I've heard that most online communities have less than 50 percent engagement, so we've made a big improvement.

Here's a quote from a participant, Zee Randolph, on the public board of one of our online pain groups to tell others about how the twelve-week community impacted him: "For the first time in my 31 years of life dominated by pain, someone gets exactly the way I feel . . . everyone's story relates to something unique that only those like us can truly comprehend. We're all at different points in our therapy and have encountered different pitfalls and obstacles, but that only adds the benefit of learning from one another. My only hope is that everyone stays in touch. . . ."

Building Your Own Community

To clearly show how to build a successful community, let's walk through an example together. Let's imagine we're creating a community to help new mothers cope with stress. No matter how much their baby projectile-vomits on the new couch, or screams at 4 a.m., this community would be there to help moms get through it, and perhaps even see the beauty in it. Having a little one myself, I'm well aware of the need for a solution. Here's what we would do to help our new mothers.

First, we need to understand the psychology of the new mothers we're trying to reach.

To identify the right peer role models, let's start by identifying some shared psychological characteristics among recent mothers who are experiencing a lot of stress. Maybe they are more likely to be first-time moms? Maybe they are younger on average? Maybe their parents or other family members are less available to help them take care of the baby? These are the types of questions that need to be addressed. We need to get a good understanding of who we are trying to reach.

Next, we'll interview some of the women we're trying to reach to make sure we have the right answers to these questions. We'll also ask them psychological questions to learn how a community could help them. We'll need to learn who they think is influential, how they like to socialize, and how they relax. We'll research whether they would prefer a community of women only versus men and women, whether they prefer to talk freely or be directed with questions, and whether they prefer it to be online or in person, or both. Because they are a group of sleep-deprived women, it might be tough for them to come to an in-person community event. For that reason, an online community is probably better for them. But we should first confirm that in the interviews.

For this exercise, let's imagine we learned that the mothers we are targeting are stressed because they feel like they don't know how to take care of a newborn baby, feel alone from sitting by themselves with the baby all day, and miss feeling like they were being productive at their jobs. If we want to build a community that gets these women engaged and helps reduce their stress, we need to address these issues.

We're now ready to build the online community. The trick is to find the best role models to spread the right message. This must happen before inviting our mothers to join. You can do this in any number of ways. It's not always necessary but it helps to have a small budget for rewards to give to your role models to thank them for helping you.

Here are the four types of role models that are typically used when building a community:

THE EXPERT. Partner with influential experts. They might be bloggers, scientists, doctors, or successful entrepreneurs who have experience satisfying the needs of new moms.

THE CELEBRITY. Get the support of celebrities who are liked by new moms. These don't have to be famous actors like Jennifer Garner or Jessica Alba. They can be small-time online celebrities who are respected among new moms, like Kate Inglis or Ciaran Blumenfeld.

THE MESSENGER. Find new moms who are social butterflies to join your community. They can help spread the word to their friends and help the community grow.

THE HOMEGROWN ROLE MODEL. In case you don't know experts or celebrities and can't find messengers, don't worry. You can still use homegrown role models. In fact, these are your best role models. Get a small group of new moms to join your online community. Find the ones who love it, are social, and are passionate about helping others. They will want to do whatever they can to help you by spreading the word. Cherish these homegrown fans and make sure they have a great experience. Because of the simplicity and cost-effectiveness of the homegrown role model, most of our HOPE studies use them.

The next to last step is to *make it easy for the role models to be role models.* Give them some basic guidelines for what new mothers will want from them. This lets your role models feel valuable and gives them direction on how they can help. For people without much time, like celebrities or experts, you might ask them to send only one message, or one message a week on Twitter about the community. For homegrown role models, you might ask them to send multiple tweets a week and give them small rewards (even as small as a personal call) as a thank-you. As I mentioned earlier with our HOPE studies, this is where we would invite the peer role models to participate in short training sessions. We'd teach them what we'd learned about the needs of the women from our interviews, and we'd give them materials like videos, websites, and blog posts that they can use to share with the mothers in the group.

Once the role models have started the group and begun sharing with each other, the final step is to *open it up to new moms*. You'll have to do some marketing to spread the word, but if you're working with the role models in the right way, many moms will already have learned about your community. Immediately after you get your first visitors, get some role models talking to these moms.

There is only one initial goal that you should have for your new visitors: to contribute something to the community within their first week of joining. It might be as simple as responding to a question, liking a post, or commenting on a picture, but getting them to contribute something will begin the process of stepladders we described in Chapter 2. It will help make the social magnet grow stronger. You'll soon find that many of the moms who join will become role models themselves. They will want to share stories and their success with the newer community members. They will want to help grow the group. By this point, you'll have created a real community. We found that after twelve weeks with this method, you'll have a homegrown community that continues to grow, and lasts for years.

Perhaps you're just trying to change your own behavior and it's too much work to create your own community. Fortunately, many communities already exist that can help you create lasting change. Let's say you want to motivate yourself to practice daily yoga. Remember that people are more influenced by communities of people they relate to, so pick a yoga studio with people similar to you. Make friends with them, and meet them outside of class. The more actively involved you are, the stronger the social magnet will be, and the more likely you will be to effect lasting change.

Applying Communities in Business
Matei Zaharia was a Google engineer working in an area called "big data analytics." His job was to develop tools to help people ana-

lyze lots of information in milliseconds. These tools would allow people to collect and immediately make sense of the billions of data points that exist but that humans can't process. They need advanced computer tools.

The current big data tool that Google was using, Hadoop Map-Reduce, wasn't solving his technical problems.[15] He left Google and created his own big data solution, called Spark. Spark quickly became a better solution than Hadoop for solving real-time data analytics problems without requiring a lot of storage space. The problem was, most people hadn't heard of Matei or Spark. But just because Spark was a better product than Hadoop didn't mean that people would immediately switch and use it. Matei had to come up with a plan for how to get people to use Spark. After brainstorming ideas, he came up with two theories. First, although he knew Spark was better than Hadoop, other engineers wouldn't realize that unless he could get them to try it. Second, he knew that though engineers were stereotyped as being socially awkward, it wasn't because they weren't social. It was because they wanted to be social on their own terms, by talking about the things they liked, such as engineering.

Matei realized that engineers needed a community. Just as we use HOPE communities to improve people's health, Matei created a community to help people learn about—and to learn to like—Spark. He established meetup groups in the Berkeley area, where he lived, and invited his friends. He enlisted the support of graduate students and friends in Berkeley to invite friends to these meetup groups. Like HOPE, Matei created a social magnet by getting engineers who joined to immediately feel connected to the community. These graduate students and friends took on the responsibility to hook newcomers into learning about and using Spark. Each person who came to a meeting was introduced to someone who had used Spark and loved it. The big data space was so new that Spark users were quickly becoming pioneers—a scientific cult of sorts—around a growing trend in computer science. This got new computer scientists interested in learning what was happening at Berkeley. Word spread. People kept coming to the community to learn more about Spark, to talk about how they were using it, and, yes, to socialize as part of a community. Spark grew into a lasting success. It not only has become a powerhouse in the big data space, but has researchers and companies knocking on Matei's door to recruit him.

If "socially awkward" engineers can be influenced by communities, so can the rest of the world. And if an engineer like Matei can create a social community to change how people act, so can you. You simply need to know how to create a community. You need to know the science. We studied this science extensively when we created the HOPE community.

Here's another business example. We talked about music in the first chapter. Now let's talk about something that goes with music. Beer.

A lot of beers taste similar. Most of them are priced pretty closely as well. So how do beer companies distinguish themselves and get customers to keep buying their products? With the tremendous growth of social media, most companies have learned that online communities like Facebook pages are a great place to start. Although companies are trying to build communities to get customers coming back, not all companies are using communities correctly.

Compare the Facebook pages of Sam Adams and Dos Equis. The Sam Adams page has a thumbnail picture of a freshly poured glass of beer, a picture of the Sam Adams bottle, and an impressively active group of fans with one million page likes.[16] Dos Equis has a picture of Senor Dos Equis taming a snow leopard, another one of him calling the NFL all-star team into a huddle, and an even more impressively engaged group of more than three million page likes.[17] That's three times as many likes as Sam Adams.

So which company do you think sold more beer in 2013?

If you're like most people, you probably guessed Dos Equis. But then you'd be wrong.[18]

People think that marketing, advertising, and, more recently, a huge social media following is the recipe to get repeat customers, but it's not. Dos Equis spent a lot of money creating a new brand around a Colombian cartel–looking, gray-bearded man in a black suit billed as "the most interesting man in the world." It built a highly engaged Facebook fan base. But Sam Adams, which spent less money, used the same boring ads they had used in previous years, and had a smaller group of Facebook fans, sold more beer. Although Sam Adams and Dos Equis both built communities, Dos Equis spent way more money and got much less out of it. So, if Sam Adams isn't creating new ad campaigns and spending lots of money on marketing, then what's its secret to getting its customers to keep buying its beer?

As we've already noted, since the growth of Facebook, most companies have learned that growing a strong community is essential for brand loyalty. They invest a lot of money and resources into creating communities, both online and offline. Sam Adams and Dos Equis are no exception: both of them knew they needed to leverage Facebook and build communities. Both of them did great jobs: they leveraged the resources that Facebook shares on how to build Facebook communities; they paid for advertisements to drive traffic to their Facebook pages; and they spent a ton of money on marketing and social media gurus to help them create engaging website content. And if you measure fan engagement, that money definitely paid off for Dos Equis. Its ads, along with its exciting Facebook community, make it—on one level—a stronger community than Sam Adams. After all, Dos Equis has demonstrably more fans and higher fan engagement. But if you're measuring the real purpose of their communities—getting fans to be loyal and supportive of the brand, and to buy the beer—then Sam Adams is the clear winner.

The point here is that you might have read the title of this chapter and thought: So what? Building a community is not a new idea in how to create lasting change. You'd be right. Even though people are learning to build communities, and some like Dos Equis and Sam Adams have even built successful communities that get people talking, those communities won't achieve their objectives (like getting people to buy beer) unless they are built with the right science. So what was it about the Sam Adams community that caused people to buy beer but was missing in the Dos Equis community? The difference lies in the *purpose* of the community, and how it was created.

Dos Equis had a brilliant marketing campaign. If you measure success by word of mouth, or by how much people talk about your brand, then Dos Equis is one of the most successful brands in the past decade. Its commercials with "the most interesting man in the world" are known around the world, have millions of YouTube hits, and have resulted in tons of parody skits, Halloween costumes, and jokes among friends. Knowing that it's important to build a strong community, and that they had a great advertising campaign, they began to build their community around this advertising campaign to let people talk about Dos Equis ads. They got all kinds of people to visit and engage with their Facebook community to see the latest ads, "like" the jokes, and post their own jokes about the ads. Many of these people didn't even like Dos Equis, or beer.

But even though Sam Adams doesn't have the word-of-mouth marketing that the Dos Equis community has—not as many people talk about Sam Adams—it formed a community to get people talking about the *right thing* to increase beer sales: their love for Sam

Adams. Sam Adams didn't have the clever commercials of Dos Equis. It didn't have engaging pictures or funny jokes like Dos Equis. All it had was a compelling story of being a microbrewing company with an old recipe for great beer—and a desire to selectively appeal to people who like beer for its taste. And that's what it leveraged to build in its Facebook community: Sam Adams Facebook fans tell stories of when they bought their beer, how good it tasted, and how they want more of it.

Take a look. On the Dos Equis page, you'll see people talking about the ads by saying things like "When he [the Senor] scores a touchdown, the opposing fans must resist the urge to cheer." You'll even see people denigrating the beer, like this one that takes the Senor's classic statement, "I don't always drink beer, but when I do I drink Dos Equis," and mocks it by turning it into "I don't always drink Dos Equis, but when I do, it's because my beverage choices were limited."

Dos Equis created a community based on talking about its *ads*. And sometimes getting people to talk about ads can actually backfire on the purpose of the ads—which is to get people to buy the beer. Although Dos Equis was correct in building a community because communities can be a powerful way to create lasting change in customer behavior, this was clearly not the effect it wanted to have on potential customers.

Compare that to the Sam Adams page, where the community is structured around the actual taste of the beer. Sam Adams fans are saying things like, "Cold Snap is the best beer. Period," and "I was just in the states and brought a bunch of SAMs home with me . . . can't get a good selection here in Canada." Sam Adams created a community around its *beer*.[*]

---

[*] I'm not saying that Dos Equis didn't do a good job of advertising. Sales of Dos Equis dramatically increased year over year as a result of the ads. But sales were still fewer than Sam Adams, who has grown consistently without rebranding or changing advertising. That is because it has a strong community.

When people express their love for Sam Adams beer, or post it on the Facebook page, they're building and reinforcing a community. When other Sam Adams fans join in the conversation and say that they like it, the strength of the community grows stronger. It makes Sam Adams's fans feel like they fit in with each other. It also makes it tough for them to stop liking Sam Adams.

The most active online meetup groups have been successful because they've built lasting communities. Take Marina Zdobnova, who got her MBA and moved from Boston to Los Angeles in 2012. She was looking for people to share ideas to form a start-up to make people happier and help promote personal development. She started a group on meetup.com called Santa Monica New Tech and opened it to the public.

Mostly through trial and error, Marina learned how to build a successful community. She started by paying out of pocket for things like free food, which got people to show up, but she later learned that if she offered them something more focused—like the opportunity to watch pitches from start-up companies, make new friends with a shared interest, and meet other entrepreneurs, users, and investors—members didn't need the free food and would even pay to attend events. Marina found that the largest growth started to occur once she had volunteers—peer leaders—who believed in the meetup and helped to market it and run meetings for her. Today Santa Monica New Tech is a self-sustainable 501c3 nonprofit with more than nine thousand members.[19] It is known in Los Angeles as a community where new start-ups are born. As one Santa Monica New Tech member said, "With mobile technology . . . people lose their interpersonal skills and opportunities to interact with others. Meetup groups like Santa Monica New Tech help to restore that lost element of human contact by drawing people together through a common purpose and interest. . . . I've met programmers who work remotely and never speak to a real person during their day job. I meet hardworking entrepreneurs who attend SMNT events to escape a lonely day at work. I meet people who are happy and fully employed who attend SMNT regularly as a way to help build their dream idea or be inspired or motivated by others. And I've met a vast number of people who are new to Los Angeles and want to make new friends. . . . The shared linkage is the energy and sense of hope and encouragement that people experience by going to SMNT meetup events. Seeing what their entrepreneur peers are doing and making new friends. So while there are business objectives that are fulfilled, I think there are personal needs that are met at the same time."[20]

Like our HOPE intervention, Santa Monica New Tech has learned how to use the science behind community to make lasting change in people's lives.

If you've tried to make a lasting change and failed, you might start to feel alone. Whether you've failed at limiting the number of sugary sweets you eat, failed to keep your new hobby of learning to cook, or failed at getting your employees to complete their work on time, you might start to feel alone and powerless over areas of your life. But you're not. One of the most profound things I've learned from studying social psychology over the years is that people are never alone. No matter how alone you might think you are when wrestling with the thoughts inside your head, there are many people who are having the exact same thoughts as you, at the same time.

We are all humans, and humans experience their thoughts and feelings in a similar way. For example, a person might feel embarrassed to have a stain on his shirt, a limp when she walks, or to have responded with what she thinks is a stupid answer to a question, but other people around don't notice because they have similar thoughts about themselves at the same time. A person might feel frustrated or depressed for failing to stick to a nutrition plan, but there are usually thousands, even millions of people around the world who are feeling the exact same way about the same problem. As humans, we share similar concerns, and similar psychological responses to those concerns. We all feel happy, sad, scared, and excited when we're put in similar situations.

This psychology can be leveraged for good. It can be used to help people feel more connected and empowered, and to help them achieve their goals. The growth and lasting success of groups like Alcoholics Anonymous, Weight Watchers, and fitness groups like CrossFit are a testament to the power of community. And our HOPE intervention studies have proven this scientifically. What do they offer to people? A sense of universality, a sense that you're not the only person who has walked down this road before, and a certain acceptance of yourself. That is how we've been able to grow them around the world and have built lasting communities. But communities aren't limited to just helping people feel more connected. If they incorporate the science of behavior change, they can become a powerful force to help people stick with change.

EXERCISE

Your exercise for this chapter is to join a community focused on something you want to change.

1. Go back to the behavior you said you wanted to change in Chapter 2. Got it?
2. Find a community you can join around this. If not an in-person one, then an online community.
3. Join it. Say you want to reduce your stress: you might join a gym with other people with the same goals.

4. Connect with other community members to create a social magnet—something that will keep you coming back. Contribute to the community, even if it's just to "like" a post someone made on an online community, or to say hi to someone at an in-person community, like a gym or hiking club. If you're feeling a little bolder and really want to build the social magnet, send a community member a private message or publicly ask the person a question.

5. As you talk to community members, notice how the comments from the other community members affect what you say and think. Notice how you begin to say things that you think will engage them. That's the power of the social magnet forming.

CHAPTER 4

IMPORTANT

D oris Levine Felner was my grandmother on my mother's side. She was a stereotypical New York Jewish *bubbe*. Born and raised in the shtetl of Brooklyn, Grandma Doris then moved to a Manhattan high-rise and lived there most of her life. Ultimately it was time to settle down in sunny Miami Beach.

My memories of Grandma Doris ranged from eating pastrami sandwiches in her Seacoast Towers apartment in Miami Beach; introducing her to In-N-Out Burger Double-Doubles when she visited us in California; taking a family road trip to Canada, where she hung her old-lady underwear to dry in the backseat; listening to her complaints about immigrants and the latest gossip about her daily soap operas during long phone calls between California and Florida; and always trying to push her politically incorrect buttons by telling her about my dating life. Despite her flaws (as every human has), I was always struck by one of her most admirable qualities: love for family.

Doris cared about family more than anything else in life. My mother was raised by her with the dual maxims "my family right or wrong" and "blood is thicker than water." Doris is the reason I am close to my cousins. She organized a yearly retreat in the Catskill Mountains so that the families of her three children could grow up knowing each other despite living, respectively, in California, New York and Maryland, and Georgia. She eagerly anticipated the several times a week she'd get the opportunity to talk to us via phone. She also helped raise one set of cousins after their mother (her daughter-in-law) passed away.

Grandma Doris was especially close to her youngest child, my aunt Meryl. From an early age, Meryl's asthma made my grandmother feel needed. Grandma Doris needed to feel needed. It gave her a reason to live.

Beatrice Young was my grandmother on my father's side. In a way, she was also a stereotypical New York Jewish grandmother, but almost a polar opposite of Doris: intellectual, cultured, and socially minded. Grandma Billie, as we called her, was also a born-and-bred New Yorker. When it was time to retire, she left New York and settled in Huntington Beach, California, near my family. I got to know her well. Despite not being as supportive a mother as my father would have preferred, Grandma Billie was passionate about something else that was very important: life.

Grandma Billie loved experiencing life to the fullest. She was a true intellectual and packed her days with pursuits that stimulated her brain. She corresponded with writers like J. D. Salinger, and frequently attended theater performances for plays like *Waiting for Godot* (in response to "How was the play, Grandma?" she joked that it was "a lot of waiting"). Bruckner, Mahler, and Bartok were always playing in the background in her home, which hosted a grand piano and walls filled with Marc Chagall paintings. She was also an ardent advocate of liberal ideals. She believed that everyone was entitled to a top education and should study or work in whatever field their hearts called them into. She believed that forcing artistic people to work commercial jobs stifled their creativity and could lead to mental illness, as she felt it did with her brother. She also had pushed progressive boundaries in her own life. Unlike most other women at that time, she kept an active dating life (she told me that she fell in love with my grandfather while they were on a date and he commented, "It's not enough that you're dating three other people while dating me; why do you have more men trying to meet you while we're on this date?!"). She also focused on getting into graduate school when other women were told to focus on taking care of their children. After graduating she first acted as a college counselor for high school students, then became an English professor at Hunter College.

Grandma Billie was also passionate about health and exercise. She played tennis every day with my grandfather, loved her routine of going for a swim first thing in the morning, and advised me that to get more exercise I should park as far away from places I was going as possible.

Billie's activities and interests kept her excited about life. She lived in an independent living senior citizen center with my grandfather, but she didn't socialize with the other seniors unless they enjoyed intellectual and fitness pursuits as ardently as she did. She told me she avoided the old people because they sat around complaining about their health (these "old people" were about twenty years younger than her). Her secret to life was 1) follow your passion, 2) exercise every day, 3) drink when you walk past a water fountain, and 4) always take the stairs instead of the elevator. When she moved to Huntington Beach she reduced her workload but never fully retired. Instead, she volunteered as a docent at a local art museum.

When Doris and Billie were around the same age, in their midseventies, they both suffered devastating losses. Doris lost her youngest daughter, Meryl. Billie lost her husband, my grandfather. Researchers have found that the way people respond to stressful life events can predict their health and longevity.[1][2] Doris and Billie responded to these tragic events in very different ways. They also had very different outcomes.

After my aunt Meryl died, Grandma Doris changed, literally overnight. She not only suffered emotionally from the loss of her daughter, but immediately began deteriorating physically. Her daily soap operas lost their allure. My mother visited her the day after Aunt Meryl's passing and discovered that Grandma Doris could no longer lift her feet to walk. Within two months, she required a wheelchair to get around. My mother would tell her to stop dragging her feet on the ground and start walking again. But it was no use. Grandma Doris began being plagued by a growing number of health problems. She started thinking she had Alzheimer's and a degenerative muscular disease. The fluid levels in her body became abnormal. Over the next two years, she was hospitalized numerous times and finally died by choking one tragic day in the hospital when no nurses were around to save her.

My grandma Billie had a very different response to her loss. She, too, was devastated. But instead of losing her ability to walk, she did the opposite: She walked, and walked, and walked. She walked the streets of Huntington Beach all day. She walked for days and weeks. She was in agony over her loss but wouldn't keep still. I remember her looking back on that time and telling me about her devastation and confusion. She didn't know how to cope with it. All she could do was continue doing what was most important to her, which was keeping herself fit and full of life. So she walked each day, walking until her feet became too calloused and painful to stand on. But she kept walking. Eventually, Grandma Billie returned to her passions in life. She went back to swimming every day. She returned to volunteering at the museum. She continued attending theater and musical performances. She ultimately passed away about twenty years later, at the age of ninety-seven, while doing what she loved to do: swimming.

What was it that caused Grandma Doris to pass away so quickly after her tragedy, while Grandma Billie was able to recover and live another twenty years? Was it genetics? Probably not. Grandma Doris's parents had lived well into their nineties, just like Grandma Billie's. Was it nutrition? Probably not that, either. Grandma Doris ate healthy food, just like Grandma Billie. So what caused the difference?

THE FORCE OF IMPORTANCE

If you've walked down the self-help aisle of a bookstore then you've probably noticed that a lot of people are trying to teach you how to be more motivated. The underlying idea, which seems obvious, is that if people are motivated to do something, they will probably do it. And if they aren't motivated, they probably won't. So self-help books and motivational gurus try to teach you to develop a *personality* that burns with motivation.

But suppose you don't have a personality like that? The good news is that people don't need to be born motivated to follow through with things. In fact, most research psychologists believe there's no such thing as a motivated personality. Instead, they say that people do things because of their *context*, by being in the right (or wrong) place at the right time. Your neighbor who gets up at 5 a.m. every day to run might seem like she was born a runner, but she probably has been surrounded by forces that make her want to keep exercising, like having parents, role models, friends, or romantic partners who make her feel good about exercising by doing it with her or telling her she looks great because of it.

How, then, do people become motivated to do things they might not want to do? One way is to incorporate the forces in the other chapters. As we showed in the last chapter, our HOPE *community* took people who didn't want to change and helped them make lasting changes. But community isn't the only reason people are motivated to change.

So, other than community, why else do people keep doing things? Because they think it's *important*.

Do you want to quit smoking? You'll have more success if stopping is *important* to you. If it is important, then tricks (like stepladders and communities) can help you cut down. If it's not important, then you probably won't stop. Telling smokers the "age of their lungs" has been found to increase long-term quit rates because the realization that you are forty-two but your lungs are sixty-two can be quite a shock. These smokers are quitting because the image of their smoke-related demise has suddenly been made tangible to them. It has become important.

The same goes for exercise. If you want to start a new routine, say getting on the rowing machine, you need to determine why it's more important to do that than what you're used to doing. For example, if you have limited time, is it more important for you to go on the rowing machine or to respond to work emails? Whichever is more important will have a big impact on what you choose to do.

That probably sounds obvious while you're reading it, but it's one of the most common mistakes people make when they're trying to change themselves, or others. They'd like to stop eating cookies but they keep doing it because tasting that cookie is more important than stopping. Or, from a business perspective, they'd like to get their customers to buy their product, but first they need

---

* If a person has a chemical or physical dependency, then change is especially tough. Seeing the importance in change is often not enough for people to have lasting change. Incorporating the other steps in this book will be needed and make it more likely the person can change.

to learn whether the customers need the product—if it's important to them. If the product doesn't solve an important need, then people will stop using it.

Fortunately, you don't have to guess what things are important to people and what things aren't. Researchers have come up with a long list of these topics. (I'll explain the top three below.) People differ on what they find important, so don't expect that all of the items on such a list will motivate yourself or others. But you only need one for it to work.

THE BIG THREE: MONEY, SOCIAL CONNECTIONS, AND HEALTH

So what are the things that researchers have found are important to people? The three top ones are money, social connections, and health.

Let's start with money. Most economists say that money is the single most important thing to people. It allows people to buy what they need and want, and makes them feel powerful and successful. Dollars (or pesos or pounds or euros) might just be made of paper, but they bring out strong emotions in people. Not just negative emotions but also positive, lasting emotions. The story of Oportunidades in Mexico is a good example.

In 1994, Mexican president Ernesto Zedillo faced an economic disaster in the making that also had far-reaching political ramifications: growing instability at home and abroad caused rapid devaluation of the Mexican peso. Called the "Mexican Shock," the decline was causing widespread panic among the Mexican people. People were in such dire straits they were going without food. President Zedillo, a trained economist, enlisted the support of two academic colleagues to address the accelerating degree of poverty throughout the country. One was a fellow economist named Santiago Levy. The other was a demographer, José Gómez de León.

Together, the team designed a social program that differed radically from previous ones.[3] Instead of giving out food stamps, they handed out cash. But they attached two critical strings to the money. First, households receiving cash would have to use public medical clinics for health care, not private doctors, and this would have to be verified by the public health clinics. Second, the cash would only be given to women. Levy and Gómez de León felt that women, rather than men, would be more likely to use the money to feed their families and keep their children healthy.

The Mexican cabinet fiercely objected to the plan. They felt that giving people cash would increase alcohol and drug use. They also thought that giving cash to women would encourage domestic violence. Sensing that the cabinet would intervene, the president and his team acted quickly and quietly. Without issuing a press release, they tested the policy in the state of Campeche. They wanted to know whether the program would work, or whether the cabinet's concerns were valid.[4]

They weren't. The program worked. The thirty-one thousand people in Campeche who received cash did not use it for drugs or alcohol, but for food, and to get medical care. The pilot was enough to convince the Mexican government to scale the program up.

The official government program, initially named Progresa, began in 1997.[5] Approximately ten times larger than the pilot, it reached more than three hundred thousand people. It also differed from the pilot in several significant ways. This time the cash was given to women only if their children attended primary and secondary school. The amount of money also increased as the kids got older. Families still had to use public health and medical facilities, but preventive care was emphasized. Finally, women had to prove that their families were eating healthy food, rather than spending the money on products that were low in nutrition.

Ultimately, the program broadened to reach more than five million people—to almost everyone who was living in extreme poverty in Mexico. Even then, more than 72 percent of the money given to women was spent on food. Families ate more fruits and vegetables than before. Fewer infants were malnourished. Educational enrollment increased. There was a dramatic increase in medical visits, and there was a more than 10 percent drop in incidents of childhood disease. Most important, these changes *stuck*. Households that kept participating continued to spend the money on food. The program still exists in Mexico today. What's the lesson here? That cash made the changes *important enough* so that people radically changed their behaviors. Cash *motivated* them when food stamps didn't.

I'm not saying that cash will do that for everybody. Money can even backfire and stop people from doing things. In fact, researchers have found something that is an even bigger motivator than money.

Here's a question I ask my students. Imagine you are given the following choices: You can either have an endless supply of money throughout your life but never any close relationships, or you can possess a small amount of money but enjoy strong, meaningful relationships with others. Which would you choose?

If you're like my students, then you probably think the answer is obvious. But it's not obvious. There are a lot of readers who would make the opposite choice from yours. (In fact, my students exhibited an interesting effect in psychology. Even though they differed in what their answers were, each of them thought their answer was the "obvious" one.)

People differ in what's important to them. These differences are caused by factors too numerous to list here. The way they were raised. The country they were born in. Their age. But two things are clear when you study the research. First, money isn't as important for happiness as people think. Second, social relationships are *more* important than they realize.

In the 1930s, a team of Harvard researchers began a study that tracked the life choices of a group of Harvard undergraduates. They continued this study for seventy-five years. One thing they found was that strong social connections were the most important factor in achieving happiness.[6]

Evidence for this shows up in our brains. The brain responds to social connections in a similar way to how it responds to the pleasantness of being warm. Researchers found this by asking people to sit in an MRI brain scanner while they read messages written by friends and family that were either kindhearted (warm) messages, like "I love you more than anything in the world," or neutral messages like "You have curly hair."[7] While reading, people were asked to hold two objects for ten seconds, first a warm pack and then a room temperature ball, or vice versa. They measured people's brain responses during these activities and then asked them how warm they felt while reading the messages and how socially connected they felt during each task. What did they find? They learned that there is truth to the metaphorical expression *heartwarming*: people actually felt warmer after reading the kind messages compared to the neutral messages, and felt more socially connected after holding the warm pack compared to the ball. They also found similar activity in the brain during these two "warm" activities. To the brain, physical warmth is similar to emotional warmth.

And social rejection has the exact opposite effect: the brain responds to it as it does to pain. Social neuroscientist Matt Lieberman (my undergraduate advisor at UCLA and a wonderful teacher) is an expert on this topic. The study lead, his wife, Naomi Eisenberger, had people play a virtual game called Cyberball while sitting in a brainwave scanner. Here's how Cyberball works. Players start by passing the ball between themselves and two virtual humans, or avatars. After a certain point, however, the two avatars stop passing the ball to the research participant. They ignore him or her while continuing to pass the ball between themselves.

You can imagine how the player might feel. Snubbed. Rejected. Like not being chosen for kickball. Or being kicked off the debate team. And that's what the researchers found. The same part of the brain lit up on the scanner when the avatars stopped passing the ball (when they socially rejected the subject) as when the person experienced physical pain.[8] They also found that the people who were the most saddened by the rejection had the greatest reaction in the pain regions of the brain.

How did they address this pain? Suppose he used a common pain reliever like Tylenol to relieve the pain of social rejection. It sounds crazy to think that a painkiller could alleviate the signs of sadness in the brain, but that's what happened. People who took Tylenol before they played the game showed less sadness in their brain scans.[9]

The point is, social connections are really important to people. Social relationships make people happy. They're sometimes even more important than money in getting people to keep doing things. That's the reason why the HOPE intervention and the force of communities are such powerful tools for change. They work because it's important for people to feel connected to others.

Take television show traditions. For more than fifty years, Saturday afternoon has been the most popular time for watching television in the Western Hemisphere, and not because of college football. In 1962, Chilean-born Don Francisco was living in the United States and learning about American television. He knew that it was important for Latin Americans to participate in group activities on Saturdays. They were social people, loved drama, and were used to socializing in each other's homes on Saturdays. While American families had grown accustomed to sitting around watching shows like *Gunsmoke* and *What's My Line?*, Latin Americans, who were culturally even more social, didn't have a show to bring them together. To address this important need, Francisco created the variety show *Sábado Gigante*.[10] For more than fifty years, it has been the most popular show in the Western Hemisphere.

Personal health is also important to people and can be used to motivate lasting change. If you are very sick or dying, getting promoted to vice president of your group doesn't matter much. But if you feel that you can improve your health through certain actions, those are the things you will do. A lot of books, technologies, and remedies falsely promise they'll improve a sufferer's health. Unfortunately, such promises are so attractive that some people cannot help but keep attempting to follow the advice, try the diets, and buy the products being promoted. In such cases, the force of importance sometimes leads us to make wrong decisions.

Money, social relationships, and personal health become important at an early age. They continue to be important to most people throughout their lives. That's why health and social relationships are good at motivating people to keep doing things. Money can incentivize a stockbroker to find new clients every month. The need for social connection can motivate romantic partners to stick together for years despite occasional arguments. The promise of health entices people to keep buying dietary supplements throughout their lives. We learn about social relationships and healthy choices early in life.

But does that mean people can't find new important things that will lead to change later on?

WHEN SOMETHING BECOMES IMPORTANT

For the past five years, nothing has been more important to Suzanne Crotty than preventing prescription drug abuse.[11] She writes a blog on the topic, is working on a book about it, and lobbies politicians to pass overdose prevention legislation. Her achievements include helping to pass the I-STOP Act, a program that requires the use of electronic medication prescriptions so that drugs can be tracked. Suzanne spends so much time trying to prevent prescription drug abuse that you'd think she was an addiction medicine physician, nurse, or other public health worker. But she's not. Far from it. She works in real estate. Why, then, has Suzanne spent the last five years of her life trying to do something that has nothing to do with her work? Because it became important to her.

When Suzanne went through some of her old family photos, she started to cry, remembering the Mother's Day cards and necklaces that her son gave her. Her son, Zach Crotty, died in 2009 of an opioid overdose at the age of nineteen.

Zach started using drugs when he was fourteen. He began by smoking marijuana with friends to relieve anxiety, but marijuana wasn't enough to satisfy him. He and his friends started stealing prescription pills like morphine and oxycodone from relatives. By the time Zach was sixteen, he was heavily addicted to opioids but could no longer get enough prescription drugs to satisfy his addiction. He started doing anything he could get his hands on, like cocaine, crack, and heroin. All this time, he was seeing a psychiatrist who gave him psychotropic medication for his anxiety. He was also going to an addiction medicine doctor who gave him Suboxone for his opioid addiction. But ultimately, the methadone he procured illegally from an older woman with a prescription killed him.

Zach had known he needed help. He wanted to stop. He also

wanted to help prevent others from experiencing similar addictions. He kept a diary of his thoughts and feelings. Here's one excerpt:

> I want to go through college. I want to have a kid, and you can't properly raise a kid when all your money goes to drugs, and you sure can't properly love a kid when all your love goes to drugs. . . . Not quite a role model. More of an example. So learn from me.

Suzanne found the diary shortly after Zach's death and was devastated by his suffering. But instead of letting his death destroy her life, she took Zach's writing and used it to spread his message. As difficult as it was for her to share the most personal experiences in her and her son's life, she began publishing Zach's journal entries on a blog at zacharycrottystory.blogspot.com. Even though her work to prevent drug abuse is a constant reminder of her sadness, the importance of it motivates her to keep doing it. Knowing that she can commemorate and memorialize her son by preventing opioid abuse in others, she finds solace.

Suzanne's story shows that life can lead people to reevaluate what is important in their lives. Life leads people to new motivations, and new reasons for doing things. Even tragic events can lead to happiness and well-being if we learn to focus on what is truly important.

A participant in one of our studies, Elizabeth Thomas, lived a life of pain but, like Suzanne, learned to cope with her tragedy by focusing on what was truly important to her. "I have something called systemic scleroderma as well as type 1 diabetes—that along with all of the secondary syndromes that follow those. ☺ I cannot work, I'm 33 almost 34 and haven't accomplished much in life. . . . There is no cure for my disease, and I don't 'fit' into any of the studies out right now to improve my quality of life. All of this seems quite dark and sad, but I can't help but be happy. I see myself as lucky in this world.

IMPORTANT

My life could be so much worse. I credit a lot of my happiness to the fact that I got sick so early in life. I grew up going to the doctors and being poked and prodded, it's my lifestyle, I wasn't bombarded with it at an age where it completely wrecked my life. . . . I've survived an insane amount of time, considering my diagnosis, and for that I have to be happy. Plus, there isn't a lot of energy in this life I live, so I find it better to conserve what I can. Being happy is much easier than being sad or angry. It's a coping thing I guess. ☺" [12]

Suzanne's and Elizabeth's stories are dramatic examples of how people make lasting changes in their lives if things are important to them. But fortunately, life events don't have to be tragic to lead people to lasting changes. There are much more mundane things in life that are still important enough to keep people doing things, like studying to get good grades, making time for friends, and keeping good oral hygiene.

Take William Addis of England. Back in 1770, he incited a riot in London and got tossed in jail. While in jail, he had a tough time keeping up with his personal oral hygiene. Fortunately, he had a lot of free time to think. He realized that prisoners weren't the only ones in England having trouble taking care of their teeth. If you think British people have bad teeth now, you should have seen people's teeth then. At the time, people would simply take a rag, put soot and salt on it, and rub it on their teeth. William didn't need four out of five dentists to tell him this wasn't the most effective way to clean teeth. But what else could he do?

He had an idea. He saved an animal bone from his meal one night and drilled some holes in it. He then talked a guard into giving him some bristles made from boar's hair. He sewed the bristles through the holes in the bone, making the bristles stick straight up. His invention? It was a way to "brush" his teeth. But when he left prison, he didn't keep this idea to himself. He knew other people would agree to the importance of dental hygiene, and so he built a company to manufacture these devices, creating the world's first mass-produced toothbrushes. His time in jail made him very rich, but it also created a new behavior that has lasted for centuries. His company, Wisdom Toothbrushes, continues to operate today. It sells more than 70 million toothbrushes each year in the United Kingdom alone.[13]

Not everyone can sell a bone with bristles to the general public and get rich from it. William Addis must have been a good salesperson in addition to inventor. But that raises the question: How do you make something important to people if it's not something they're naturally interested in?

There are few products that are harder to sell than life insurance. First, you have to talk to people about death. Most people don't want to do that, and they really don't want to shell out cash after having a depressing conversation about when they expect to die. Life insurance is also a tough sell because you have to get people to plan for their future when most people want immediate gratification.[14] That's one reason why only about half of Americans have enough savings to cover their credit card debts and about half have less than three months' worth of savings.[15] But even among more affluent people, it's still tough to sell life insurance. Why would people buy life insurance? They don't get any pleasure from buying it. They won't get pleasure in the future because they'll be dead. The cards are heavily stacked against the life insurance agent.

Challenge accepted. A few years ago I decided to tackle this problem head-on. I wanted to learn how people perceived risk. I also wanted to learn whether people could be convinced of the importance of something that was toward the bottom of their list of priorities. And I wanted to be the first academic professor that I knew to become a life insurance agent.

Turns out, I didn't do too badly. Within three months I was the top-selling agent in the company's West Coast region. How did I get them to keep paying money each month into something that they didn't (initially) think was important? In my case, I had both the force of importance, as well as some plain luck on my side. I told my friends about it and they quickly agreed it was an important investment. I only pitched them on the two products I believed in and had bought myself—which were designed as investments more than insurance—and they agreed that these products were valuable. I was successful selling these two products because I believed in them—they were important to me so I wanted to tell others about them—and because I was lucky to have friends with money and who trusted me. A few of my friends who invested had a lot of money to give and that, along with the fact that I was working for a small to midsize company, made me the top-selling agent.

But more than luck is needed to make a career as a life insurance agent. I went into insurance to learn about sales and risk more than I did to become a career agent, so I can't speak based on my experience as to what gets people to keep buying insurance. That's why I asked thirty-year veteran salesman and trainer Tom Pugmire what his secret to success has been over the past thirty years. Tom started selling insurance when he was twenty-eight years old. In his first year he was the top-selling agent in the company and was promoted to national sales director. He soon left to launch his own company, which became one of the top ten life insurance brokerages in the country from 1991 until he sold it in 2000. He then returned as an insurance agent and coach, and has been the top-selling agent in his company for nine of the last ten years.

Tom's success in sales has less to do with selling the product than with selling himself. Just like some of the most successful political campaigns and organizational leaders, Tom appeals to people's emotions, rather than their intellect. When something is important to people, they feel it. They have a need to follow through with it. That's how Tom is successful in getting customers to see the importance of his products: because he makes them *feel* the importance of the products. He gets them to emotionally connect with him and the products by doing a few things.[16] First, he gets clients to believe in him by showing them that he's one of the biggest customers of the product he's selling. "If I don't get them to believe in me, how do I get them to believe in a product I'm selling?" He said he can't convincingly advocate that people invest in something if he doesn't believe in it himself, so he shows them, "I've got two on me, two on my wife, and two on my son, my daughter-in-law, my son, my grandkids . . . here are all the policies. I've got 12 of them." This gets most clients to *feel* they can trust Tom when he says this is a good product.

He also tells customers stories about common mistakes people have made in planning for their retirement. These factual but dramatic stories resonate with many customers and get them to feel the need for having the product. One story he tells is about a woman who invested in a retirement plan her whole life and was ready to use this money to retire in 2008, but because of the stock market crash that year she lost half of the account value and had to wait for years to get it back. He also tells a story about a man who invested in a 401(k) plan through his work. The account accrued over a million dollars. But when it came time for him to withdraw the funds at retirement, the man learned that after taxes he was left with barely half of it. These stories emotionally resonate with people. They teach them that their assumptions about retirement funds are incorrect and that they need to plan for their retirement differently. Tom then teaches them about financial products that can prevent these types of problems by allowing people to have guaranteed tax-free returns each year. By that point, customers are ready to see the importance of these products.

Tom also keeps the product message simple: "How would you like the opportunity to make double-digit returns with no market risk, and it's free from federal and state taxes?" He said that much of his success is based on his background in education, which taught him the value of teachers and how to communicate with people from all educational backgrounds, like staff, teachers, principals, and school board administrators. Just as teachers are able to create an emotional experience with students and leave a positive mark on them, Tom sees a successful encounter with a client as one where he has created an emotional experience by teaching them something they wanted to learn. "Most [agents] try to impress others with how smart they are. They usually overcomplicate things and over talk about their knowledge and ability. The client doesn't care about their knowledge and ability. They care about the product. I'm able to take complicated concepts and explain it in a way that people understand. And when it's very complicated and something they don't know, you know why they love me, because at the end of the day the light goes on and they say 'You know what. I get it.' And that person likes me a whole lot more than the one I impressed with all my knowledge."

But just getting someone to understand and feel that something is important isn't enough to get them to stick with it. What's important to someone now might not be important to them tomorrow or next year. For most insurance products to work, people need not just to feel it's important now and pay into it once, but to keep paying for many years.

How does Tom get clients to keep paying into it? Once clients are interested, Tom uses stepladders (along with a number of other forces we'll discuss later). To find out how much they can afford to invest, he asks them how much they could afford to lose from their monthly income without hurting their lifestyle. Knowing that people usually offer to give more than they can afford—they're focused on the dream of making a lot of money from the investment, rather than the step of what it will take to make their first payment—he advises they invest less than they think they can afford so that they don't feel trapped making payments. "If people aren't happy doing what they planned to do, then they'll stop doing it." He tells them to save that extra money in the bank and check in with him later in the year; if they still have the money in their account and want to invest it then they can add more. When he follows up with them later in the year, most clients have spent the money. But this process of starting with a small investment is what gets clients to keep paying for the policy each year and keeps them trusting and coming back to Tom.

Psychologists have designed scientific "interventions" to motivate people to keep doing things. For example, Hal Hershfield studied how to make something important to someone who is not interested. He came up with some interesting findings: people have a tough time making long-term changes for things where the reward is far in the future. But with a simple exercise, he was able to change this.

Remember the ghost of Christmas future from Dickens's *A Christmas Carol*? That ghost convinced the terrible Scrooge to change his current behavior. Hal tried using this "ghost intervention" to change people's long-term behaviors. He and his research team gave people a retirement savings tool to determine how much money they should allocate each year to retirement. Everyone saw a picture of themselves while they were deciding. But while some of the people saw a picture of themselves at their current age, others saw a picture of themselves that had been morphed to make them look older. People who made their retirement decisions while seeing the older version of themselves put aside more money for retirement. It makes sense. In fact, Merrill Lynch is now using this idea on its website.[17]

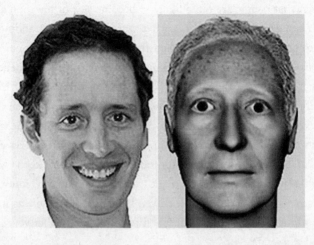

Figure 5. The Future Self-Intervention (Hal, current and future). Photo courtesy of Hal Hershfield.

Hal is highly sought after by insurance and financial services companies to help them sell their more difficult-to-market products. But his work doesn't just apply to those areas. The future-self intervention could get people to change dietary patterns, exercise routines, and work routines because of its ability to make things important to people that otherwise would not be. Seeing a future (thin) self could get people to put down that cookie in favor of a healthier option. It could get people to get off the couch and go for a run. People reminded of their future selves (the ones who get bonus paychecks) could be more likely to stay focused at work. The future-self intervention shows that people can change their behaviors even if the rewards are far away. So what should you do? Visit the ghost of your future self.

Before we end the chapter, I want to return to the earlier Grandma and Grandma story. It's well documented in research that people are more likely to become sick or die soon after their spouse passes away.[18] But what caused one of my grandmothers to pass before the other when they both lost a loved one? We discussed that it probably wasn't genetics or nutrition. My belief is that it's because different things were important to each of them in life. While family was the most important thing to Grandma Doris, I think living life—and keeping her hobbies—was the most important thing to Grandma Billie. There are no proven psychological tests to measure how important it is for people to keep trying to live after they experience a tragic event. I therefore can't know for certain that my grandma Billie lived longer because life was more important to her, but here are my final thoughts on that very personal story.

I questioned why my grandma Doris would have passed so quickly after her loss, while my other grandma lived so much longer. Although Doris had a lot to live for, I don't think she saw it that way. I think she felt alone. Her husband had passed away long before, leaving her with her three children and seven grandchildren. When the youngest of her children (the one who relied on her the most) passed away, I think she stopped feeling needed. Her other two children and her grandchildren lived farther away and didn't see her frequently. Her day-to-day hobbies, watching television or sitting by the pool, weren't enough for her to keep going.

As for Grandma Billie, I was fortunate enough to spend a lot of time with her. I got to know her life story. When we would have lunch I would sometimes interview her, recording her stories. Here's what I learned about her, and it makes me think that she survived simply because she felt it was important to keep living.

IMPORTANT

1. She told me that after my grandfather died she felt devastated. With no answers to her suffering she decided to walk for miles and miles.

2. She looked around her community, and saw the seniors playing board games day after day. She'd be damned, she said to herself (and to me), if she was going to sit around playing mahjong for the rest of her days.

3. She told me that her secrets to life were to park far away from your destination—so you have to walk; to always take the stairs instead of the elevator; to drink from water fountains when you passed them; and most important, to always do what you love to do.

4. She loved to recite quotes from the Dylan Thomas poem "Do Not Go Gentle into That Good Night."

5. She continued being an art docent and actively participated in book clubs. When we got together, she couldn't stop talking to me about the latest book she was reading or a painting she had recently seen.

6. She loved to swim every day, and always talked about it. She ultimately died at ninety-seven years old. She was found in a swimming pool, doing what she loved.

I've learned to use the lesson of Grandma and Grandma as a reminder to keep my life focused on things that are important to me—including my work and hobbies, spiritual connection with loved ones who have passed away, and most important, relationships with my loved ones who are still living today.

Focusing on what is important keeps me excited about living and doing things. I hope you'll find that it helps you, too.

Even though this chapter mentions death, it's not meant to be depressing. Rather, I wanted to use a theme that would be important to everyone. I chose these examples because avoiding death is pretty high up there in importance for most people. If you watched *Seinfeld* you might remember Jerry saying that death is the second-scariest thing. What's the first? Public speaking.[19]

C onventional wisdom says there are "motivated people" and others who are, well, "lazy." If you've been unable to stick with things you want to change, like going to bed early or going out more frequently to social events, then conventional wisdom says you've failed because you're lazy. That's a pretty sad view of others, and for people to have of themselves and the world.

Fortunately, scientific research shows that it's wrong. You're not doomed to failure if you haven't been able to stick to things in the past. The problem might have been that you didn't see the importance of doing it. But that's in the past. That doesn't mean you're unable to see the importance of it, just that you need a more important reason to change. You need to figure out how to make something important enough to you that you're willing to change for it. Would you do it for better health, for more money, to become closer to family or friends? Once you find what is truly important, you can use the other forces in this book to leverage the force of importance and you will be able to stick with your goal.

EXERCISE

1. Choose two things to do this week that involve a change to your usual routine. One of these actions should be very important to you. (Earn more money. Get in touch with a friend.) The other should be less important. (Floss your teeth. Do the dishes right after dinner.)
2. Make an effort to do both these things throughout the week.

IMPORTANT

3. Notice how much easier it is to keep doing the activity that is more important to you.

4. Now mix things up a little to make it more interesting: Make the less important activity more important. How might you do that? We've already discussed two possible techniques you can use: join a community (as we learned in Chapter 3) or use the ghost of the future to either motivate or scare you into making something more important.

   We'll also be learning another way to make things important in the next chapter, "Easy."

CHAPTER 5

EASY

When he graduated from the Stanford Graduate School of Business, Joseph Coulombe thought the road to success would be an easy one. His first few years working at the grocery chain Owl-Rexall were smooth. He was so successful that Owl-Rexall asked him to take over managing a new chain of stores called Pronto. But then things turned south. Pronto was struggling and Coulombe was told to sell it. But instead, Joseph sold his own home and used the money to buy the stores himself in an attempt to rescue them.[1]

The problem was that a fast-growing competitor, 7-Eleven, was devouring the market for convenience stores. 7-Eleven had already developed a recognizable brand, offered just about every product that people could want when they didn't have the time to go to the conventional grocery—or liquor—store, and was open at unprecedented hours for those days, from 7 a.m. to 11 p.m.[2] How could Joseph possibly compete? To recover his investment and save Pronto, he had to address a familiar sales and marketing problem: How could he get people to routinely patronize Pronto stores? Or more broadly, how could he change customer behavior and make it last? Joe didn't know what to do—so he took a vacation. He went to the land of calypso music, rum cocktails, and easy living—the Caribbean. And it was there that he found his answer.

Life in the Caribbean was easy. It was easy to think, easy to drink, and easy to make decisions. There was one restaurant within walking distance from his hotel, drinking alcohol on the island was practically mandatory, and the Hawaiian-shirted waiters were friendly and happy to direct him to the limited list of places to visit as a sightseer.

Joseph realized that it was this lifestyle that he needed to bring to his stores. The Caribbean tourist industry was designed to give visitors what they needed to be happy. People weren't coming to the Caribbean to work. They were coming to the Caribbean to stop working, and the Caribbean made it easy to do that. What could Joe do to bring this lifestyle back to his convenience stores?

How about getting rid of a bunch of products?

Joe realized he needed to make it easy for his customers to purchase what they wanted without having to think. While other stores were trying to cater to the *desires* of their customers by offering a wide and extensive selection of products, Joseph decided to limit his stores by including a small and targeted selection. While other stores were stocked with all types of drinks, Joseph's stores would have a small number of high-quality ones and would feature the selection to attract the wine-loving academic community living in nearby Pasadena. With this new plan, Joseph rebranded the Pronto stores, calling them Trader Joe's.

His strategy worked. Trader Joe's changed the way people shop and where they shop. Giving people a limited number of choices made it easy for customers to purchase products at Trader Joe's and to continue coming back. Instead of ten kinds of granola to choose from, customers see just one: Trader Joe's own brand. Instead of five kinds of butter it has one. Ditto peanut butter, tortilla chips, pasta, and spices. Even its toilet paper is Trader Joe's branded. This strategy enabled Trader Joe's to create changes in customer behavior that have lasted more than forty-five years. It formed the brand as it is today.

Here's how Trader Joe's is different: whereas grocery stores today typically carry 50,000 stock keeping units (SKUs), Trader Joe's makes it easy for its customers by offering about one-tenth of that selection (or 4,000 SKUs). Yet TJ's sells more than double the merchandise per square foot than its biggest competitor, Whole Foods.[3][4] Trader Joe's has been written down in history as a company that created lasting changes in customer behavior. And so now when you shop at TJ's, the flowered shirts of TJ's employees will remind you it was all inspired by Joe's trip to the Caribbean.

THE PSYCHOLOGY BEHIND EASY

People want things to be easy for them to do. They enjoy things that are easy for them to do. And they'll keep doing things that are easy to do.

When I was in high school, I used to tutor elementary and middle school kids. On an almost daily basis, I'd have the same conversation with my students.

"What subject should we work on today?" I'd ask.

"History!" was the response I'd get from a student.

"Okay, before we start. Tell me how you did on your math and history tests last week," I'd say.

A typical answer from a seventh grader pulling out his history book: "Well, I aced my history test, but my teacher said I'm failing math."

Students wanted to study subjects that were easy for them to study, and it was easy to get them to keep studying things that were already easy for them. Grown-ups are not much different. Most people want to keep learning languages that are easy for them to speak, keep working at jobs that are easy for them to do, and keep managing employees who are easy to manage.

There's a lot of science supporting this fact. It's based on the idea that competing forces are constantly driving people to do different things. Should you go for a run or have a glass of wine instead? Should I keep writing this chapter or answer the phone and talk to a friend? Forces like these are constantly pushing and pulling at people. The easier it is for the person to do something, the stronger the force will be for that person to do it. People will be driven to do (and keep doing) things that are easy.

Have you ever been driving when construction workers or police start to close one of the lanes? What happens? As soon as the construction person lays the cones down in that far left lane, everyone puts on their turn signals and moves to the right open lanes. Traffic backs up, people start cutting each other off, and you'll hear a lot of cussing and "Dude! WTF!" (At least that's what happens in Southern California.) As soon as the construction workers remove the cones, people charge back into the left lane and the traffic goes away.

This is the psychology behind Easy: Navigating through the barriers and driving on a closed traffic lane is like trying to study for a math test after failing math. It's difficult to do. When barriers are in front of people, they quickly stop doing something. The flip side of that is, if you learn how to remove barriers, you'll easily be able to keep doing things.

There are three main areas of science on how to make things easy. You can control the environment, limit choices, or use a road map. These ideas all have to do with removing barriers and making things easier, but each of them requires a slightly different psychology, so I separate them into categories below.

CONTROL THE ENVIRONMENT

Small changes in your environment can lead to big changes in behavior. In one study, more than one thousand smokers who wanted to quit were tracked for six months to see what strategies would be successful for them. The researchers found that the most effective methods for quitting were removing all tobacco products from the house (making it easy to quit) and choosing a specific date to quit (Stepladders).[5]

Changing people's environments to make it easier for them to do something will get them to do those things. People who live in neighborhoods with more liquor stores drink more alcohol than people who live in neighborhoods with fewer liquor stores.[6] People who live near marijuana dispensaries or delivery services consume more marijuana than people who don't.[7]

People can even keep doing "evil" things if it's easy for them to do those things (or difficult to not do those things). In the famous Milgram psychology studies, people were invited to participate in a study in the basement of a building at Yale University. When they arrived, they were introduced to two other individuals. One was the experimenter, and the other was introduced as another study participant. Unbeknownst to the participant, however, the other participant was actually a "confederate" working for the study. Both the study participant and the confederate were then asked to draw slips of papers that would describe their role in the study, either as "a teacher" or "a learner." The study was rigged so that the participant would always draw the slip saying he or she was the teacher. The professor running the experiment would walk both students to a room where the confederate was strapped up to electrodes. The participant was then taken back to the main room, leaving the confederate alone. The participant, who couldn't see the confederate in the side room, was instructed by the professor to call out questions to the confederate. When the confederate answered incorrectly, the professor ordered the participant to administer a shock. Each time the confederate responded to a question incorrectly, the professor instructed the participant to increase the shock. A prerecorded audio would play each time the participant "shocked" the confederate. The participant would push the button and hear a scream of intense pain, then hear the confederate begging to please stop. The screams increased in intensity with each increasing shock, until ultimately, they stopped. The participant was led to believe the learner may have died from the shocks.

The purpose of the study? To see how far people would go in torturing others.

The findings of the study were astounding: although almost all participants were uncomfortable administering the shocks, and many participants showed tremendous distress (three of them experienced full-blown seizures), 65 percent of participants continued to keep shocking the confederate until they believed the confederate had died.[8] What was it that made them keep going?

The answer is that the professor running the experiment made it difficult for the participant to stop. As absurd as that sounds, people shocked each other because it was easier to shock than to protest. That's how powerful the force of Easy is in getting people to keep doing things. If at any point the participant would refuse to shock the confederate, the professor, wearing a lab coat, would say this series of replies to the objections:

1. Please *continue*.
2. The experiment requires that you *continue*.

3. It is absolutely essential that you *continue*.

4. You have no other choice, you *must* go on.

The experimenter even told the participant that he would take the blame instead of the participant in case anything happened to the confederate. By creating an environment where it was not easy for the participant to disagree, researchers learned that people can be led to do almost anything.

In follow-up studies, scientists changed different variables, like locating the experimenter in another room instead of standing over the participant, and having the participant see another "participant"—actually yet another confederate—refuse to shock the victim. By changing these variables and making it easier for the participant to refuse to continue, rates of shocking the learner dramatically dropped.[9] [10]

One of the most classic studies on this topic in social psychology looked at how people form and maintain friendships. The researchers asked students at the Massachusetts Institute of Technology who were living in a complex of seventeen two-story buildings to name their three closest friends in the complex (the study was later named the Westgate studies because the complex was named Westgate). They found that 65 percent of people's friends lived in the same building as they did. The most common friends were next-door neighbors, people living two doors down, or people living across the hall.[11]

The researchers didn't discover this effect because MIT students are lazy; they found it because "Easy" is a core aspect of human psychology. People choose to form and maintain friendships that are easy. In Los Angeles, for example, we have the 405 freeway, which effectively separates West Los Angeles from the rest of the city. It's an almost universally accepted phenomenon that if you live east or west of the 405 and move to the other side, you're not going to see your friends again in your lifetime (or at least not for a long time).

This effect doesn't just hold up for friendships. I've been to a lot of weddings recently and keep hearing stories about how my friends met their romantic partners. There's always a need at weddings to have an exciting story of how the couple met each other. While it's nice to believe that romantic partners are chosen because they're meant for each other, science paints a more practical picture. A study by Match.com showcased the familiar statistic from their ads that one in five people in relationships meet online, but that same study also found that more than one in three people met at work or school, places that are easy to meet others in because people already spend most of their time there.[12]

But just because people are choosing partners who are easy to meet doesn't mean that it can't still be romantic. I went to a wedding recently of my friend Chaya. He met his wife through a Cinderella story by finding her sock and returning it to her. How'd he get her sock? She was living in the same building and had left her sock in the laundry machine. She was an easy catch.

LIMIT CHOICES

Speaking of meeting romantic partners, do you ever wonder why, despite all these technologies making it (supposedly) easier to meet people, the age of getting married keeps increasing? With all the ways you can quickly swipe, click, or Grindr your perfect match, wouldn't you think people would have more success finding their true loves?

One reason is that people have too many choices.[13] The science of "choice paralysis" isn't limited to romantic partners, though. It also explains why people find it tough to do almost anything in life, whether it's going for a run, going to sleep early, or calling grandma to say hi.

In one study, researchers took over an aisle of a grocery store in Menlo Park, California, to offer customers samples of jams along with coupons to purchase a full jar of the ones they liked.[14] The researchers wanted to see whether the number of choices people had would affect their interest in the jam, and likelihood of purchasing it. They set up an experiment over the course of two Sundays in which they offered customers a choice of either six or twenty-four different jams. They found that customers who were offered fewer choices (six instead of twenty-four) were more interested in the jams and more likely to purchase them. The researchers ran a similar study where they offered participants a sample from a group of either six or thirty different chocolates. Participants were then paid for their time (not a bad study to get paid for eating chocolate) and told they could receive their pay in money or chocolates. Those who had been offered samples from the group of six chocolates were more likely to choose chocolate over money compared to those who had seen thirty different chocolates.

People bought jams or chocolates when they had fewer choices because it's tough making choices. When you give people a smaller number of choices, it becomes easier for them to make a decision to do something, and to keep doing it. Although people think they want to have a lot of choices, too many choices actually makes it tough for people to do things. Researchers continue running studies on this effect. For example, people are more likely to participate in a 401(k) plan if they have only a handful of plan choices compared to ten or more plan choices.[15]

CREATE A ROAD MAP

As you know from Chapter 2, having a plan of steps can help people keep doing things. A road map or plan is helpful because it makes it easier for people so that they don't have to think about how to get from point A to B.

Take entrepreneurship. Getting a start-up off the ground is a daunting experience. A lot of entrepreneurs give up along the way. A common emotion I hear among many cofounders is the experience of feeling frustrated and lost. Not surprisingly, having a clear road map and plan can help start-ups stay on track. There's a classic psychology/public health study that illustrates this concept.

Students at Yale University (as if those poor students didn't suffer enough trauma from the Milgram shock study) were contacted and invited to help evaluate a public health pamphlet. When they came into the study room, they were provided with a booklet describing tetanus and suggesting that students get inoculated for it. However, about half of the students also read detailed instructions including a map of the health clinic, a list of available times to get the shot, and a request to access their weekly schedules to find a convenient appointment time.

This additional text was an action plan, or a road map, of how and when students could get their tetanus shot. The other half of students did not see this additional text. Students then completed some questions about their experience reading the pamphlet and left. The researchers followed up with the university health clinic to determine whether students in the study had gotten tetanus shots.

Although all students knew the location of the health clinic and could have scheduled an appointment, students who saw the action plan were more likely to get a tetanus shot than were those who didn't see it.[16] This effect generalizes to more than students getting tetanus shots: having an action plan makes it easier (and more likely) that people will do *anything*. People choosing a new career path will be more likely to stick to it if they have a plan for what they will do and how to do it. People trying a new fitness plan will be more likely to stick to it if they have a plan for how they will do it and when. People trying to get their employees to turn in assignments on time will have more success if they have a clear and easy strategy for how employees can do that. Easy to do means more likely to do.

APPLYING EASY TO YOUR PERSONAL LIFE

Technologies like smartphone apps and mobile devices have increased productivity by making it easier for people to do things. They help people to keep in touch with their friends, get their work done faster, and stick to their routines. But technological innovation isn't the only way to make people's lives easier. There are plenty of low- or non-tech ways people can make their lives easier, too.

Take clothing. People spend a lot of their lives thinking about what clothes they should wear. One study found that women spend about fifteen minutes per day deciding what they should wear. That adds up to a total of about one year of their lives.[17] Even for people who spend only a couple of minutes each day, that can quickly add up to a lot of time spent deciding between wearing your dark blue pants or medium blue pants. While some people enjoy spending time choosing their outfit, many people would prefer to use this time doing something else.

Having a clothing routine, or a uniform, makes it easier for people to know what to wear so they can focus on other things they want to do. Many of the most successful people, including Steve Jobs, Mark Zuckerberg, and Albert Einstein, decided to wear the same clothing style every day to make their lives easier.[18] And this isn't limited to science and tech people who are comfortable looking like a character from *The Big Bang Theory*. Look around and you'll see that former president Barack Obama defaults to a blue or gray suit; Karl Lagerfeld, the creative director of Chanel, often wears a black suit, white shirt, sunglasses, and gloves; and film director Christopher Nolan wears his signature dark jacket, blue dress shirt with a lightly fraying collar, and scuffed shoes. This isn't unique to men, either. Matilda Kahl, the art director at Saatchi & Saatchi, wrote an article about how her daily white silk shirt and black trousers dramatically reduced her stress and made it easier to focus on things in her life other than people's opinions about her clothes (she also shared how she found the outfit at Zara and negotiated on the price, as she says everyone should).[19] [20]

THE CURSE OF KNOWLEDGE AND THE DAY TRADER EFFECT

It's pretty intuitive, or maybe even obvious at this point, that people will keep doing things that are easy for them to do. But knowing that hasn't helped. People *still* have trouble sticking to things. They *still* have trouble making things easy. So why do people make things tough for themselves or others?

There's a classic study that my graduate school advisor, Lee Ross, used to describe that was conducted by one of his former students, Elizabeth Newton. Stanford University undergraduates were invited into a research lab and randomly divided into one of two groups: half were assigned as "tappers," who would find a song from a list of 125 common songs like "America the Beautiful" and "Rock Around the Clock" and tap the melody of that song on a table. The other half were told to listen to the tapped song and identify the name of it. "Tappers" were asked to report the likelihood that the "listener" would identify the song, as well as the proportion of students who would be able to identify the song if they heard it.

It was pretty obvious to the tappers that it would be easy for the listeners to identify the songs they tapped. The tappers predicted that about 50 percent of students who heard their tapping would be able to identify their song. But it turns out that they were pretty far off: only three out of 125 tapped songs (about 2.5 percent) were correctly identified.[21] What happened?

The tappers had suffered from something called the Curse of Knowledge.[22] They had too much knowledge of how the song sounded. They used this knowledge to try really hard to communicate all aspects of the song through their taps: while they were tapping they heard the melody of the song, orchestral arrangements, and lyrics, and did their best to communicate all this through outstanding tapping skills. But the problem is that the listeners just heard taps. Even though the tappers thought it would be easy for the listeners, it was too tough. You might have had this problem if you've played a game like charades or Pictionary and thought you had stupid people on your team. "What's wrong with Jason that he doesn't realize I'm acting out Stewie Griffin from *Family Guy*?! Doesn't he realize that I'm miming myself inside Lois's uterus?!"

People make the same mistake when they're trying to get other people to do things. Technology start-up product developers have discussed the ins and outs of their product thousands of times. They know every special feature and the exact location of every button. Because of their knowledge of the product, they often assume that users will have more knowledge than they actually do and would be able to easily navigate through the interface. New managers who have worked their way up through ranks often assume their employees have more knowledge than they actually have and will understand assignments. New salespeople who have recently learned about a product often assume that their pitches are clearly understood. Each of these issues results from people suffering from too much knowledge, which makes it tough for them to make things easy for others.

People don't just make things too complicated for others, however; they also overcomplicate things for themselves, which makes them less likely to follow through with their own plans. People sign up for gyms that are far away from their homes. They like the gym and think they'll be able to keep going, but it's not easy to keep going so they quit. Software developers plan a timeline for the completion of their own work but often dramatically underestimate how long it will actually take for them to do it, causing team arguments and sometimes even the abandonment of projects. The reason for this is often less about being too much of an expert and more about people incorrectly thinking they know themselves better than they actually do.

I call this the "Day Trader Effect," and most people suffer from it. I spend my mornings trading in the stock, commodities, and futures markets and constantly hear predictions from day traders and market analysts about which direction the market is going and what securities people should buy or sell. They might have confident voices, but these traders are typically wrong, just like the majority of people who trade in the market.[23] In fact, even the professionals are right at best 50 percent of the time[24] (that's one reason why I trade mostly options instead of stocks or futures; options are more directly based on human psychology and therefore more predictable than stocks). This effect isn't just limited to the stock market, though. People confidently make all kinds of predictions. A famous one, for example, was *Variety* in 1955 predicting that rock and roll "will be gone by June." Then came Elvis and the Beatles.

People are also overconfident in their predictions about how they or others will act in the future. For example, studies have asked people to make predictions about how well they know their friends and how those friends will act in different situations. People are then asked to rate their confidence in their own predictions. By looking back on whether their predictions were correct, researchers can learn whether people are accurate in them. Although most people think they are really good at making these predictions, they don't do much better than chance.[25]

Recently this effect has been used to explain a lot about people's behavior, including CEO and management performance,[26] entrepreneurship,[27] and of course stock trading.[28] For example, one study of engineers found that more than 30 percent believed they were in the top 5 percent of their peers; more than 60 percent believed they were in the top 10 percent; and almost 90 percent believed they were in the top 25 percent.[29] The entrepreneurial engineers in this group showed the strongest bias. Other studies of entrepreneurs have shown similar results. Although a common stereotype is that entrepreneurs are risk seekers, they are actually just as risk-seeking or risk-averse as wage-earning employees. The difference is that entrepreneurs are overconfident about their skills.[30]

People are also poor predictors of their own emotions.[31][32] For example, students were asked how happy they think their lives would have been if they had won a housing lottery to pick housing. Although students reported thinking it would lead to big changes in their happiness, one year later there were no meaningful differences.[33]

The overall psychology behind the "Day Trader Effect" can be applied to teach us why people are also poor at sticking with things. People make plans for themselves or others, such as wanting to make a career change or learn a new language, but because they are poor predictors of themselves, they underestimate how difficult it will be for them to follow through with their plans, and as a result, they frequently wind up quitting things they had planned to do.

So how do people overcome these problems and make things easy?

HOW TO MAKE THINGS EASY

Remember the E-Trade commercials of the baby in a crib who clicked on his phone and said he just bought a stock? Those commercials might have been silly, but the idea stuck: E-Trade is so easy to use to trade in the stock market that a baby could do it (although I'm still waiting for my toddler to trade stocks and I have a feeling it might be a while . . .). People can follow this example and use the "E-Trade test" to see whether something is easy to do. For example, instead of an engineer or product developer assuming that their users will share their knowledge and intuitively know how to use a software application, they can try to put themselves in the shoes of someone with less knowledge (imagine creating the software for a child), and that will help make it easier to use. Below, you can view Table 1, which will give you examples of things that are easy versus not easy, to help you understand how to make things pass the E-Trade test.

Behavior	Easy	Not Easy
Getting yourself to exercise	Signing up for a gym across the street from your home or work	Your gym requires a 15+ minute commute
Getting yourself to eat healthier	You've removed all of the junk food from your house and have a lot of healthier foods stocked up	Your home is filled with junk food but you rely on your willpower to stop you from eating it
Getting yourself to learn a new instrument	You blocked off time in your calendar to practice every day and set an alarm to remind you	You rely on yourself being motivated to want to learn each day
Getting your employees to show up on time	You have a daily two-minute motivational check-in with new employees every day, first thing in the morning, that is on their calendars	You assume they will be there on time
Getting your website visitors to view another page	You have a big button that leads them to the page you want them to visit	The page is completely filled with text
Table 1. The E-Trade test: How do I know if something is easy enough for me to stick to it? Here are some examples.		

In addition to the E-Trade test, other tools can make things easier. You can incorporate the science behind Easy that we described earlier: control the environment, limit choices, and use a road map. You can also harness the other forces in this book. Although this chapter is focused specifically on Easy, the forces in the other chapters can make things easier for people to keep doing them. For example, you can use the model of stepladders from Chapter 2 on steps, goals, and dreams to make things easy for people to keep doing things. Small steps are easier to achieve than goals or dreams. You can also surround yourself with other people who are doing the thing you want to do (Community, Chapter 3).

APPLYING EASY TO BUSINESS

Or Arbel, an Israeli app developer, had an April Fool's Day joke he wanted to spring on the world. He decided to release an iPhone and Android app with an intentionally stupid idea. In just eight hours, he built the app and released it on April 1, 2014. Three months later, it had hit number three in the Apple store, had more than one million downloads, and the fifty thousand most active users had used it more than four million times. Arbel, shocked by his success, quit his job in Israel, packed his bags, and moved to the United States, where he raised his first million dollars in financing. Now, if this were 2006, when apps were first being created, people might be able to understand this type of success resulting from a "joke" app. Back then, as I saw from my graduate school friends and colleagues, people became overnight millionaires from making apps like "What's your porn name?" (an app that would rename you with a porn star name). But the novelty from those joke apps had worn off by 2014. How could an app in 2014, designed as an April Fool's joke, get such high rates of user engagement? The answer was that it was easy to use. Stupid easy.

The entire purpose of Arbel's app was to allow users to send the word *Yo!* to other users. That was it. There was a big button that would allow people to send a Yo! notification to friends to invite them to download the app. But the fact that it was easy to use got a lot of people using it. Since Yo!, a number of copycat apps have been released, like an Indian version that sends the word *aiyo*, and a more practical adaptation of Yo! that warns Israeli citizens of missile strikes on Israel.[34] By being one of the easiest apps to use, Yo! quickly became successful. It's too early to tell, but my prediction is that the Yo! copycats won't experience the same level of success that Yo! had, because so many people have copied Yo!'s design that an even easier design needs to be created to cut through the competition. Yo! did make one thing certain: no matter how stupid something might seem, if it's easy to use, people will use it.

But start-ups aren't the only ones using the force of Easy to change people's behaviors. Bigger companies like Amazon and Google are also using it. By revolutionizing how easy it can be to shop, Amazon has become a lasting success and gained a market value of greater than a hundred billion dollars along the way.[35] When Amazon first started Prime, people were skeptical whether customers would be willing to pay the $79 a year subscription to be able to buy products online.[36] But Amazon knew that making shopping easier for customers would pay off. At the time Prime was created, people were paying for shipping and then still had to wait a week to receive the product. Amazon knew that providing customers with free shipping and two-day delivery would make it easier for them to shop and keep them coming back. A decade later, Prime subscriptions are in the tens of millions and still growing quickly. And four out of five of the tens of thousands who joined on the first day of Prime are still subscribing.

The vice president of Amazon Prime Global, Greg Greeley, said "everyone is trying to analyze the financials" to decide whether to implement a new product or service like Prime. But Greeley learned, "It's really about the convenience." Make things easy for people and they'll keep doing them. Amazon continues to leverage the force of Easy to keep their customers engaged. Its latest tool? Amazon Dash connects with home devices like a thermostat. When your air filter needs to be replaced Amazon will be notified and the part will be automatically reordered and shipped to your door.[37]

Google has made it easy to change employee behavior, too. One of the perks of working at Google has always been the fact that food is never more than 150 feet away. But easy access to food has caused some Google employees to gain too much weight. It's not uncommon for people to gain fifteen pounds after starting work.[38] Google decided to tackle the issue by making it harder for their employees to eat unhealthy foods and easier to eat healthier substitutes. They restructured their kitchens by moving the salad bar front and center to the entrance, swapped their big plates and takeout containers for smaller ones to reduce people's consumption, and moved their M&M's from clear bins to opaque jars so that people had to search for the candies. By making it easier for their employees to eat healthier, Google employees' calories from candies dropped 9 percent (from 29 percent to 20 percent) and consumed fat dropped 11 percent (from 26 percent to 15 percent).

Having graded papers from high school, college, and graduate students, I find many students start using bigger words in their essays once they get to college. Maybe it happens after they study for the SATs and learn bigger words, or maybe it happens because they feel like they need to sound more sophisticated now that they're in college. The problem is, the bigger words are often less precise than the smaller ones they formerly used. The sentence "I plan to utilize my computer" can be more simply and appropriately replaced with "I plan to use my computer." The problem gets worse as students progress to graduate school and write scientific research papers. I'll see papers with "College students were recruited to join a study" instead of the simpler and more familiar active voice, "We recruited college students to join a study." The idea that we need to make something complicated for it to be smart extends past writing, to many things in life, like creating complicated fitness routines or complicated business plans. But this is wrong.

The psychology behind Easy teaches that we need to retrain ourselves. Making something simple and easy is smart and will help people stick with things.

More than two thousand years ago, Aristotle said, "We may assume the superiority *ceteris paribus* [other things being equal] of the demonstration which derives from fewer postulates or hypotheses." In other words, the simplest idea is usually the best. Throughout the years, many philosophers and scientists—like Ptolemy,[39] William of Occam, and Isaac Newton,[40] as well as contemporary scientists—have said something similar. So if the smartest people agree that simple is better, it's time for us to listen to history and stop trying to make things so difficult for ourselves.

The father of social psychology, Kurt Lewin, first applied a similar theory to behavior to explain the conflicts that prevent people from doing things.[41] Lewin said, "A conflict is to be characterized psychologically as a situation in which oppositely directed, simultaneously acting forces of approximately equal strength work upon the individual."[42] The idea behind much of his work was that a lot of different things affect whether and how people will act. Simply put, if you're having trouble sticking with something, remove whatever is stopping you from doing it. It's that easy.

EASY

Your homework for this chapter is simple, but not easy.

1. Think about the behavior you plan to change.
2. Using the tools provided in this chapter, try to make it easier for you to change it. For example, think about whether you're suffering from the Curse of Knowledge or the Day Trader Effect.
3. Acknowledge that your plan to change the behavior may not be as easy as you believe.
4. Think about ways to strip down its complexity and make it as easy as possible for you to stick to it.

CHAPTER 6

NEUROHACKS

I n 2011, Mauricio Estrella was going through a rough time. His recent divorce had led him to sink into a severe depression. Although he was fortunate enough to have friends and a strong support network, he felt like his life had spiraled out of control. Every day he asked himself, "How could she do something like this to me?" He needed a solution, fast.

While sitting at work in front of his computer, he got the familiarly annoying prompt when he tried to log into his email, "Your password has expired. Click 'Change password' to change your password." But he suddenly had a crazy idea.

"I'm going to use a password to change my life."[1]

Remembering that his boss had used passwords as to-do lists, Mauricio decided that he would use his password as a to-do list to regain control of his life. Instead of using a typical password like his birth date, favorite food, or location where he grew up, Mauricio changed his password to "Forgive@h3r." This simple action changed the way he thought of his ex-wife. It literally changed his life. Instead of holding hostility toward her, he was reminded to forgive her. In fact, this was more than just a reminder. Because he had consciously picked this as his password, something that he would have to type on a daily basis, he realized that he was ready to act on it and forgive her. Each day he typed it helped to solidify in his mind and body that he was healing. Mauricio said he felt better almost immediately. He wasn't just unlocking his computer. He was unlocking his mind and heart. He had learned an important psychological trick on how to reset the brain. It's called a neurohack.

Mauricio didn't return to his old ways of creating passwords. A month later, when he was asked to change his password again, he changed it to "Quit@smoking4ever." This led him to stop smoking, overnight. Five years later, he's been happily remarried for two years, has a child arriving in a few months, and hasn't smoked since.[2]

How could changing a password make you quit smoking? How could borrowing a book from someone antagonistic to you turn them into a friend? How could accepting little or no money for work make you enjoy your job *more*? How could making consistent purchases of a stock make you unwilling to sell it? How could going to "Halloween Horror Night" help you win the love of your life? The answer? Neurohacks.

Conventional wisdom teaches that behavior change begins in the mind. Pick up a self-help or business psychology book and they'll tell you that if you want to overcome your fears, be a better salesperson, or be happier, you need to change the way you think. An old-style psychotherapist might teach people who want to feel better about themselves that they should stop their negative self-talk by creating a self-mantra like "I'm good enough, I'm smart enough, and doggone it, people like me" (courtesy of the old Al Franken *Saturday Night Live* skits with unlicensed therapist Stuart Smalley).

But after years of Freudian psychotherapy and self-help books, people still struggle with how to control their minds. They find it can take years, or an eternity, to learn how to change their minds in order to change their behavior. That's because conventional wisdom is wrong. Fortunately, there's a much quicker and simpler way to hack your brain to help you keep doing the things you want to do, and it's backed up by science. I call them neurohacks.

NEUROHACKS

Conventional wisdom has it backward: lasting behavior change doesn't typically start with the mind telling the body to make lasting change; it starts by making a small change in behavior and letting the mind reflect on that change.

Self-identity is a key part of this process. People often decide whether to do something based on how they think of themselves.[3] Will you finish writing a blog post or stop and have a cocktail instead? Will you push yourself to run another ten minutes or call it quits and walk? Will a person keep sober another day or give in to temptation and have a drink?

The answer depends in part on how people think of themselves and what they've done in the past in similar situations. If you usually keep writing a blog post until you finish then you'll probably finish this one instead of stopping to have a drink. Part of the reason is that it's become a routine for you. Another big reason is that by finishing your blog posts you have formed a self-identity that you're a "closer." Your past behavior shows that you complete your work before taking a break, and you need to remain consistent with that self-image of getting the job done before you play. Similarly, the answer to whether a person sticks it out for another ten minutes on her run or keeps sober another day depends on how she thinks of herself after looking back at past behavior. If her past behavior signals she's a fighter, then she'll want to maintain that self-image and stick it out and fight.

Similarly, people say to themselves "all my past businesses

have failed so I must be a failure." That type of thinking, self-identifying as being a failure as a person, makes it much more likely that the person will actually fail at business in the future. It's tough to change that pattern through self-help books that say to tell yourself you're not a failure, because if you start a new business and things get tough the mind will automatically revert to remembering the last time this happened and the business failed. Instead of self-talk, neurohacks start with behavior and use it to reset the mind so that the person doesn't think of himself as a failure anymore.

For example, if you want to become a nicer person, instead of *telling* yourself you're a good person, simply start helping people in need and then you'll *become* a good person, and that self-identity will make it a lot easier for you to stay a good person.

Conventional Wisdom (Change begins in the mind)	Neurohacks (Change begins with action)
Change the Mind ⟶ Actions Will Follow	Change Actions ⟶ The Mind Will Follow

This is the idea behind neurohacks. Neurohacks are a set of psychological tricks—quick and easy ways to reset the mind. They get people to think about themselves in ways they couldn't do before and get them to keep doing things they weren't able to do before. We can apply neurohacks to get ourselves to do things we want to do, and also to get others to do things that are good for them to do.*

---

* Neurohacks are powerful mind tricks. If you're using them on others, please use them for social good.

Have you ever had hours of pain from a toothache, headache, or other part of your body in pain but decided to hold off on taking pain meds, hoping it would go away on its own, and it didn't? It stays with you for such a long time that you start feeling like the pain is never going to end. You just had your birthday and realized that this lingering pain is a sign that you're getting old. This is what old people feel like, and this pain is going to be here for the rest of your aging life. You give in to your unfortunate reality of your old body and decide you should give up the idea of trying to let your body fix itself without medication. You take a painkiller, and oh what a feeling . . . the pain subsides. The next morning you wake up expecting to have it back as strong as ever but to your surprise you find the pain is still gone, or at least much less than you felt the previous day.

Now how is that possible? The aspirin was only supposed to last a few hours, so the pain should be back in full force. But the pain didn't come back. Why? Because the pain medication was a neuro-hack. While you were struggling in pain, you might have thought the pain could take days or weeks to go away, but that little pill got you to see a new way of thinking. It reset your mind to remember what it felt like just days before when you didn't have pain. It gave you a fresh way to think about the world and about your identity. You quickly changed from viewing yourself as an old person with chronic pain to realizing that you're still the same pain-free person you were a few days ago who doesn't need to rely on taking pain-killers. And that transformation didn't happen because you tried to retake control of your mind and convince yourself to stop feeling pain; it also didn't happen because of the ingredients in the pill, as those ingredients wore off long before. It happened because that little pill was a neurohack.

A colleague of mine is a board-certified addiction medicine physician. We work on studies together to find ways to reduce addiction and chronic pain. He told me that addiction patients who failed medical therapies, such as longtime heroin addicts, will sometimes call him a year after seeing him to tell him that they miraculously became clean because they one day woke up and saw the world differently. They had "an epiphany moment" where they realized they didn't need to be addicted to heroin anymore and they haven't used since. These types of stories are rare but they illustrate that epiphany moments do exist, and they've motivated us to study how to artificially create such moments within people. One way (not recommended) is by working with drugs like hallucinogens that are designed to alter your brain. Since most of you are trying to get yourself to stick to your gym class or get your customers to buy products rather than quit a life-threatening addiction, a risky drug like LSD is definitely not the recommended treatment. Instead, I'll touch on some of the more legal and less harmful ways (compared to mind-altering drugs) to change your behavior and your mind using neurohacks.

If I had been asked when I was twenty-one to describe one of my worst fears, I would have said that it would be finding myself in a country where I didn't speak the language, had no money, and didn't know anyone. Not long after giving this answer, I found myself in that exact situation.

As a graduating college senior, I was having a tough time. I had just had a rough breakup with a girlfriend, and to top it off, I had no idea what I was going to do with my life. I thought it would have something to do with music, but after taking psychology classes for fun and being encouraged by my psychology professors and mentors that I should apply to graduate school in psychology, I decided I'd give it a shot even though being an ethnomusicology major wouldn't help my chances. I wrote and submitted my application, got two of the three required letters of support (I later found out that my UCLA ethnomusicology counselor never sent his in to the schools), and left on January 18 for Caracas, Venezuela, to travel around South America and play music. My plan was to have a "motorcycle diaries style" trip, except instead of riding on a bike like Che Guevara I would ride on anything that would get me across the continent, which turned out to be buses, boats down the Amazon, and hitchhiking. Along the way, I'd wait to hear back from graduate schools to see if I'd get in anywhere and keep my one-way ticket open in case I was rejected from all of them.

I had my first location mapped out—staying at a friend of a friend's place in Caracas—but after that I'd decide my plans based on how I felt when I woke up each morning. After staying in Caracas for a few days, I came back to their home one night only to find that all the money I had saved for the trip was missing from my wallet. Angry and unaware of what to do or whom to fall back on for support (Caracas has one of the highest murder rates in the country, so the police have bigger problems than an American losing his money), I fortunately still had a credit card and used that to catch a bus down to the Brazilian Amazon. It was there that I realized my worst fear: I was just learning Portuguese, was all alone, my only money was on a credit card in a jungle with no credit card machines, and I was surrounded by roaches and flies the size of my hands.

Yet things ended up not being so bad, and in fact, they turned out great. During the remaining two and a half months of my trip, I was welcomed by strangers who took me in to live with them, learned to play samba on my ukulele and cavaquinho, and overcame my fears. I remember walking down the streets of Rio de Janeiro one day reflecting on my past fears of being in an unknown land with no money. Reflecting on what I had been through, I realized I was no longer afraid of those things because I had already experienced them and actually enjoyed them. In fact, I now saw myself as a different person, one capable of doing things I hadn't been able to do before, like travel to a new place with no money, plans, or friends. Without realizing it, I had used neurohacks.[†]

Neurohacks can do the same thing for others. By getting people to look back on their past behavior, neurohacks can get people to see themselves differently, allowing them to follow through with things they couldn't do previously.

So neurohacks aren't just for changing our own behaviors; they can also get other people to keep doing things. For example, they can get people to take on an identity of a person who uses only certain types of products, like premium services, and get them to keep using premium products to keep with their view of being a premium user.

Neurohacks get people to stick with things through two psychological processes: 1) people convince themselves that if they're doing something without being pressured to do it, it must be because it's important to them (people will then stick with that behavior to remain consistent with what's important to them) and 2) people form an identity of themselves by looking back on things they've done in the past (people will continue doing that behavior because it is part of their self-image).[4]

I'll now give you the science behind how and why neurohacks work, along with some of my own ideas on how you can apply neu-

---

[†] I define neurohacks as psychological tricks that get people to reset their brains by looking back on their past behavior. Because of that broad definition, there are many types of neurohacks. In fact, the forces in the rest of the book can be neurohacks, if they get people to reflect on their past behavior and make conclusions about who they are based on their reflections. For example, a person who thinks he is not capable of following through with a hobby might use Stepladders or Community to stick to a new hobby. Once he does that hobby a few times and reflects back on doing it, his brain can be reset to realize he is a different person than he initially thought; he is someone who can stick to a hobby. That's how the other forces can also be neurohacks.

rohacks to your life and work. I group neurohacks into different categories to help you understand the different types: neurohacks based on behavior, body movement, physiology and emotions, speech, and thoughts.

BEHAVIOR

When Benjamin Franklin was running for his second term as a clerk, one of his peers delivered a long speech that attempted to ruin Ben's reputation. Ben realized that simply firing back insults might help in the short term but could ultimately harm his own career. But he had to win this detractor to be on his side. What did Ben do? He used a neurohack to change his enemy's mind and win him over.

Knowing the man proudly owned a rare book, Ben contacted the man and asked to borrow it. Flattered by the request, the man quickly sent the book over. Ben wrote a nice thank-you note in return. This small act forever changed their relationship dynamic—and helped Ben's career. It created a major shift in the rival's mind. It reset his brain to make him realize that Ben wasn't an enemy, because enemies don't loan each other books and act graciously. When the legislature met the next time, the man approached Ben for the first time. After that day, the two of them became friends. And their friendship didn't just last for a week or two. This one little request led to a friendship that lasted throughout their lives. Ben admitted he learned an important lesson about how to use neurohacks on rivals instead of fighting with them: "He that has once done you a kindness will be more ready to do you another, than he whom you yourself have obliged. And it shows how much more profitable it is prudently to remove, than to resent, return, and continue inimical proceedings."[5]

Ben had gotten the rival to act in a way that changed how he thought of himself and his relationship with Ben. He gave the rival a new identity and helped him think of himself as being Ben's friend rather than his foe. To be consistent with this new self-image, the rival was now committed to doing nice things for his friend Ben.

Ben Franklin's case is an example of how to get someone to do nice things (in this case, make new friends). However, the same concept of getting people to act and reflect on their actions can be applied to get people to do almost anything, even things that aren't so nice, like getting educated, well-meaning people like Janja Lalich (see Chapter 3) to join a cult. For example, terrorist organizations use neurohacks to get their recruits more committed to their cause.[6] If an organization can get someone to voluntarily take a simple action like visiting a website, or registering on the site to gain access and learn more information, then they can get her to think of herself in a different way. They can get her to start thinking of herself as the type of person who is interested in learning more about that terrorist organization. This might not mean she sees herself as a terrorist or willing to commit harmful acts, but she may start to view herself as and become someone more sympathetic to their cause. That new identity makes it more likely that she'll increase her involvement with the organization.

Another way for people to create a neurohack is to jump straight into their fears. Just as I learned I could overcome my fears in South America by being thrown into them, science supports exposing people to what they fear, or at least a light version of it. In one study, researchers invited a group of heterosexual men who felt anxious, socially awkward, and unattractive because they couldn't get dates to participate in a study. The researchers wanted to see if they could hack the men's brains to get them to feel better about themselves and improve their dating life. After being paired up with women to have twelve-minute conversations, the men reported feeling less anxious and less socially awkward.

This effect didn't go away the next day: they followed up with the men six months later and found that they felt much more socially comfortable than they originally had, and were going out on a lot more dates.[7][8]

BODY MOVEMENTS

Did you know that your decisions, like whether you like a person or agree with things he says, depends on how your body moves while he is talking? In one study, people were told to listen to an advertisement on why students should carry identification cards with them. Half of them were instructed to nod their heads up and down while listening, while the other half were told to shake their heads side to side during the recording.[9] They were then asked whether they agreed with the recommendations in the advertisement to carry cards. The researchers found that people's agreements about the ads depended on how they were told to shake their heads while listening to it: people told to move their heads up and down (as if they were nodding in agreement) were more likely to agree with the advertisement, compared to people who were told to shake their heads side to side (as if they were disagreeing). Why did researchers find this result? They had purposely asked people to either move their heads the way people do when they agree with someone (nodding up and down) or disagree with something (shaking the head side to side). The people in the study hadn't been aware of the purpose of the study but they intuitively knew that they nod when they agree with something. Because they had been nodding, they intuitively thought they must have agreed with the statements. Scientists had learned that simply getting people to move their bodies the way they do when they agree with something gets them to be more agreeable.

A similar study looked at whether people's self-esteem could be influenced by something as seemingly unrelated as which hand they used to write responses to questions. Students were asked to write down their best qualities as future career professionals. Half of them were asked to write down their qualities using their (dominant) right hand while the other half were asked to write them down using their (nondominant) left hand. They wrote down things like being a hard worker, having a positive attitude, and being flexible. They were then asked to rate their overall self-esteem as well as confidence in the skills they had listed about themselves.

You may know what it feels like to write something down with your nondominant hand. Perhaps you've been in a situation where you are holding a sandwich or some messy food in your dominant hand when an important call comes through. You answer and have to write down a message but your dominant hand is full of hummus and avocado (or whatever delicious toppings you prefer on your sandwich). You put the phone on speaker and lay it down so you can write the message with your nondominant hand. What a mess. You realize your writing looks like it did when you were in second grade and got a "U" for Unsatisfactory on handwriting on your report card (or maybe it's just me who got that grade). Good thing no one will be evaluating your writing skills, because you aren't feeling proud of yourself right now.

This is exactly what the researchers found. People who wrote about their positive qualities using their right hand had higher ratings of self-esteem compared to students who wrote using their left hand. The reason for this was that people reflected back on their work, and if their writing was sloppier and appeared less confidently written then it made them feel less confident about themselves. Similar to the study on shaking your head, the researchers found that people's confidence and self-esteem are affected by things as seemingly irrelevant as which hand they use to complete tasks.

Most people typically think about self-esteem as something entirely internal. The common belief is that people either have high or low self-esteem and that the secret to improving self-esteem is to grab control of the mind and stop thinking negative thoughts about yourself. But these studies on neurohacks suggest we use a different, even simpler approach. Instead of trying to control your thoughts, just make small changes in your behavior and your mind will follow. Using a neurohack as simple as choosing which hand to use to write a note, which foot to kick a ball with, or which style of dance to do to music can determine people's self-esteem. More broadly, we learn that body movements can be used as neurohacks to change the way people think about themselves.

PHYSIOLOGY AND EMOTIONS

You've probably heard of people taking dates to horror movies in the hope that the date will get scared and hug them. This tactic might sound ridiculous, but there's actually some science to back it up.

If people become physiologically aroused, for instance, by watching a scary movie, they sometimes mistake their arousal by the movie as being caused by something else, like being nervous about whether their date is going well. It turns out that downloading and watching *Saw III* instead of *Star Wars: Episode III* can make the difference in whether people keep dating.

Some of the strongest research on this topic was done years ago using methods that might not pass the research ethical boards, but bear with me because they did teach us some interesting things about people. For example, one study asked men to look at pictures of "seminude" women while being hooked up to physiological equipment and listening to prerecorded sounds so that the men (incorrectly) thought they were hearing their heartbeats. One group of men heard the heartbeats increasing or decreasing in speed as they viewed the pictures, while another group heard a steady heartbeat speed throughout their viewing of the pictures. The men were then asked to rate the attractiveness of the women in the pictures.

Stop for a second and see if you can get where I'm going with this. . . . Similar to the conventional wisdom that self-esteem shouldn't be affected by seemingly tiny things like whether a person writes with her left or right hand, there is a belief that attraction is completely subjective and shouldn't be affected by little, seemingly unrelated things like how fast a sound is pulsing. But that's not what the study found. The researchers found that men rated the women in the pictures as more attractive if the men had seen them while hearing the (fake) heartbeat increasing or decreasing in speed. This effect didn't go away after the study ended; it had a lasting effect: researchers interviewed the participants four to five weeks later (disguised as visiting the men for a different reason) and learned that the men still preferred the women they had picked.[10] [11] This study took place back in the 1960s, and a number of people did not believe the results. More recent studies in the past ten years attempted to retest this phenomenon and found similar results.[12] There is even neuroscience research showing that the brain acts differently when people are asked to do something while listening to their own heart rate (even if it's actually a fake recording).[13]

In fact, there has been a lot of research showing that people look to their physiological and emotional signs to learn who they are, what to think, and how to act. For example, people look back on their emotional expressions to learn whether they were happy or sad during an event. The idea behind this work is that emotional expressions, like smiling or frowning, can get people to feel emotions even if they aren't aware they are making those faces.[14]

Take smiling. If you were going to teach someone how to smile you might tell them to move the sides of their lips up toward their eyes. Or you might give them an object like a pencil to hold between their teeth, because that forces the muscles to mimic how they move when people smile. Researchers have done very similar studies. Rather than asking people to smile, one study split people up into two groups. They asked the first group of people to hold a pen between their teeth to mimic the expression people make when they smile (the participants weren't told the reason they were holding the pen between their teeth). They wanted the other group to not smile, so they told them to hold the pen tightly between their lips (try smiling with a pen held tightly between your lips and you'll see it's not easy). They then had them do different activities like look at cartoons and asked them to report how funny they found the cartoons.[15]

You're probably sensing a theme by now. Although people's ratings of how funny they find something seemingly shouldn't be influenced by whether the person has a pen between her lips versus her teeth, the researchers found that the people with the pen between their teeth thought the comics were funnier. The participants weren't even aware that they were smiling or being prevented from smiling. This all happened without their knowledge.

Other studies have had similar effects by getting people to speak using words that have vowels or sounds that force people to move their facial muscles a certain way. German words that use the two-dotted umlaut are a popular research tool for this because words with the umlaut prevent smiling.[16] Botox, which makes it difficult for muscles to move, has more recently been used by psychologists and physicians studying this effect. Botox, if applied in certain places in the face, can prevent the face from making frowns or angry faces. Studies found similar results: People who were asked to frown after getting Botox (compared to before they got it) had decreased activation in the brain areas that show emotion. In other words, people reported being less angry about things after they got Botox and were unable to frown. It has also been shown to reduce depression.[17] (Being a proud weirdo who likes to find odd ways to study people, I'm proud to say that the theory and method behind facial expressions was created by one of my graduate advisers, Bob Zajonc, a pioneer in the field of psychology.)

As you can tell by now, these methods are pretty powerful because of their simplicity. Instead of working hard to gain control over the thoughts that come up in our minds, we can apply a small physiological or emotional neurohack that can lead to big changes in our mind and behavior. It's no surprise then that scientists have begun studying how to apply this work. They've shown that physiological and emotional neurohacks can help to improve patients' mood[18] and even reduce racism.[19]

SPEECH AND COGNITIVE NEUROHACKS

Speech neurohacks are based on the idea that little changes in speech can affect how people think of themselves and what they do. Take the old *SNL* reference we made earlier. Remember Al Franken playing the unlicensed therapist Stuart Smalley? If you haven't seen any of these I'll give a little background (and I recommend watching them because they're pretty funny). In the typical episode, Stuart Smalley gives a therapy session with a patient (usually the host, for example sports great Michael Jordan). Stuart gives Michael an intervention to help him feel better about himself. He tells Michael to look into the mirror and repeat out loud, "I'm good enough, I'm smart enough, and doggone it, people like me!" While the skit is a spoof of bad and unlicensed therapists, at a high level it highlights something that psychologists have learned: the words people use affect how they feel about themselves and what they'll do in the future.

For example, one set of studies asked people to answer questions about their likelihood of voting. The questions were phrased in one of two ways: "How important is it for you to vote?" or "How important is it for you to be a voter?" While people who saw the first question were asked to think about how important it is for them to *do* something, people who saw the latter were asked to think about how important it is for them to *be* someone, the type of person who votes. By asking people to take on the identity of *being* a voter, rather than just to say they care about voting, the researchers believed they could get people to act differently. They found it worked, too: voting rates were higher for the group saying it was important for them to be voters.[20]

This effect has been found in other areas, like cheating. People were given the opportunity to take money that wasn't theirs at someone else's expense after being instructed either "Please don't cheat" or "Please don't be a cheater." While the people instructed to not cheat took a lot of money, the people who saw the message to not be a cheater (linked to their identity) didn't cheat at all.[21]

Cognitive neurohacks, the last type of neurohack, let people learn about their behaviors by looking back at their thoughts. If they can change their thoughts, then they can change their behavior.

Take mind wandering. In a series of studies, people were given instructions on things to think about and then asked to do activities, like putting together a puzzle. They were then asked how much they enjoyed the activity, whether their mind wandered while doing it, and if so, to which topics. The researchers found that people looked back at their mind wandering as a clue as to whether they had enjoyed the activity they were doing. If they had been frequently thinking about other, positive unrelated things while they were doing the activity, then they reported that they didn't enjoy the activity very much.[22] In other words, they had looked back at their mind wandering and expected that for activities they enjoy they would be able to keep focused. Similar to the examples above on other types of neurohacks, we find that even though we think people know what they like and don't like, you can change these preferences by getting people's minds to wander in different ways. If people are able to focus while doing an activity, they'll enjoy it more than if they find their mind wandering.

Cognitive neurohacks are the hardest to implement, however. Why? It's tough to control your mind.‡ It's much easier to use one of the other types of neurohacks, where you simply need to make small changes in your behavior, or how you move your body or your facial expression, rather than trying to control your mind.

Now that you've learned the science behind the different types of neurohacks, how do you apply this science into your life and work?

APPLYING NEUROHACKS TO YOUR PERSONAL LIFE

I'm a big fan of Cesar Millan, "the dog whisperer." I like his show for a few reasons. Even though he's not a trained psychologist, he intuitively understands psychology and how to apply it. I also love animals. It's really cute to see a Lab who was scared to go to the beach being able to happily run in the sand alongside his owner. But also, I like the show because it gives me ideas for new types of neurohacks that I can test.

Take Nora Jones, my sixty-pound black Lab–white German shepherd mix. She's about three years old now but still rambunctious enough to steal and chomp on our toddler's toys or run head-first through a screen door to greet my parents when they arrive. Fortunately, I have a never-fail method to get her to listen when she gets out of control. I do this with a neurohack.

---

‡ This is also why I talk about neurohacks versus conventional wisdom. The conventional wisdom approach is that people can change their actions by changing their minds. I don't think that's wrong or impossible, but it is really tough. For example, if people want to overcome their fear of speaking, it's much easier to do this by starting with a short presentation online or to a friend (neurohack) than by trying to tell yourself that it's irrational to be scared of speaking.

Nora's body does very specific things when she is submissive and wants to listen to me. For example, when I arrive home, she greets me at the door by putting her head down while looking up at me, wagging her tail, and getting her giant satellite dish–size German shepherd ears to fall backward and down. I find the ears are the secret for the neurohack.

When Nora starts getting crazy, whether by inappropriately barking at the old woman in the wheelchair driving down our street in the morning, or by starting to do figure eights in our living room like she's a horse in a barrel racing championship, I try to get her to listen to me like she does when she's in her submissive mode. My secret is to move her body in the position it goes to when she's naturally submissive. I gently push her ears back and down just like she does to herself when she's greeting me at the door. Without fail, as soon as I push her ears back and down, Nora becomes submissive. Her mind becomes clear of whatever craziness was just telling her to open and eat a bottle of antibiotics on the table. She becomes immediately ready to calm down and listen to me.

Although there's a lot of research on the science behind neurohacks, there isn't much work on how to apply it in your own life. That's because I created the concept of neurohacks by distilling years of research across different areas of psychology. In the section below, I give some examples of how you might apply neurohacks to different situations. Although these are not (yet) scientifically proven, my hope is that these examples will give you a better understanding of neurohacks so that you can think of new ways to test and find out which neurohacks work best for you in your own life.

WANT TO FEEL MORE CONTROL OVER YOUR BODY? A participant in one of our studies, Kayla Martin, had been plagued by intense chronic pain. She'd been growing increasingly unable to move after years of debilitating pain. She made a small change in her behavior—by going to a physical therapy session for the first time in years—and described to another participant how it reset her brain and made her feel like she had more control over her body and her pain: "[It's] crazy how the universe validates things. I was reading the posts in our group & read yours . . . it made me smile because lately, I'm kind of feeling like I'm turning a corner . . . feels like things are a little more positive. I credit this to physical therapy. I can't describe the encouragement I feel each time I see/feel a little strength coming back into my leg/arm. ☺ I'm not me yet, but it feels like I'm headed in that direction—finally! Before p.t. I tried everything the drs suggested, trigger point injections, u/s guided injections, epidurals, acupuncture, yoga, went to a head shrinker . . . all the while I kept getting worse. So in a strange way PHYSI-CAL therapy has been really good 4 my mind, body & spirit. Yay!" Kayla's quote shows that physical therapy was a neurohack that let her reflect back on being able to make her body do things that she couldn't do before. That reset her brain and is allowing her to again feel hopeful and on track toward health.

DO YOU WANT YOUR KIDS TO BE MORE APPRECIATIVE? One neurohack that might help is to get your kids to do activities that "appreciative people" do, like volunteering. In one study, adolescents who were made to volunteer were found to be more caring toward others.[23] Getting kids to volunteer (especially if you can get them to do it willingly) helps to create an identity for themselves that they are the type of people who care about volunteering. That can make them more appreciative and keep them volunteering.

WANT TO STOP PROCRASTINATING? Start a self-help group or podcast on how to stop procrastinating. It's tough to be the leader of a group that teaches people to not procrastinate if you're a procrastinator yourself. Leading other people in how to stop procrastinating can make it easier for the leader to stop procrastinating, too.

Think of your therapist (like many Southern Californians, let's assume you have one). Just think how relaxed your therapist seems and you'll realize that much of your therapist's tranquility comes from taking on the role of being a mental health expert. This "fake it till you make it" approach creates a neurohack that you wouldn't be creating and leading people on preventing procrastination if you weren't good enough at it yourself to be able to lead them.[§] It also helps people to see a new side of themselves and to stop procrastinating.

WANT TO BE MORE IN THE MOMENT? Take an improv class. Improv requires people to go with the flow because the first rule of improv is to agree and go along with everyone's statements.[24] Taking an improv class and learning that you can adapt to any situation creates a neurohack to reset the mind. It allows people to gain a new realization that they are capable of going with the flow of life. Or, if you don't like improv but do like music, you could try something similar by listening to jazz, or by learning to play jazz if you're a musician. Jazz is based heavily on improvisation and acting in the moment. If people can learn to appreciate the freedom and seeming lack of structure in jazz music, they can also learn that they must be the type of person who can enjoy spontaneity. This neurohack for becoming more present-minded isn't limited to using improv or jazz. There are a lot of other possible neurohacks to achieve the

---

[§] As in all cases, there are exceptions to the idea that leading a group means that you will embody all the characteristics of the group. People often bring up the hypocrisy of the immoral priest or teacher who should be leading other people in moral ways but is actually immoral. These neurohacks aren't 100 percent guaranteed to change people's minds and behaviors. Just like all of the other chapters, they will move the lever up to make it more likely for people to change, especially if they're combined with other forces in the book.

~e, such as changing fashion styles, workplace demea-
~nows you watch on television.

WANT TO FEEL MORE SOCIAL AND CONNECTED TO OTHERS?
Many people feel lonely when they reflect on their friendships. Conventional wisdom tells people to change their thoughts to realize they aren't alone. But it's hard to change your thoughts. The neurohack approach tells people that instead of changing your thoughts to feel closer to others, *do* something that will actually make you closer to others. People should pick something that "social people" do, like sharing personal things with friends, community members (online or offline), or even strangers. The act of sharing makes people feel more connected to each other and the world. People who openly share and reflect back on themselves realize that they must be connected to others; otherwise they wouldn't be sharing personal information with them.[25]

HOW ARE RELIGIOUS GROUPS ABLE TO KEEP FOLLOWERS ENGAGED? Regardless of your thoughts about religion, or whether or not you're a spiritual or religious person, there's no denying that religion has been a powerful and lasting tradition throughout history. How do religious leaders keep their followers engaged? Other than promoting a belief in a higher power, many religious groups also do an excellent job of applying neurohacks.

Rabbi Mendel Cunin, a rabbi for the Orthodox Jewish organization Chabad, taught me how neurohacks are part of the process that has kept Jews engaged for thousands of years. Chabad rabbis aren't concerned if Jews don't initially believe in God. If they can get Jews to follow the prescribed religious behaviors, then belief in God will follow. Chabad encourages all Jews to show up to temple (shul) to pray. During silent prayer time, congregants are instructed to mouth the words or prayers, even if they don't connect with the prayers or with God. The mere act of mouthing and sounding the words is a neurohack. As people repeatedly practice this ritual, they will be able to reflect on their behavior and realize that they must care enough about the religion to keep mouthing the prayers. It helps to reinforce their Jewish identity, allowing many people to open up to the possibility of belief in God. Mouthing prayer is just one of many neurohacks that helps to reinforce a Jew's identity. As Jews reflect on other behaviors, like being part of a community, wearing traditional religious clothing, and eating kosher food, the power of neurohacks grows even stronger.

I think it's important to note that just because religious groups like Chabad are able to leverage neurohacks doesn't in and of itself make these groups good or bad, it just makes them smart for intuitively understanding human psychology. Many other engaging groups have been successful using similar processes, like political parties (Republicans and Democrats, for example). What ultimately matters then is not whether a person or group uses neurohacks, but whether they use them for social good. Fortunately, I've witnessed Rabbi Cunin using them for good. I first met him when I was in college. He would stand on campus trying to unite people from all races and religions to do "random acts of goodness and kindness in the world"—like getting people to make cards for kids in the hospital or food for homeless people, and to visit people with drug addictions. And by getting people to reflect back on the good they did for others in the world, he was using neurohacks to make the world a better place.

GETTING CHOICE BUY-IN

Getting people to indicate they want something can be an important neurohack. People who voluntarily decide they want something, for example, deciding they want one job over another or choosing the date they plan to complete an assignment, are more likely to follow through in trying to achieve that outcome. I call this getting choice buy-in. But how do you get people to give their buy-in that they want something? One way is to give people a small number of choices and ask them to pick one of them. If it was their decision, not yours, then they'll be more likely to stick with that choice. That's one reason why in Chapter 5 (Easy) we talked about limiting the number of choices people have because it makes it easier for them to choose something and stick to their choice. If you remember back to Chapter 2, MyFitnessPal immediately gets users engaged through the onboarding process. They show new users a small number of choices and ask them whether they're using the app for "losing weight," "maintaining weight," or "gaining weight." My guess is that most people aren't choosing to download an app like that because they want to maintain or gain weight, but that doesn't matter. What matters is that people choose *something*. If they can get the user to choose one of the options, then they've started to create a neurohack by getting the user to commit to that decision. When people reflect back on their action of saying they're using the app to lose weight they are committing themselves to want to keep using the app to lose weight. The app has successfully gotten user buy-in by getting people to make a choice.

Getting choice buy-in isn't just helpful for businesses. Parents can use choice buy-in to influence children's decisions. For instance, if you're trying to get your kids to eat breakfast, instead of opening the refrigerator and asking them what they want (too many choices), you can try giving them a choice between two or three things, like cereal or eggs. If you can get them to respond that they want one of those choices then they'll be more likely to follow through and eat it. An important thing about getting choice buy-in is that people have to feel that they made their choice voluntarily. If people feel they were forced to have chosen to do something, like a kid feeling like his parents would punish him if he didn't choose to eat cereal, then it can actually backfire and make them not want to follow through with the decision.

CREATING CHAIN LINKS

In Chapter 2 we said we'd revisit stepladders in a later chapter. Well, here it is. . . . One reason why stepladders works is that each step people complete increases their commitment to keep doing something. The more days in a row a person goes swimming, the more committed she'll be to continue swimming every day. This commitment tricks the brain into not being able to give up. Think about how much harder it becomes to put down a book as you read more chapters. I call this creating a "chain link" because the more days in a row a person does something, the stronger the chain link becomes. Neurohacks are therefore more successful if they're done more than once, ideally at least a handful of times. If people do something once, like going to one improv class with the goal of becoming more present-minded, then it's tougher to gain a new identity as "the type of person who does improv," because that implies the person goes to improv multiple times out of her own interest. If a person goes to a larger number of classes, say five, then the mind starts to believe that she must be doing it because she enjoys the classes and is the type of person who likes going to improv; otherwise she would have quit.[26] This identity reflection really improves the strength of neurohacks. It helps to reset the mind and get someone to keep doing things. People need to do the same thing over and over for them to change their self-image.

Combining neurohacks with other forces helps to accomplish this and make them engrained in people's brains (more about that in the next chapter).

S ome of the biggest battles in people's lives and in the world can't be seen, because they're happening in people's minds. Low self-esteem, depression, addiction, and pain cause people great suffering, but they're all happening within people's heads. Conventional wisdom says that people—whether they're suffering from mental health issues like anxiety, or more benign behavioral issues like not being able to stick with a hobby—need to change their mind. If they can change their thoughts then their actions will follow. But much like the laws of physics and inertia—an object in motion stays in motion; an object at rest stays at rest—lasting behavior change won't start until an action has occurred. Lasting behavior change starts with an actual physical change in behavior, not a change in mind. Change starts not by contemplating putting on running shoes but by actually putting them on. This is the science behind neurohacks. Guided by similar forces of physics that have been known for hundreds of years and have been used to help people construct airplanes, computers, and new vaccines, neurohacks are a behavioral force that people can use to change their lives and change the world through action.

EXERCISE

1. Choose one of the neurohacks in this chapter (behavioral, body movement, physiological and emotional) and think of a way to apply it to the behavior you want to change. For example, if you want to become more present-minded, go to an improv class. If you want to get others to do something, like getting your employees to become more unified, at your next meeting

plan an exercise where each employee is asked to reflect and share on a positive experience working with the team.

2. Try to combine this homework with some of the forces from the other chapters, for example, incorporating community. You'll start to see how creating a plan that integrates multiple forces will lead to lasting change.

CHAPTER 7

CAPTIVATING

Christy Rakoczy was a self-described "extreme coupon shopper" between 2007 and 2010.[1] She was obsessed with combining store sales with cutting out coupons to get the best deals. Often she got things completely free—top food brands, personal hygiene and household products, and cleaning supplies.

But what exactly did she end up buying? A random assortment of things like diabetes monitors, toothpaste, and cold medicine, as she haunted coupon-rich retailers like Walgreens, CVS, and Rite Aid. If she found a coupon good for ten jars of spaghetti sauce, she would buy ten jars. Over time, these things stockpiled on her shelves. She had to spend time organizing and rotating the goods so they could be easily accessed. Sometimes food items spoiled. At one point she had one hundred jars of Robitussin cough syrup, and she purchased more than sixty diabetes monitors even though she doesn't have diabetes.[2]

"The problem, of course, is that I didn't need the items I was buying," wrote Rakoczy in a blog post. "The coupon craze created an incentive to buy unnecessary goods." She found herself stockpiling items, buying unhealthy foods, and just generally wasting a lot of time and money until she quit cold turkey in 2011.

"When I spent about eight hours after a Black Friday after Thanksgiving shopping for free toothpaste and toothbrushes and things that I already had an entire room full of stuff, I said, you know, I'm not going to do this anymore," she said in an NPR radio interview with Michel Martin. "This is just a waste of time."

Rakoczy is not alone in her addiction to couponing. Ninety-six percent of U.S. consumers use coupons.[3] In the digital era, this means they spend less time with scissors cutting paper coupons from newspapers, and more time trawling the Web for deals. In the first half of 2016, the average face value of digital coupons increased by 21.2 percent compared to the same period last year, far outpacing the increase of 0.6 percent registered by print coupons.[4] Overall paperless coupon distribution has grown 373 percent over the last four years.[5] There are so many ads online, and it's so easy to pass time searching through them, that digital couponers might even spend more time searching for deals than people did when only paper coupons existed.

But regardless of media, we're a coupon nation. Why do retailers love to offer coupons so much?

Because they work in businesses' favor.

Thirty-six percent of shoppers purchased the product sooner than they would have otherwise. And 29 percent of shoppers bought more of the promoted product than they originally planned.[6]

If the whole point of coupons is to save money, why do consumers actually spend more than they intended? And, ironically, why do the wealthiest people use coupons the most? A full 65 percent of the wealthiest consumer shoppers—with incomes of more than $150,000—would not have purchased an item without the coupon, compared to 51 percent of shoppers earning less than $40,000.[7]

Because it's fun. Beyond fun. Addicting. Captivating.

WHAT'S THE DEAL?

The idea is simple. People will keep doing things if they feel rewarded for doing them. I call this the *captivating* element of sticking to a behavior.

Think about it. Why do people shop after their base necessities are met? Why do they continue to shop, spending money on accessories, tchotchkes, or other things that they don't need and might never use? Because they enjoy the shopping experience itself. Stores like Nordstrom realize this, making sure that the experience is even more pleasurable for its customers by providing live piano music, coffee bars, a café with fresh salads and other enticing snacks, and, above all, helpful and attentive salespeople.

Alternatively, you've probably seen the people addicted to metal detecting. They're usually found on the beach or at historic sites with their rolled-up dungarees and large metal wands, carefully covering every inch of ground. Why do they do it? It's debatable that it's a profitable enterprise. After all, you have to shell out $500 or $1,000 in equipment up front. Most people never recover even a fraction of that back. Ask people why they do it and they talk about the pleasure of the activity, the anticipation of *maybe* finding something valuable. It's a hobby—and an immensely enjoyable one for many people. As one experienced hobbyist wrote to a newbie on an online forum:[8]

> If you're going to look upon it as a task and an economic proposition don't even bother. Those who buy equipment hoping to clean the countryside of coins usually have their gear on eBay in no time.

You could ask the same question about mobile phones. Why do so many people spend so much time consuming content on them? U.S. citizens are far and away the largest consumers of online data in the world—spending an astonishing 4.7 hours a day watching or reading it on their mobile devices.[9] There seems to be something more than just pleasurable—or, as we would call it, *captivating*—about the activity that keeps people doing it beyond what might be considered reasonable.

This chapter will show you that making boring things fun and rewarding can help you stick to your goals, whatever they might be.

THE SCIENCE BEHIND CAPTIVATING

Research on making something captivating goes back about a century. It began with work by people who unfortunately weren't very nice to animals. Called behaviorists, these scientists trapped animals like cats, rats, dogs, and monkeys in cages, and gave them rewards or punishments to try to understand what motivated them to do things. Specifically, their theories about *operant conditioning* assumed that learning would occur through giving and taking away reward and punishment.

Take Edward Lee Thorndike. In the early 1900s, he trapped cats in "puzzle boxes" to study how they learn. He gave them a non-obvious way to get out of the boxes, and learned that although the cats were confused at first, they soon learned that pulling a cord or pushing a pole would get them out.

Imagine that a mad scientist with an enormous mustache trapped *you* in a box. If you escaped, you'd probably feel pretty good. Freedom, after being scared you were going to remain captive in a box, would probably feel much better than most rewards you've gotten, like money for work or points for moving up a level on your favorite video game. That's probably how it made the cats feel, too, and so they quickly learned what they needed to do to get that reward again. After being put back in the box, they quickly pulled the cord or pushed the pole to get out again.[10]

The renowned behaviorist B. F. Skinner believed that all actions depend on a previous action—that is, there is no such thing as free will. We are simply conditioned to behave in a certain way. If consequences of doing something are bad, then we don't do it again. If consequences are good, we will repeat the action or behavior.[11]

Skinner didn't want to use Thorndike's puzzle boxes. So he made the famous Skinner box, in which he trapped and isolated animals like pigeons and rats and tried to get them to push levers and perform other tricks by rewarding them with food and punishing them with electric shocks. He found they learned based on these consequences.

A side note (and not a particularly inspiring story for animal lovers) on a practical application of Skinner's research: during World War II, the U.S. military needed to improve missile targeting systems. Skinner created missiles with pigeons inside them. By using pigeon conditioning, the pigeons guided the missiles to the correct targets.

How did Skinner do this? Through operant conditioning, he trained pigeons to recognize, and respond to, missiles' targets. The pigeons were placed in the front of the missile, right in front of the target screen. As they were conditioned to do, between one and three pigeons would peck at the target with their beaks. If the target remained centered on the screen, the missile would stay on its current course. But if the missile started to track wrongly, the target image would move to the edge of the screen. The pecking of the pigeons would signal to the controls that something was wrong and help the missile to get back on course.

Although this technique worked, and the National Defense Research Committee contributed $25,000 to Skinner's pet project, Skinner complained that "our problem was no one would take us seriously."[12] The program was canceled on October 8, 1944.

Recently, a lot of popular books have been written on "habit science." Although the "habit books" I've read say this is a new area of research, their theories are actually the same ones that were endorsed by Skinner and other behaviorists more than seventy-five years ago. Psychologists long ago abandoned this purely behaviorist psychology in favor of other theories because it doesn't work. The reason: these theories about people came from watching how caged animals act, but most people don't live in cages or act like caged animals. In fact, if you take animals out of cages, they don't act that way anymore.[13] That's why habit science doesn't work on people. People have a lot more freedom and choice than caged animals, and that makes them much more complicated.

What psychologists believe now: people will still respond to rewards, but not to just any reward.

The trick (it's not that easy) is that *the reward needs to feel just as powerful as it would feel if the person were actually in a cage yearning to get out or get fed.* Just as a caged rat waiting all day for food would be willing to press a lever a thousand times to get the food, people need to feel that a reward they will get is so powerful that they'd be willing to keep doing something—like running, eating healthy, sticking with a new instrument—a thousand times just like a caged animal.

The reward needs to be truly captivating! For that reason, we don't call this chapter "Rewarding." We want to separate captivating rewards from the typical advice that simply handing out rewards for an action is sufficient to get someone to stick to something. The difference between "just any reward" and something that is truly captivating is the difference between someone doing something once and feeling compelled to keep doing it.

Here's a quote from a participant on one of our online pain forums: "First, WOW. Reading everyone's stories has been so captivating that I canceled my plans and stayed glued to my monitor for the entire evening."

APPLYING CAPTIVATING TO YOUR LIFE

By 2011, more than 30 million people were living with HIV and almost three million people had been infected in the past year alone. Many of the top scientists believed that identifying a crystal structure of an AIDS-causing virus—the Mason-Pfizer monkey virus (M-PMV)—would bring us a step closer to the cure. But after fifteen years, the top scientists weren't much closer to finding the answer. The University of Washington's Center for Game Science had an idea. They suggested that scientists "crowdsource" the problem—that is, ask people to help them solve it. They knew from their research that making an activity into a puzzle is one way to engage large numbers of people to solve difficult problems. However, M-PMV was not a riveting topic among gamers. Moreover, only a limited number of people had sophisticated enough knowledge about biochemistry to even know what this monkey virus was.

Enter Foldit, an online puzzle video game created in a collaboration between the Center for Game Science and the university's biochemistry department. The game had an instructional session that taught players how to build, move, and complete biochemistry puzzles and gave them scores for how well they did.

A Foldit puzzle was created with the goal of identifying the structure of the monkey virus. The game was open for three weeks. But three weeks wasn't needed. More than 240,000 players on Foldit signed up to play the puzzle game. They completed the puzzle, and, unlike the scientists who had been trying for fifteen years, the gamers completed it in only ten days.

So how do you make something captivating enough for people to do something not just once, but repeatedly?

First, find something that is a captivating reward for the individual.

To do this, think back to Chapter 4 (Important) and try to discover what is truly important to the person (or group of people) you are trying to reach.

Is it money? Social environment and approval from peers? Self-improvement? Self-esteem? Health? Whatever is truly important can be a captivating reward.

As we discussed, studies have found the following things to be important—that is, rewarding—to people:

- Financial rewards (up to a point; after a while, they matter less)
- Social rewards (including belonging to a community, having people support you, competing successfully against others)
- Certain psychological states (feeling in control of a situation, feeling calm and tranquil)
- Good health
- Freedom/independence

The list could go on and on . . . but you get the idea.

People differ in which of these things are most important and how they want to be rewarded. The difference between *any* reward and a *captivating* reward lies in whether the reward is important to the person. The tough part is knowing ourselves or others well enough to know what's important.

FIVE THINGS YOU CAN DO TO MAKE SOMETHING CAPTIVATING

If the idea of captivating is so simple, why don't people use it correctly to get themselves or others to follow through with things? Because we have some engrained beliefs that don't stand up to facts when examined closely. Here are five ways to make something captivating that may contradict what you expect.

Make Doing the "Right Thing" Fun

Most people simply don't believe that things we "have" to do can be pleasurable. For example, most people believe that eating healthily can't be fun. If we want to eat healthy we have to give up enjoying life. We have to endure being put off, or at least bored, by our food. Yet some people do very creative things with healthy food—things that make mealtime enjoyable, and even fun.

Or take what we call the "workweek:" The very term engrains in us the attitude that we can't have fun during the week—that good times and pleasurable activities are relegated to the weekend. It's a perspective thing, however, as a study of German and American work habits found. Germans worked fewer hours per week (thirty-five hours) yet were more productive than Americans (forty-seven hours average). That's because to Germans, "work means work" and writing or answering personal emails, surfing the Web, or interacting with Facebook is culturally frowned upon. In other words, they don't waste time around the proverbial water cooler. Then, when the 5 p.m. bell rings, Germans are off work! They participate in clubs, musical groups, have family dinners or gatherings with friends, and truly put work behind them. Whereas Americans "waste" a lot of time at work. As a result, their work bleeds over into nights and weekends. Bottom line: Germans arguably have a better work-life balance than their American counterparts—and having fun during the "workweek" is a big part of that.[14]

Use the Carrot Instead of the Stick

Although fear can motivate people to do things for a little while, research shows that it's not sustainable. If people are taught to do something out of fear—like fear of losing a job, having a heart attack, or getting attacked by terrorists—and that feared event doesn't start happening to them or someone they know, then most people will stop doing what they were doing out of fear. For fear to work long-term, employees and their coworkers would need to start losing jobs, or citizens of a country would need to hear about terrorist attacks. Fortunately, other than with totalitarian organizations, it's not possible to force people to experience their fears. That's why it's more effective to use captivating rewards to get people to keep doing things, rather than fear and punishment.

A study of "fear" literature showed that although fear could appear to motivate people to change their behavior for the short term, in the long term it simply scares them into reactive mode by triggering avoidance of the topic in question as well as denial.[15] For example, much research has focused on whether fear-based campaigns that attempt to reduce HIV/AIDS risk are effective. For a long time, public health officials and activists avoided such campaigns because of ethical concerns about targeting vulnerable populations. But when such techniques were eventually used, the results were illuminating. Although there was an increased "perception of risk," knowledge of HIV/AIDS and condom use actually *declined* among the target populations. Why? Because the fear induced by the campaigns caused participants to avoid the issue or even deny any problem existed. However, using HIV testing and counseling to resolve rather than excite fear resulted in higher knowledge and condom use when subjects were questioned at both the intermediate and delayed follow-ups. The conclusion: inducing fear is *not* an effective long-term strategy to change people's health behaviors, whereas positive outlets like counseling are.[16]

Prison reformers are also finding that the carrot is more powerful than the stick. Take the case of Stacey Torres. A resident of one of Colorado's toughest prisons, Torres racked up more than sixty violations for fighting and dealing drugs while he was incarcerated. He was given the choice of doing more time at the maximum-security

Colorado State Penitentiary, or trying a new "good behavior" incentive program the prison had started called STAR (for Security Threat Administrative Review).[17]

Torres chose STAR. He now takes cognitive behavior classes that give him "homework" to complete and provide incentives for good behavior. Rewards include padded chairs, early meals, a large flat-screen TV, and DVDs of movies such as *Avatar* and *Rambo*. Since joining the program, Torres hasn't committed a single violation of prison rules. No more fighting with other prisoners. No more insubordination to security guards.

Other evidence shows that offering positive incentives rather than punishments works for some of the most hardened murderers and criminals in the Colorado justice system.

The Limon, Colorado–based penitentiary is no stranger to inmate violence. Over the past five years, there were two fatal stabbings of inmates and a correctional officer was beaten to death. Yet within a fourteen-month period, the 260 prisoners participating in the "Incentive Unit"—which makes up nearly 30 percent of the inmate population—committed just 2 percent of the more than 1,200 total violations.

Previously, inmates like Torres frequently found themselves in a downward spiral, where punishments were dealt out with each successive violation. Their living conditions would be progressively more restrictive until they eventually ended up at the state's maximum-security prison in Canon City. But through classes designed to teach inmates how to better control their emotions, STAR gives them a chance to gradually earn their way back into the general population and avoid that steady slide.

At the same time, the new incentive program at Limon allows inmates in the general population to trade up through good behavior into better living conditions. Prison officials are currently looking at how to expand the STAR program to other penitentiaries in the state.

Don't Assume Money Is the Best Reward

There's also the incorrect belief that money is the best way to reward people. That rational people simply want more money and will keep doing something—as long as they are paid for doing it.

There's a certain basis in fact to this. Yes, money can be rewarding—but not for everyone, and only to a certain point. What's more, the feeling of being rewarded by money can wear off.

A Princeton study by Nobel Prize winner Daniel Kahneman found that once a person earns $75,000 per year, the emotional benefits of income wear off. He analyzed more than 450,000 responses to the Gallup-Healthways Well-Being Index, a daily survey of 1,000 U.S. residents conducted by the Gallup Organization, and discovered that emotional well-being rises with income—but not beyond an annual income of $75,000.[18] Lower income is associated with divorce, ill health, and being alone.[19] What is the significance of $75,000? It's not a magic number. It appears to be the income considered "adequate" to meet people's basic needs. And the researchers found that lower income did not in itself cause sadness, but made people feel more burdened by the problems they already had.

In other words, that old adage "money can't buy happiness" turns out to be true.

There's a similar study with kids. Most elementary school–aged kids don't care about money, but they certainly like rewards like badges and ribbons. Will giving kids rewards get them to keep doing things? The answer is, it depends. . . .

In one study, kids who enjoyed a coloring activity were approached and put into one of three conditions.[20] In one condition, the kids were offered a "good player" reward if they kept coloring. In the other two conditions, the kids were either offered no reward or were not told they would be rewarded for coloring but were given a reward at the end of their activity. The researchers learned that the kids who were explicitly rewarded for coloring spent less time coloring than the kids who were either not rewarded for coloring or not rewarded at all. Why would rewarding kids for coloring make them want to color less?

The answer is that the reward changed what they thought of coloring. In a sense, it was a neurohack that worked in the opposite direction. Because the kids already enjoyed coloring, adding a reward to do what they already enjoyed doing got them to not want to color anymore; that activity seemed less interesting if it needed a reward. People don't need rewards for things they already find rewarding. If you start giving them rewards for these activities, they may start to think the activity isn't as fun as they had thought, because people need to be rewarded for doing it.

This same reasoning has been found in a lot of other areas, such as employee management. If you give a large reward to people for doing things they already enjoy doing, they'll often lose their motivation to keep doing them.[21][22] Think carefully before you increase the salary of an employee who already loves what he does. It might reset his brain to stop thinking of the work as pleasurable and start thinking of it as a tedious task that requires a lot of compensation to keep people motivated.

Forget Using Education by Itself

Then there's the belief that education is what really can change people's minds and behavior. This again goes back to the idea that people are rational. Once they know the benefits of eating healthily, or getting a colonoscopy, or whatever you are trying to get them to do, they will respond by acting appropriately.

But information has been proven time and time again to not be enough. People know that smoking is bad for their health. Yet they keep smoking, drinking too much alcohol, and doing other things that they know aren't good for them.

"We've known for over 50 years that providing information alone to people does not change their behavior," said Victor Strecher, a professor at the University of Michigan's School of Public Health, in a *New York* magazine article.[23]

Take the so-called war on drugs. The National Institute on Drug Abuse (NIDA) commissioned evaluations of the National Youth Anti-Drug Media Campaign, which spent more than $1 billion educating young people on the dangers of drug use. The results showed that education not only didn't deter drug use—it made young people even more likely to use drugs by glamorizing it.[24]

Another example: people suffering from diabetes have twice the likelihood of experiencing an acute coronary syndrome (ACS) and twice the rate of death after ACS compared with patients who do not have diabetes. You'd think these numbers would scare anyone into lifestyle changes.

Yet believing that this issue could be addressed with education, one group of researchers investigated the relationship between patients' diabetes knowledge and their efforts to control their conditions and improve their health incomes. There was no correlation.[25]

The moral: instead of attempting to educate people, you need to appeal to people's psychology and emotions to get them to keep doing things.

Make the Activity Itself Rewarding

There's also the incorrect belief that if people are simply *given* rewards they will keep doing things. People try to come up with theories and models on how accumulating points, badges, and other goodies—including money, of course—will get themselves or others motivated enough to keep doing things.

However, like negative fearmongering, simply handing out

rewards does little but encourage "temporary compliance" with a course of action. The fact is, *the activity itself has to be rewarding.*

This is a subtle but important difference.

Research has shown repeatedly that once the rewards stop flowing, people's behaviors will revert to what they were before. They are *extrinsic*, not intrinsic, to what commits us to act in certain ways.

Dozens of studies back this, especially when it comes to workplace productivity and rewards.[26] One of the most comprehensive studies of how incentive programs impact employee productivity—a "meta analysis" of ninety-eight individual studies—found no impact overall statistically between the productivity of employees who were given incentives and those who weren't.[27] However, the survey found that training and goal-setting programs affected worker productivity to a far greater extent than so-called pay-for-performance plans.[28]

For a while in Silicon Valley there was the manic compulsion to "gamify" everything—provide rewards, levels of achievement, "leaderboards," and other reward systems taken from computer games to entice people to keep doing something. But rewards like gamification will only work if they're designed correctly. A leaderboard isn't a panacea for a lack of engagement. You have to be careful when to gamify, and why.

So why are enterprises deploying gamification? Because of the dismal state of employee engagement. Gallup measured employee engagement in 2015 and came up with a figure of 31.7 percent.[29] That means that almost 70 percent of U.S. employees are disengaged. No wonder that employers are grabbing at sticks to solve the problem. As articulated by Brian Burke, vice president of research at Gartner:[30]

The focus is on the obvious game mechanics, such as points, badges and leader boards, rather than the more subtle and more important game design elements, such as balancing competition and collaboration, or defining a meaningful game economy. As a result, in many cases, organizations are simply counting points, slapping meaningless badges on activities and creating gamified applications that are simply not engaging for the target audience.

The rage for gamification has dropped off somewhat. Gartner—which predicted back in 2011 that by the beginning of 2015 more than 70 percent of Global 2000 enterprises would deploy at least one gamified application[31]—was warning of a failure rate of 80 percent of those applications because of poor design one year later.[32]

In most cases, a *simplistic* way of introducing some form of gamification failed. The common causes:

- An emphasis on extrinsic motivators without including intrinsic motivators
- No consideration of the players' motivations
- Introducing competition in an environment where collaboration, creativity, or learning were more important
- A primary focus on managerial goals rather than employee motivations

As an example of something that did *not* work, Wuppermann, a steel company headquartered in the Netherlands, created a computer dashboard—a graphical display that showed up on employees' screens—that highlighted safety problems and work stoppages. The software also rated individual workers, with management hoping that would improve productivity. But employee scores were mainly based on negative events such as mistakes and accidents.[33] Wuppermann employees found it *highly* discouraging to be constantly reminded of what they were doing wrong. This negative "gamification" of the workplace also encouraged competition between teams that resulted in unprofessional behavior, such as workers leaving problems for the next shift so their scores wouldn't be affected. This obviously didn't help with safety or productivity!

What researchers have learned: gamification can't be just about competition (after all, in many cases the same people keep winning every time, and the people who don't win get discouraged and disengage) but needs to provide both individual and team feedback in real time to combine what Gartner calls the key elements—social capital, self-esteem, and fun—into a seamless experience.

Disneyland tried to gamify work for its hotel laundry workers in Anaheim, California, by creating a "leaderboard" that tracked employee productivity, but while it might have increased productivity it also led to unintended negative consequences. The firm installed giant screens in its basement laundry facilities at the Disneyland and Paradise Pier hotels. Workers toiled under large flat-screen monitors that were placed prominently on the walls of the room in which they sorted, loaded, and folded laundry. Each worker's speed was compared to all the others'. And employees were listed by name, so everyone could see who was quickest at moving pillowcases, sheets, and towels through the laundry system.[34]

One longtime Disneyland hotel laundry worker began calling the new system the "electronic whip" and the name stuck.

Keeping track of worker productivity is fairly standard in the hospitality industry. But until the huge leaderboards were installed, only manual counts of productivity were kept, and they were confidential to management. The new leaderboards broadcast every single worker's productivity numbers. For example, it might show that R. Alvez is working at only 37 percent of expected production. Workers who were meeting the efficiency numbers set by management had their names displayed in green; workers underperforming were displayed in red.

The display did lead to some competition and increased engagement as certain workers tried hard to get to the top of the leaderboard. But it also led to increased stress and discord among employees. According to the local union, employees began skipping bathroom breaks and lunches to keep their numbers high. They began feeling that their jobs—which paid $8 to $14 per hour—involved a race to the bottom at a time when the company was recording profits of approximately $4 billion. Although the leaderboard display might therefore have led to increased productivity, it was unfortunately at the expense of workers. This was not a success story.

TWO TYPES OF CAPTIVATING "FIXES"

There are two things you can do once you've established what is important to an individual: the Quick Fix and the Trick Fix.

The Quick Fix

If you've ever walked into a casino, one of the first things you'll notice is the barrage of energy and noise. "Ka-ching! Ka-ching! Jackpot!" You can't go a minute without hearing someone winning on the slot machines. And it's designed that way by casino owners who have mastered the Quick Fix. The Quick Fix is the immediate reinforcement people need for doing something. If you just entered a casino, immediately hearing the clanging of coins dropping out of a winning slot machine is an example of a Quick Fix. It immediately teaches people that they can win, too—and that they should keep walking in, put some money down, and let it roll. An important thing about the Quick Fix is that people need to get it quickly after they start something. If it takes a while to get the Quick Fix—making it no longer quick—then people won't connect the reward to the behavior.

For example, imagine you're training a dog to sit. You get him to sit, wait an hour, and then give him a treat and say, "Good boy!" What happens when you tell him to sit next time? Nothing. The reason is that he got the treat an hour after he sat. Too much time has passed for him to realize that the treat was a reward for sitting. Unless he can connect the pleasure of the food to the act of sitting, the dog won't learn to sit. Giving the dog a Quick Fix—a treat immediately after sitting—helps him to learn that he's supposed to sit next time. A Quick Fix also helps people to keep doing things, like hearing the sound that an email or text was sent after pushing the send button, feeling compelled to keep reading a book after an engaging first paragraph, or getting a sugar rush to the brain after a first bite of a chocolate bar.

The reward also needs to be *appropriate* for people to keep doing something. A leaderboard of "top employees" isn't an appropriate reward for an employee who is motivated by supporting coworkers rather than competing with them. She simply wouldn't find that captivating. The reward has to be tailored to what she needs, like having peers congratulate her on helping to finish a project on time and under budget.

Perhaps you want to learn an instrument. You want to do it for the long term—years and years rather than just quitting after a few months. Yet you know you have a tendency to initially get excited and then drop things as the newness wears off. How do you *stick to it*?

Using the advice from Chapter 2 (Stepladders) and Chapter 5 (Easy), pick a very easy song to learn as a tiny first step. The very act of mastering it should be a *captivating* experience—you'll feel rewarded by it. Then, each time you practice, play that song to re-inforce that pleasure.

If you find performing in front of others captivating (some people do, others don't), reward yourself by playing that song in front of an audience. Even an audience of one should suffice.

The Trick Fix

The "Trick Fix" involves *intermittent* reinforcement. The science behind this goes back to B. F. Skinner, who discovered that rats that were intermittently rewarded with pellets by pushing a lever would push the lever more frequently than rats that were always rewarded. In effect, you're "weaning" yourself off the reward by getting it when you don't expect it. So once you feel that you're on a good path to sticking to something, gradually taper off your reward.

How do casinos use the Trick Fix? They make sure people win, but not every time they play. They let gamblers win occasionally, when they least expect it. Studies have shown that people actually become more addicted to gambling when they intermittently win than if they win every time. If rewarded every time they play, they soon get bored and stop playing, but if they win intermittently then they keep gambling until they run out of money or are stopped.[35]

How do you apply this to your own life? Take the instrument example. You can use the Trick Fix to gradually stop playing your easy "reward" song. You can still play it sometimes, but not every time you practice. Learn to play other songs that are more difficult. Then, every once in a while, return to playing your easy song to feel a reward. Or set a new goal with a new reward, and begin the process all over again.

More than 90 percent of high schools offer foreign language classes to students.[36] These classes are time-consuming and expensive—approximately one-twelfth of a student's high school education is spent on language classes.[37] But guess how many students wind up being proficient in the language they study? Less than 1 percent.[38] Clearly, people have trouble sticking with learning new languages.

Former president of the World Bank Paul Wolfowitz speaks six languages: Arabic, German, French, Hebrew, Indonesian, and

English. He told me his process for learning languages, using Indonesian as an example, which he learned while he was the U.S. ambassador there. Unlike the previous U.S. ambassador to Indonesia, or the European ambassadors to Indonesia, he didn't want to rely on translators. So how did he learn to speak it?

Wolfowitz said that the learning *process* needs to be immediately rewarding in order for him—or any student—to keep learning. He started learning by reading his favorite Indonesian book, *Twilight in Jakarta*, which he had read a number of times in English, alongside the Indonesian version. He would read a few pages at a time, just enough to understand the gist of it and pick up some basic words. He said this process was important to ensure that he immediately enjoyed learning the language (a Quick Fix), compared to a more tedious process of stopping to look up every word in a dictionary the way many people are taught to learn. One day, while purchasing food in a local market, he tried using some of the words he had learned at the checkout. He was immediately rewarded by the cashier's surprise that he cared to learn their language when other visitors and diplomats had not.

After a while, however, the pleasure from Quick Fixes began to plateau, and he needed a bigger challenge, a Trick Fix, to keep him motivated.

Wolfowitz committed himself to giving a speech six months later on the cultural and religious tensions in Indonesia. He knew this topic might offend the current authoritarian government, but that, if delivered correctly, it would win the support and trust of the Indonesian people. For the speech to have the influence he intended, he knew he needed to speak entirely in Indonesian and for him to understand every word of it.

After months of studying, Wolfowitz delivered the speech and received a standing ovation. A young man who had felt hopeless in the current political regime, saw him on the street after the speech and told Wolfowitz that the speech had inspired him to stand up against the current government. Wolfowitz began earning the respect of the Indonesian people, a captivating reward that inspired him to keep learning the language. It became easier for him to continue learning Indonesian as other forces like Community, Easy, and Important became integrated into his learning process. His driver, a local man who was inspired by the speech, decided to only communicate with Wolfowitz in Indonesian. During those drives, Wolfowitz started keeping flash cards with him so that he could respond to the driver and study when he was waiting in the car before a political meeting.

Wolfowitz continued using Trick Fix reinforcement to keep himself motivated to learn the language. The intermittent praise he got from meeting Indonesians who told him in Indonesian that he truly understood the people and their cultural issues compelled him to keep learning and become fluent. Paul Wolfowitz didn't quit learning or forget how to speak Indonesian after completing his term as ambassador. Despite living outside of Indonesia for more than twenty-five years, he remains fluent and keeps practicing.[39]

APPLYING CAPTIVATING TO BUSINESS

A few months before the 2014 Winter Olympics in Sochi, Russia, if you'd gone down into the Vystavochnaya subway station in Moscow, you would have been greeted by a strange sight: people standing in line, bundled up against the winter chill, one by one shedding their hats, scarves, and outer clothes to perform squats in front of a machine outfitted with sensors. People yelled encouragement as one person after another attempted to perform thirty squats within a twenty-second period. When someone succeeded, the crowd cheered as he or she was handed a paper ticket by an official-looking person overseeing the operation.

What was going on? Simply an example of making something *captivating* in action. To encourage Russians to get more physically fit, as well as get into the Olympic spirit for the upcoming games, the Russian government was giving out free subway tickets (worth thirty rubles, or about one dollar) if the challenge was successfully completed. The first person to earn her ticket was gymnast Elena Zamolodchikova, winner of two gold medals at the Sydney Olympics.[40]

Other initiatives along the same lines included removing the handles on buses and replacing them with exercise bands. The Russian government even placed bikes on the streets that Russian citizens could ride to produce electricity for their mobile phones. Said Alexander Zhukov, president of the Russian Olympic Committee, to Russia's state-run news agency: "We wanted to show the Olympic Games are not just an international competition that people watch on TV, but are also about getting everyone involved in a sporting lifestyle."

Loyalty programs, if designed correctly, work for a similar reason. They reward people for something they already really want or need—something that already captivates them—and gives them a justification for why they should get more of it.

Take frequent flyer rewards. They've become an economy of their own, with more than $16 billion worth of reward points and miles going unredeemed in 2011 alone.[41] There's something about the allure of free flights (or upgrades, or hotels, or rental cars) that captivates people and gets them to do anything to accrue more points. More than 40 million frequent flyer tickets were issued in 2014. Two hundred million people—that's nearly half of all U.S. households—participate in at least one program. And 39 billion miles expire annually, never to be used.

Industry analysts estimate that about a million trips are taken each year just to add miles to one's account.[42] One survey of participants in FlyerTalk, an online community for frequent flyers, found 24 percent admitted taking unnecessary trips to get extra miles. Experts estimate that abuses like this add up to a full 8 percent of annual business travel costs.[43]

It is not just about earning points. It's about imagining what you can do with those points. Fantasizing about that free trip to Hawaii or Mallorca. And the way you're treated when you accrue enough miles. Frequent flyer programs have created their own international caste system. Elite travelers get their own priority lines at the airport, are given aisle seats and bumped up to first class. If a flight is oversold, they're not the ones who get shoved off the plane. Good flier programs also capitalize on the Quick Fix and Trick Fix: they reward people immediately for joining the program and gradually taper off the rewards so that customers don't know when to expect their next reward, making a surprise upgrade feel like winning on the slot machines!

For the businesses, these programs are a way to successfully differentiate what are essentially commodity services. And people eat them up.

In fact, it's rare to find a business that *doesn't* have a loyalty program. Take coffee. Not being a coffee drinker, each morning I feel like I'm in the middle of *28 Days Later* surrounded by zombies. My coworkers are all coffee drinkers and nothing will stand in their way of getting their morning fix. Clearly, coffee is a captivating reward that people give to themselves for waking up and getting ready to start the day. Starbucks does a great job capitalizing on using this reward, not just by selling it, but by creating an additional system to reward people for buying what they already want, or in the case of caffeine, need.

The My Starbucks Rewards campaign has made a big difference in Starbucks's record growth. Starbucks claims that the program played a key role in its 26 percent rise in profit and 11 percent jump in total revenue to $3.6 billion in 2013's second quarter fiscal results.[44]

Best Buy also turned to customer loyalty after experiencing stagnant revenue growth year after year in its brick-and-mortar stores. To keep up with major online retailers like Amazon and eBay, Best Buy increased reward points from 4 percent to 5 percent last year to motivate customers to keep coming back.[45] This helped the company's stock more than double within twelve months.[46]

Businesses can make purchasing experiences socially rewarding as well. This is a captivating reward for the growing number of young people who value leaving a positive impact on their world over more traditional rewards like money.[47]

Take the company Toms. Buying shoes, eyewear, coffee, apparel, or bags from Toms contributes something tangible to impoverished people. Toms founder Blake Mycoskie calls it the "One for One" model. Every time a Toms product is purchased, someone in need is helped.

Mycoskie got the idea from his travels around the world when he was in his twenties. While in Buenos Aires, he helped a woman deliver shoes to children in poor rural areas. Mycoskie called the experience "life changing." He wanted to help. But rather than go the traditional nonprofit route, he decided to start a for-profit company based on the buy-one, give-one idea. In 2006 he started the firm in his apartment, naming it "Shoes for Tomorrow," shortened to Toms so that the name would fit on a tag on the shoes.[48]

By the end of its first five years in business, Toms had a compound annual growth rate of 300 percent and had given away its 10 millionth pair of shoes.[49] The One for One model, which had been pooh-poohed by traditional businesspeople as not financially feasible, had worked. Mycoskie decided to expand it to eyewear, giving away pairs of glasses or medical treatments to restore sight for each pair of sunglasses sold. It sold more than 150,000 pairs in the past two years—and, in keeping with the One for One model, has helped deliver eye care to more than 150,000 people.

So successful was Toms at making buying its products captivating that it spent virtually nothing on traditional advertising. Instead, its more than five million social media followers spread the news about the company via word of mouth.

People differ in what they find rewarding. To some people, money might be the strongest reward, to others it might be community, and to others it might be personal health. Rewards change over time, too. People might find money to be a captivating reward when they're younger but spending time with family might become more important as they get older.[50] If you can understand the difference between giving just *any reward* compared to one that you or someone else truly finds *captivating*, then you'll have the power to make change stick.

But the ability to know what people find captivating extends far beyond being able to get someone to stick with something, such as a plan to eat healthier food. It allows us to truly understand ourselves and others on a deeper psychological level by learning what people value and find meaningful. Through that process of learning what people find captivating, we're able to not only change behavior but also to develop a deeper bond with humanity.

EXERCISE

1. Continue working with the goal that you chose in an earlier chapter, whether that is attracting more customers to your product, becoming healthier, or earning more money.
2. Remember from Chapter 2 that people often aren't excited about planning to accomplish small steps leading to a goal. If you want to learn to be a jazz

bass player, you might not be excited about the mundane steps of getting sheet music and blocking off time in the calendar to practice tomorrow. But the stepladders model explained why it's necessary to focus not only on the dream of being onstage and playing like jazz great Ray Brown, but on the small steps that lead up to it. How can you get yourself excited about completing such small steps? Start by thinking about a "reward" that would make you feel great for accomplishing a step toward that goal. Make sure it's not just any reward, but one that is *captivating*, based on what's truly important to you. For example, does receiving praise or a smile from a certain friend, significant other, family member, or coworker make you feel great? If so, ask that person to be involved in making you feel good when you complete your steps. Are you motivated by money? If so, create a commitment contract where you earn money if you complete steps or you have to pay someone if you don't. Determine what's important to you and then use that as a captivating reward to motivate you.

3. Use both the Quick Fix and the Trick Fix. Make sure you're rewarded with the reward you chose in number two immediately after you complete your step. Continue getting that reward as you complete more steps, but gradually taper it off so you don't get it as frequently. If possible, begin to get rewarded only periodically, and when you least expect it.

CHAPTER 8

ENGRAINED

After enduring seven long days of drug treatment at a halfway house, Michael Richards had made it through the early phases of cocaine withdrawal. By clinical standards, he was stable and drug-free. By general standards, he was considered "clean." A longtime cocaine addict, Michael had known he needed to quit drugs and had been searching for a way to do it. While in the program, he heard about a research experiment designed to simultaneously help recovering cocaine addicts and study how cocaine addiction affects the brain. The study required participants to be free from cocaine for a week. Because of his stint in the halfway house, Michael was accepted. Participating in the study would also put some much-needed cash in his pocket.

As part of the study, Michael consented to be placed in a device called a functional magnetic resonance imaging machine, or fMRI. The fMRI is effectively a giant magnet. It measures brain activity by seeing where blood flows throughout the organ.

The actual procedure was simple. Michael lay in the fMRI machine while researchers showed him pictures of gray screens with black crosses displayed on them. As he looked at the pictures, they monitored his brain activity.[1] All Michael had to do was keep his eyes open and watch.

But approximately ten minutes after the pictures began to flash in front of him, Michael began to feel strange. He recognized the sensation. It had taken over his life for nine long years. His cocaine cravings were back. After about twenty minutes of looking at crosses, Michael was finished. He needed to get out of there. He'd do anything to get hold of some powder. But why was he suddenly feeling like this again?

What Michael didn't realize is that in between pictures of crosses, researchers were flashing images of cocaine and crack pipes. The images were displayed for just 33 milliseconds—a split second that can't be recognized by the human eye. Yet the images had *become engrained* in Michael's brain, arousing his craving once again. The brain scans from the fMRI proved this. While Michael unknowingly viewed pictures of cocaine, his brain showed activity in places that had long been established as related to addiction: the amygdala (which shows preferences for liking or disliking things); the ventral striatum and ventral pallidum (areas that recognize rewards); the insula (linked to addiction and emotional states); and the temporal poles (classically linked to cocaine).

Two days later, Michael was again shown pictures of cocaine, but this time he could see them. He was then assessed psychologically to see how those pictures made him feel. Using the fMRI brain scans that had been taken two days earlier, the researchers were able to predict how good he would feel seeing these cocaine images again.

Michael's story illustrates what happens when something—in this case, cocaine addiction—has been engrained in the brain. It becomes easier for it to stick, and to return, at a hair-trigger.

That's why, if you repeatedly do things that are good for you—like eating healthier, working safer, and being more present-minded—these activities can become engrained in your brain, making it easier to keep doing them. Or, as in Michael's case, they can make it tough for someone to quit doing things they don't want to do. The urge to use cocaine was so engrained in Michael's brain that mere images of cocaine caused his brain to immediately return to its old familiar state. Even though the pictures of drugs were first shown without his awareness, his brain let him know it was time to get high again.

On the surface, Michael's story appears to be a disheartening one. Are we powerless to overcome our history because our brains are programmed? Does this imply that people can't change—that once a behavior gets engrained in the brain, we are forever doomed to repeat it?

No. In Michael's case, there was good news: the researchers who conducted that study later discovered that taking baclofen—a medication commonly used to treat spastic disorders like spinal cord injuries and cerebral palsy—could block the brain's response to unconscious cocaine triggers and reduce cravings.[2]

But the real question is, can the human brain change even after habits have already been engrained? Gabrielle Giffords's story answers that question.

On January 8, 2011, Gabrielle Giffords, a representative from Arizona's eighth congressional district, was hosting her first "Congress at your Corner" initiative outside of a Safeway store in a suburb of Tucson.[3] She invited voters to meet her and ask questions about her political reform ideas. She was particularly excited to discuss her thoughts on security along the U.S.-Mexico border, an issue of great importance to citizens in her district.

Midway through her speech, Giffords was suddenly interrupted by gunshots. A young man with a long history of antigovernment protest burst through the crowd. He used a 9mm Glock 19 semiautomatic pistol to send streams of bullets in every direction. He headed straight toward Giffords, shooting all the way. In a clear assassination attempt, he pointed the gun straight at Giffords and put a bullet through her head. Along the way, he killed six people and wounded twelve. Giffords was the thirteenth. Shot through the brain, she was rushed to the emergency room, critically injured but alive.

Later that day, doctors performed emergency surgery on Giffords, removing part of her skull and some brain tissue to reduce swelling. She was placed in an induced coma to give her time to rest. When she woke, the doctors performed a thorough examination. Because she was on a ventilator, she couldn't talk. She only had limited ability to move her arms. Although a complete recovery seemed unlikely, her chief neurologist, U.S. Army Dr. Geoffrey Ling, said that "her prognosis for maintaining the function that she has is very good. It's over 50 percent." In other words, she probably wouldn't get any worse. But she might not get any better, either.

Among other things, it seemed highly unlikely that Giffords would ever be able to coherently speak again, much less serve out her term in Congress.

But with science on her side, Giffords's story took a miraculous turn. Giffords's brain had been severely damaged by both the shooting and the surgery performed to save her life. But although the damage erased her engrained set of daily habits like walking, talking, and campaigning, Giffords didn't just accept the prognosis that she wouldn't regain these important skills.

Under the care of an outstanding rehabilitation team at TIRR Memorial Hermann, a rehabilitation hospital in Houston, she began putting her body into situations that demanded it to return to her original state. The plan to rehabilitate Giffords started with the basics of learning to count, and reciting her name and the days of the week. Giffords had always been a music lover, and music therapy played a large role in her recovery. A therapist would play the song "Happy Birthday," stopping at the last word of each stanza to encourage Giffords to respond, "Happy birthday to *you*."[4] After being released from the hospital, Giffords continued intensive physical therapy, occupational therapy, and speech therapy through an outpatient rehabilitation program. A monumental point was her ability to speak her first sentence, directed toward her husband: "I love you, Mark."

Over time, with this kind of repetitive physical, psychological, and speech rehabilitation, Giffords's brain learned to adapt. She learned new habits—to not just lie there motionless, but to move. And at the same time, inside her brain, new neural connections were being formed to engrain the progress she had made in her speech, movement, and thought, and to facilitate further improvement.

Giffords soon was able to sit up on command. She learned how to breathe on her own. Her doctors began saying she "had great rehabilitation potential." With more time, Giffords learned to speak short sentences and use her left arm to write. Giffords's husband, Mark Kelly, the space commander of NASA's space shuttle Endeavour, began to hope that Giffords might be well enough to come to Florida to attend the launch of his final space shuttle mission, STS-134.

By April 2011, just three months after the accident, Giffords had recovered enough to be temporarily discharged from the hospital to attend her husband's launch. On August 1, 2011, she received a standing ovation from Congress for making an appearance on the House floor to vote in favor of raising the debt ceiling.

On January 22, 2012, Gabrielle Giffords announced that she was resigning from Congress to focus on her recovery. She has continued to improve and retrain her brain. She even went skydiving in 2014 to mark the three-year anniversary of the shooting, and has become a fervent advocate of gun control.

Giffords's story is a remarkable example of how habits that appear to be stuck—whether due to familiar routines like eating late-night desserts, or to biological and chemical changes in the brain—can be replaced with others for a lasting change. Her case dramatized an important theory of how the brain engrains knowledge and behaviors. Called "plasticity" by psychologists and neuroscientists, this theory refers to the ability of the brain to change and adapt to new situations.[5]

Fortunately, most people will never experience brain trauma. Still, it is uplifting. We realize that if Gabrielle Giffords can make lasting rehabilitative changes to her brain and behavior in the face of extreme adversity, then the rest of us have the potential to win the smaller battles in life.

But the question remains: How do you engrain something in the brain to create lasting change? We'll begin answering that question by teaching you why the brain forms habits.

WHY DO WE FORM HABITS?

The human brain is amazingly efficient. It is designed so people can do things without having to think. It rewards people for sticking to routines.[6] We learned in Chapter 5 that people keep doing things that are easy to do. The brain works the same way. It tries to make tasks easy. For example, when people see, hear, or smell something repeatedly (even if they aren't aware of it), the brain stores this information to recognize it quickly.[7] When people are learning to do something new, such as learning to repeatedly play the first few notes of a song, the brain rewards these efforts by releasing neurotransmitters like dopamine, which makes us want to do it again.[8]

Brains are like cars. Driving them in manual mode takes a lot of awareness and effort. But brains prefer to be in automatic mode. They do this by storing things that frequently occur so they can be easily accessed. Think of it like your computer storing your username and password for a site you visit often. That way, you can log in effortlessly, without thinking, allowing you to concentrate on other things.

That is exactly how the brain works. It constantly seeks out ways to make tasks easy to do. It turns repeated behaviors into habits that require little thought. Once habits have been built, the brain achieves homeostasis—a stable sort of equilibrium—and is able to relax. That habit then becomes a go-to default behavior.[9]

The bad news is that habits—such as addiction to drugs—can be destructive and exceedingly hard to change.[10] [11]

The good news is that, with the right efforts, undesirable patterns *can* be changed. And once people change their habits, strong forces will then be in place to make the new behavior last.

I use the word *engrain* to describe the process the brain uses to create lasting change. When the brain believes it needs to remember information or a behavior—usually because the thing happens repeatedly—the brain engrains that information or behavior to make it easy to remember so it can do it again.

Take newborn babies. Babies prefer their own mother's voices to the voices of other women. This is because from the early days in the womb, a mother's voice becomes engrained in a baby's brain. The mother's voice becomes a familiar, safe, and recognizable sound that makes a baby happy when she or he hears it.[12]

In one study, babies were given pacifiers that made sounds when they sucked on them. If they sucked in a certain way, they'd hear recordings of their mother's voice. If they sucked another way, they'd hear another woman's voice. The babies quickly learned to control the sound of the voice. They chose to suck on the pacifier in the way that would recreate their mother's voice.[13]

When we brought our newborn girl home from the hospital, I used my knowledge of this effect to forge a bond between her and our dog, Nora Jones. I put a recording of my wife's voice on Nora to make it sound like it was coming from the dog. I also wrapped a dog bone in the baby blanket and gave it to Nora so Nora thought the baby had given it to her. Baby Melody was soon snuggling with Nora Jones. In fact, Nora took on a protective mother role and would guard Melody from unwanted visitors like the mailman.

And this effect between babies and their mothers' voices isn't something that happens only in human brains. Researchers have found that animal brains also become engrained to identify sounds. It starts even before they are born. Researchers played two musical tones, one to each of two different sets of unhatched chicken eggs. When the eggs hatched, the researchers played both of the tones for each of the chicklets. Chicklets made fewer distressed cries when they heard the tone that had been played before they were born, and thus showed their preference for this tone.[14]

Because the brain wants to be hyperefficient, it doesn't stop there. In addition to engraining information about sounds, smells, and sights, the brain also engrains what people *do* repeatedly. If you take the same route to work each day, the brain encodes this information so you can easily take the same route again. The more you take that route to work, the more it becomes engrained and the less you have to think about how to get to work. The brain follows this pattern across all things in life, even for things that we are not aware of seeing or doing.

The secret to making things engrained in the brain is based on this *repetition*: repeating behaviors, especially if it can be done every day, in the same place, and at the same time, will teach the brain that it needs to remember this behavior to make it easier to keep doing it. It will engrain this behavior.

It's actually pretty amazing how much the brain engrains. The brain even engrains information that might appear useless on the surface. It was designed to do this to save time in the future.

For example, in one study, two groups of Americans were subliminally shown images of Chinese characters. The characters were flashed too quickly for people to consciously be aware of what they saw, but their brains were able to catch them. One group was shown each of the unknown Chinese characters just once. The second group was shown them five times, making them subliminally much more familiar.

All participants were then given pictures to look at of the Chinese characters they had been shown as well as new Chinese characters they had never seen. They were asked to rate how much they liked each character.

The people in the group who saw the characters five times pointed to those ones as preferred more than the group who saw those images only once.[15] Even though they hadn't been aware they had seen the images, their brains engrained this information to make it easier for them to recognize the images later. This familiarity also made the characters more likable.

This effect explains how repeated subliminal advertising can get people to like and buy a product. The familiarity engrained in the brain causes people to have a positive association with the product.

More broadly, this process of how the brain engrains repeated things explains why people act the way they do. It provides a framework for understanding reasons behind important social, political, and public health issues like discrimination, racism, political extremism, and depression.

Take racism. From birth, people's brains are designed to engrain things that are familiar to them. Just as babies prefer the sounds of their mothers' voices or the faces of their mothers compared to others, they also learn to prefer their own race. Although newborns show no preferences for people based on race, three-month-old babies show clear preferences for people in their own racial or ethnic groups.[16]

This psychological effect extends to kids and older adults, too. When kids repeatedly see people who look similar to them—for example, people with a similar skin color—the brain engrains this information that people with this skin color are more familiar, safe, and preferable to people who look different. This process causes people to favor things that are familiar—whether race, religion, or clothing style.

It might sound like this logic is moving toward a justification of racism and other social problems, so let me pause here to avoid that misinterpreation. Just because there's a psychological explanation for why people become racist doesn't mean that people are *destined* to be racist. Having insight into how the brain forms preferences allows us to be able to guide and change preferences. In fact, this research supports arguments for why we need diversity in schools and society at an early age so that people feel safe and comfortable around others who are different than themselves.[17]

But what if kids aren't exposed to other races at an early age? Or, perhaps more important, how can people retrain their brains to change, even at later stages in life?

APPLYING ENGRAINED IN YOUR LIFE

There is no process better designed to engrain habits than training to become a soldier. A rigorous retraining of the brain and behavior is needed to teach civilians how to calmly and mechanically follow instructions, especially during life-threatening situations. The military has shown that even the most basic human response—the desire to protect yourself over others—can be retrained to create people who will sacrifice their own lives for others they met just months earlier. When civilians complete the transition from premilitary habits to this new set of responses, they are truly soldiers.

The secret to this process is repetition. By requiring certain behaviors to occur every day at the same time and place, the military is creating a unit of people with habits that are firmly engrained in the brain so that they can occur practically automatically. That's why soldiers in basic training are taught to spring up at 4:30 a.m. every day. If most of the rest of us were awakened at that time we might feel around for the snooze button or have to pull back our eyelids and moan before getting up. This process explains how soldiers can automatically march in unison. It explains how they can intuitively follow commands while being fired at on a battlefield when most people would be frozen with fear. Soldiers can do these things because the repetitive practicing of these behaviors engrains them in their brains. Despite this intense training and how firmly engrained behaviors are in their brains, some soldiers lose the ability to respond as they were trained. This can happen because of trauma.

As we learned through Gabrielle Giffords's story, previously engrained behaviors like knowing how to walk, talk, and sing can become lost if the brain is damaged, as hers was from gunshots. Her brain damage caused her to forget her old behaviors and required new repetitive training to re-engrain her old behaviors. But physical trauma to the brain isn't the only way people can forget behaviors that were already engrained in their brains. Psychological damage can also do it.

Soldiers who experience psychological trauma, such as from watching fellow soldiers die or from near-death experiences, can be affected by post-traumatic stress disorder, or PTSD. *Trauma* is the key word in PTSD. It can lead soldiers to behave differently than they have been trained. A soldier who experiences PTSD on the battlefield might suddenly become frozen with fear or overly reactive. It can lead them to become overly reactive in situations in the future that feel similar to how they felt when they experienced the trauma. By engraining a new set of unhealthy behaviors, PTSD can make it incredibly difficult for soldiers to reintegrate into civilian life when they return home.

Take David George, one of the first troops to enter Iraq in 2003 and a former specialist in the 101st Airborne Division of the army.[18] While he was deployed at a town north of Baghdad, insurgents detonated a car packed with explosives next to his barracks. George says that this "kicked everything off." The screams that George heard that day became engrained in his brain. The traumatic event established a new set of habits that would become a familiar part of his life. When George was discharged and returned to his parents' home in Maryland, he continued to hear the screams he'd heard in the barracks.

PTSD affects not only soldiers, but anyone who has experienced a traumatic event, such as war, witnessing a murder, experiencing the death of a loved one, or even the stress of starting a new career. Flashbacks, or dreamlike reminders of the event, are a hallmark symptom of PTSD. For a soldier like David George, bright flashing lights at a nightclub might trigger these flashbacks and remind him of his experience at the barracks.

Just like other things that the brain does, PTSD has a purpose. And one of the "psychological purposes" of PTSD is to engrain responses in the brain to make it easier for someone to deal with a similar event in the future.[19] In other words, PTSD is an extreme version of an adaptive response that engrains behaviors in the brain to prepare people in case the traumatic event occurs again. Being able to quickly and automatically drop to the ground when seeing flashing lights could be the difference between life and death for a soldier. PTSD could help to train this sort of behavioral response. The problem with PTSD, however—and the reason it is a psychological disorder—is that it's not healthy or adaptive to feel retraumatized every time you experience a reminder of the event. Fortunately, most people's lives aren't at risk every time lights flash.

Most soldiers return home and need to readjust to a world where civilian habits dominate—not the habits they needed to survive on the battlefield.

This was the problem for David George. His PTSD led to dramatic changes in his thoughts and behaviors. At his parents' home, he carried a rifle and moved from one room to the next, scanning the corners to ensure the house was safe. His anxiety and depression became so severe that he was almost driven to suicide. In desperation, he tried a number of different medications, but none of them worked. David appeared to be hopelessly off track, at risk for a life spent continually struggling with PTSD symptoms, or an early death. What could be done to help David George?

On June 6, 1984, a Russian programmer named Alexey Pajitnov was working at the Dorodnitsyn Computing Centre of the Academy of Science of the USSR, in Moscow. He released a video game that he'd created in his spare time. Named after a mix of Alexey's favorite sport—tennis—and the Greek numerical prefix *tetra*, Tetris contained four segments of geometric pieces that needed to be manipulated like a puzzle. Although that doesn't sound like much fun today in our world of three-dimensional games with sensory feedback, Tetris was revolutionary for its time.

We know that making things gamelike can be a captivating reward for people, so it's no surprise that Tetris remains a classic. In fact, it's the best-selling game of all time. It continues to sell after thirty years.

What *is* surprising, however, is that Tetris shows promise in helping people with psychological trauma, like PTSD. How? By changing their brains.[20]

Although many PTSD patients experience traumatic flashbacks and trauma-related behaviors, if the brain can be interfered with before these flashbacks and new habits become engrained, then

PTSD can be prevented. In other words, a "cognitive vaccine" can be developed to prevent the brain from developing unwanted habits.

Tetris is one of these cognitive vaccines. Researchers found that people who played Tetris immediately—within six hours—after a traumatic event experienced dramatically lower rates of flashbacks compared to those who didn't play it. People had to play Tetris for only ten minutes, but that was enough to disrupt the brain from engraining trauma into their brains. This research helps people learn how they can use distractions, such as captivating games, to stop unwanted habits from forming. Cognitive vaccines can be really helpful if you know a habit is about to be formed and you want to prevent it from being engrained in your brain.

Unfortunately, people often can't treat a traumatic event soon enough to give the brain a cognitive vaccine to stop the event from being engrained. For soldiers on the battlefield, for example, it may not be practical for them to leave the war zone and return to barracks immediately to play video games. David George was not able to do this, either. His PTSD-related behaviors were already engrained in his brain. A distraction like Tetris couldn't cure his already engrained PTSD. How, then, can people retrain their brain to get rid of older engrained behaviors and create new ones?

In the last five years, researchers have made remarkable advancements in understanding how meditation affects the brain. Meditation not only increases patience, but it can actually change the way the brain works. It can increase awareness, improve concentration, and even retrain the brain by engraining a new set of psychological responses. Meditation can lead to lasting changes in people's health, happiness, relationships, and productivity, and in the structural anatomy of their brain. [21] [22] [23] [24]

Meditation helped David George relieve his PTSD symptoms. He learned about it when responding to an invitation to a research study. For the study, he was taught to sit and meditate for twenty minutes while focusing on a mantra—repeating a word or statement to himself. After his first meditation session, David experienced a "quiet mind" for the first time in five years. He determined he would continue the practice every day of his life.

A year later, David reflected on his new ability to keep meditating every day. He was healthier and happier, with a new and lasting set of behaviors that had been engrained in his brain. He could even look back on his time in Iraq and calmly describe his experiences there. And he had begun working for Operation Warrior Wellness, a group committed to getting thirty thousand vets to practice meditation within three years.

I can attest to the lasting benefits of meditation. In high school, after soccer, volleyball, and track practice, my hands would lose blood flow and turn purple, as a result of a condition called Raynaud's disease. When I went to the doctor, he saw my constricted blood vessels, guessed that it was due to smoking, and asked me how many packs of cigarettes I smoked each day. He didn't believe I didn't smoke (he sent my mother out of the room thinking I would tell him the *real* truth).

Seeking a remedy, I began reading books on meditation and biofeedback. I learned how monks would control the temperatures of their hands through meditation. I started meditating regularly. The symptom of Raynaud's disappeared. I've continued meditating every day to engrain the practice in my brain.

On a typical morning, I'm developing stock market algorithms or am in HIV-prevention research meetings, but I stop whatever I'm doing when I hear my alarm at 8:40 a.m. to take twenty minutes to meditate. I continue to feel the benefits of this practice in both my personal well-being and my work productivity.

People are more likely to stick with meditating if they can make it a daily routine that becomes engrained in their brain. This isn't unique to meditation, but part of the psychology that making any behavior routine helps to engrain it in the brain and increases "stickiness" so that it's easy to keep doing it. Zane Lewis, a participant in one of our research studies, described how he has learned to take his medications every day: "Through software and hardware of my own creation, I have the unique ability to monitor my medication use religiously. I know precisely when and where I take my medications and am reminded not to skip doses. I can even tell whether or not it is safe for me to take extra breakthrough medication based not only on time, but also very basic vital signs . . . and yes, I have patented parts of this & am working on turning it into a viable product."[25]

MAGNETIC BEHAVIORS

While meditation is one tool that can be used to retrain the brain, there are others. Take "magnetic behaviors." People can pair similar behaviors together so that if they get themselves to do one thing they can easily do, then it will make them more likely to do the other thing that is hard to do. For example, a person might have trouble motivating himself or herself to go for a daily run but can pair this with something he or she already does on a daily basis, like putting on shoes.

Think about it. Because we already put shoes on every day, it is already engrained in our brains. Without much effort, we can substitute the typical work or casual shoes we put on with running shoes. Because running shoes are automatically paired with running, we find it increasingly easier to run. I call this a magnetic behavior because doing one behavior (putting on running shoes) can be a magnet that causes another related and desired behavior (running) to occur.

Successful people make use of magnetic behaviors all the time.

For example, it's no surprise that all-time Olympic gold medalist record holder Michael Phelps has a highly disciplined prerace ritual. Since he was twelve years old, the Olympic champion swimmer has done the same thing before he swims. He always stretches a certain way, listens to hip-hop, and flaps his arms back and forth around his chest and back before getting up on the blocks.[26] He had tremendous success with this ritual beginning as a young swimmer. As a result, he has developed a lot of confidence in it.[27]

While hopeful athletes seek out Phelps's music playlist, thinking that the songs are his secret to success,[28] they don't realize that it's not about the playlist. It's that this playlist and the rest of his routine are magnetic behaviors.

It's easy for Phelps to listen to music, stretch, and slap his arms together. The hard part is acquiring the motivation to swim on days when he feels tired or has other things he wants to do. But his familiar routine is engrained in his brain and used as a magnetic behavior. Sticking with that easy-to-do routine that has led to his success in the past helps him follow through and reach similar success in the future.

If you look back on your past experiences you might think you've failed at changing. Maybe you failed at learning a new language or sticking with playing an instrument. Maybe you failed at getting people to buy a new product or technology you created. But don't worry about what has happened in the past. It's not important now. We know it's possible to replace old behaviors with new ones. What's important today is not what you've experienced in the past—forget that—but that you now have some clues and processes so that the next time you try to change something you'll be more likely to stick with it. Engrained is a powerful force to help you do this. If you want to get yourself to exercise every day, determine a time you'll do it (tomorrow), set an alarm or reminder, and follow through. The more you stick to it, the more it will become engrained in your brain, and the easier it will be for you to keep doing.

---

1. You now have all of the forces you need to stick with the behavior you wanted to change. By making it something you do routinely, you'll be able to engrain it in your brain and make it even more likely to stick.
2. Make the behavior a routine. Plan a time and day to do the behavior. Make this time as regular as possible, like every day at 8 a.m., or every Saturday and Sunday as soon as you wake up.
3. Set an alarm to help remind you to establish the routine.
4. Experiment by adding some of the other forces while you're doing the routine to see how much easier it will become to keep the routine with those forces. For example, if you're trying to go for a daily run, add community by getting someone else or a group of others to join you for your running routine. If you want to make exercise a routine for you first thing in the morning, put your running shoes next to your bed so that it's easy to remember your plan (and don't forget to add a captivating reward to make you want to keep doing it).

CHAPTER 9

PUTTING IT ALL TOGETHER

Charlie Bracke had always loved playing video games. Even as a child, he loved the feeling of losing himself in the moment. But as he grew older, his enjoyment from gaming started to turn into a need to escape his real life. He was becoming an addict.[1]

As an adolescent bullied by his older brother, Charlie would escape and play between four and five hours of games a day on weekdays and another ten on weekend days.[2] He took a hiatus from gaming in middle school when he started making more friends, but after a series of high school girlfriends cheated on him, he found himself compelled to escape back to gaming. And things got worse. When his grandmother died during his junior year in college, Charlie fell into a depression. He was prescribed medication from a doctor, but also self-medicated by gaming for fifty or sixty hours a week.

After that, he tried to change his life. He left his college in Indiana to live with his brother and work in real estate in Virginia. But a change in location couldn't keep him from gaming. His gaming addiction wasn't the result of what city he lived in; it was happening because he couldn't beat his urge. He would convince himself that it was okay for him to play just one game, but that would lead to hours at a time. He reached a low point in his life when his brother went on vacation and asked him to house-sit. During that ten-day period, Charlie left the house just three times, so that he could quickly get food to keep gaming. Shortly after, during the lowest point in his life, his parents found he had stopped taking his depression medication and was planning his own suicide. Charlie needed help.

Fortunately, Charlie was able to get help. His story has a happy ending, but we'll get to that later. . . .

Although new technologies are making people's lives more entertaining and efficient, they're also harming people's health. New tools like smartphones, messaging apps, and video games allow people to communicate faster and easier and keep them entertained, but they also make people stressed, impatient, and addicted. We now expect to get responses immediately for things we previously had to wait days or weeks for.[3]

As in Charlie's case, "distractive technologies" are creating new types of addictions. What did people used to do before? They would get bored, and had to actively seek hobbies or other kinds of entertainment—reading, playing a sport, or getting together with others.[4] No more. Companies are getting smarter at learning the psychology behind how to distract us.[5]

And it's happening to kids at younger and younger ages. Parents can leverage distractive technologies to make it easier to parent. They can give devices to their kids so that they don't get bored or upset.[6] New technologies are therefore promoting impatience.

People use their smartphones and tablets to pass time and distract their minds when they used to have to patiently wait for friends or coworkers to arrive to a meeting, for a light to change at the crosswalk, or for a car or bus to get them to their destination.

Yet the ability to stick with things takes patience. By making people less patient, distractive technologies are also making it harder for people to stick to things they want to do. Not surprisingly, many of the people who have had the most intimate knowledge of distractive technologies—such as Steve Jobs and other technology founders—have restricted their kids' use of the tools they themselves created.

Walter Isaacson, author of the book *Steve Jobs*, commented, "Every evening Steve made a point of having dinner at the big long table in their kitchen, discussing books and history and a variety of things. No one ever pulled out an iPad or computer. The kids did not seem addicted at all to devices."[7] It sounds like Steve Jobs, by leveraging the force of Easy and restricting the use of technology devices in the home, was able to prevent technology addiction in his family.

Resisting an urge to play a video game or check your phone is only one example of people wanting to change behavior. An even more common one involves getting motivated to go to work every day. After a late night or a relaxing weekend, the sound of the Monday morning alarm can sometimes feel like a lightning bolt driving straight into your body. But some jobs are harder than others to wake up to.

Take being a recruiter for the U.S. Army. Army recruiters are tasked with the difficult job of getting a sufficient number of people to enlist. Where does that number come from? It starts with Congress, which determines how many soldiers are required. Next, those numbers get divided across the country and then assigned down to the level of local recruiting centers. Army recruiters at each of those centers are expected to hit those numbers. And they experience tremendous stress in the process.

It's stressful enough trying to get people to join an organization as politically charged as the army, where there may be people protesting the very work you're trying to do. The stigma around army recruiters lying to people to get them to join makes it even more stressful. But according to Sergeant Joshua Morrison, an army recruiter I interviewed, by far the biggest challenge is trying to find candidates who are both eligible and interested: "Seventy-one percent of Americans don't qualify for the military, and only one percent ever end up joining the military. Finding that needle in the haystack can prove difficult. Contrary to popular belief, this is not a 'one size fits all' career. The analogy I have used in the past is this: If the Boston Red Sox need a first baseman, even though they have more outfielders than they require, they don't just move an outfielder to first base. They go out and recruit a new first baseman. The army is no different. We cannot just 'plug and play' an individual into a vacancy."[8] That means army recruiters have to experience failure multiple times a day, as they're approaching people and often going weeks without being able to enlist anyone. And if you add to that failure the pressure from their commanding officers if they fail to reach recruitment numbers at the end of the month, it's no surprise that this is a job that can be tough to stick with.

So how does the army get recruiters to stick with their job? I'll answer that, along with the solution for Charlie Bracke, in a minute.

PUTTING IT ALL TOGETHER

Is it possible that one solution can be used to help people to stick with anything and everything they want to change? Is it possible that only one of the seven forces is all Charlie Bracke, army recruiters, and the rest of us need to stick with things?

Most books on behavior change say the answer is yes. Most of them describe a quality that successful people have. They suggest that if you get that quality, and become like that person, then you'll be successful, too. One popular solution given is that people should form habits. That sounds like good advice. Some books even describe a habit science you can use to form habits. But why can't people change their habits even after reading these books?

There are two reasons. First, although reading a book, much like a motivational speech, can get people to *feel* motivated to change, that motivation won't last unless people quickly act on it. One of the basic ideas in this book, as you learned in the neurohacks chapter, is that lasting behavior change doesn't start in the mind by trying to convince yourself to change. Lasting change starts by changing behavior first (starting small, of course), like by discussing this book with a community of people instead of reading it alone.

But there's a second reason. The science described in habit books is based on a seventy-five-year-old principle called conditioning. Researchers studied the "conditions" needed for animals like rats to change their behavior. To learn a new behavior, they found that animals need a stimulus (or a trigger), a response (the behavior), and then a reinforcement (a reward that would make the animal want to do it again).[9] If they wanted to teach a cat to get out of a box, they would find something the cat needed, like food, and use it to reward the cat after it pulled a lever to get out of the box. That way the cat learned when it was in the cage and saw the lever (stimulus) that it should pull the lever (response) to get out of the cage and get food (reward). Hopefully this sounds familiar: we learned about conditioning as one element in the chapter on the force of Captivating.

So why doesn't conditioning (or habit science) work to create lasting behaviors? If conditioning were the only solution needed for behavior change, then why would this book spend only a few pages of the Captivating chapter teaching you about conditioning? Obviously it's because I don't think it's the only solution. And neither do most scientists in the field of psychology. In fact, many psychologists think the field of behaviorism is dead.[10] Why? First, people aren't caged animals, so the research on conditioning that was done on animals often doesn't apply because people's minds and lives are more complicated than animals. Second, not all behaviors are the same. There are different types. Each type of behavior requires a different set of forces to change it. Captivating is one tool, but *we need more than one tool in our toolkit to make behaviors stick.*

Take learning. Conditioning works well if you want to teach people *how* to do something. If a student studies hard, earning an A grade on an exam will let her know that she correctly learned how to study for that class.* The next time she's assigned a test (stimulus), she'll know how many hours and what method she should use to study (response) because getting the A grade (reward) taught her, just like food taught the cat to pull the lever. Although rewarding the girl with the A grade taught her *how* to study, it doesn't mean that she'll keep doing it, because she's also influenced by other things, like whether her friends think it's cool to study, and whether she has sports, work, or other things taking up her time. So conditioning was enough to teach her *how* to study to get an A, but more forces than just Captivating (which includes conditioning) are needed to get her to follow through and actually keep studying for each test.

Conditioning can also help to change habits—short-term, simple behaviors that can be done automatically and unconsciously. But conditioning doesn't work for all behaviors. It won't work as well

---

* While getting an A grade rewards people for knowing something (the answers to an exam), what it really does is reward the behavior that led them to know the answers (studying). When students get an A, they have learned that if they want to get the A again they should do the same behavior that they previously did to get the A (studying the same way they did the last time). This is the idea of conditioning.

if you want to change behaviors that are more complicated and involve more thought. For those types, other forces are needed.

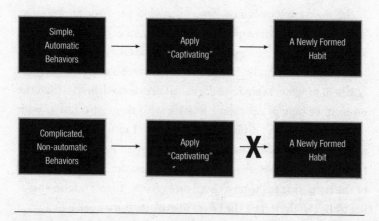

Figure 6. Different types of behaviors need different forces. Using conditioning, which is a part of the force of Captivating, can help to change habits, but it doesn't work on all types of behaviors. If a behavior is not a habit, then other forces are needed.

Take going running a few times a week. You can't use conditioning to make that a "habit," because it will never be a quick, automatic, and unconscious behavior. People have to consciously go through a number of steps to go for a run. When is the last time you realized you had gone for a run without thinking about it? In the middle of a conversation with your friend, you mindlessly stopped talking, changed into your running clothes, put on running shoes, got your music, dog, or whatever you needed to accompany you, and ran for thirty minutes? Then, after you returned home, you suddenly became aware that you had just gone for a run? Not likely.

On days when it's hard to get motivated, I wish that could happen to me, but it never has. I'm guessing it's never happened to you, either. Although individual parts of this process could become habits—like a few minutes in the middle of the run when the body is automatically moving and the mind begins to wander—the larger process is not a habit.

Humans are complicated. Not all behaviors people do are the same. The psychology behind whether people remember to floss is very different from the psychology behind why people take and post selfies.

To return to Charlie Bracke and the army recruiter, the psychology behind why people have digital addictions is different than the problem of how to get people to stick with their jobs. Just as with other things in life, different problems need different solutions. A music teacher wouldn't use a book to solve every problem that music students have. If a student has trouble understanding music theory, or the notes that make up a chord progression, then a teacher might use a book or draw it on the board to explain. But a book isn't always the best tool. If a bass player is having trouble hearing the bass in songs, then giving the student a book won't help solve the problem. They need to listen to music together so the student can learn to hear the bass. Behavior change works the same way. We need different solutions—or different forces—to solve different problems.

Treating digital addiction is a completely different problem than getting a recruiter to stay motivated. And both of these problems seem completely different than other types of problems with lasting change, like sticking to a fitness routine or remembering to stand up straight. When we think about the gazillion different problems with lasting change, it seems like we'd need to have a gazillion different solutions, one for every problem, right? That sounds exhausting, and hopeless.

Fortunately, we don't. Yes, there are a lot of differences between people's behaviors and problems they want to change. But there's only one difference we need to know. There's only one important difference between treating digital addiction and getting someone to stick with a job—or any other type of behavior.

The difference is the extent to which people are mindful of their behavior—or realize what they're doing at the time—and therefore are able to stop it. Army recruiters are fully aware of what they're doing when they're trying to enlist recruits. They consciously pick up the phone, walk up to people, or send them an email with the hope that they'll find someone qualified and interested in joining the army. On the other hand, Charlie Bracke and others with digital addiction might also be aware that they want to start playing video games but feel virtually powerless to stop. The problems are different because one of them is done *consciously* the other is done *unconsciously*. That also determines what forces should be used to stop them.

Take a resolution to keep good posture, compared to one to exercise daily. People often start slouching or lose good posture unconsciously, without their awareness. That makes it difficult to apply certain forces to keeping good posture—for instance Stepladders, which would have people plan small, gradual steps. If you're not even aware that you're slouching when you're doing it, it's difficult to take small steps to stop doing it. Getting yourself motivated to exercise is a different type of problem, though. People are often aware of what they're doing when they want to get themselves to exercise. They just need more motivation to do it at that moment. Forces like Stepladders *can* be helpful here. A person could take the first step of going for a two-minute walk. The difference in which forces to use depends on people's *awareness* when they're doing something they want to change and how *capable* they are of changing it.

As we're nearing the end of this book, I'm hoping to leave you with two things: First, as a general rule, people will be more likely to follow through with things if they use as many of the seven forces of lasting change as they can. But the second thing is that not all seven forces are always needed: knowing *when* and *how* to use the seven forces will lead to greater follow-through.

Different problems require different solutions. And it takes "different muscles in your mind" to fix different types of problem behaviors. The seven forces is your box of tools for fixing different types of problems with behavior. You can use this toolbox to get behaviors to stick. But as with anything else, certain tools will be more helpful depending on which types of problems you're trying to fix. And people are complicated, so it's especially important with behavior change that you pick the right tools to address that problem.

We therefore need a better model of behavior than to just rely on creating habits. The new model needs to be designed to apply unique approaches for creating and changing the many different types of behaviors that people engage in.

Working with some of the top psychologists and neuroscientists over the years, I've created the model of SCIENCE to address this issue. It will teach you when and how to use the seven forces of lasting change. That's the final thing I want to share with you so that you have a detailed understanding of how to apply SCIENCE to change your lives. But to understand the model, we first need to learn about what I call the A, B, and C's of behavior.

THE SCIENCE MODEL OF LASTING CHANGE

Before we get into this final section, let's do a quick recap to describe the seven forces of lasting change.

1. Stepladders: Take *really* small steps and use the model of Steps, Goals, and Dreams. For example, if you're planning goals for a new business, don't plan to lock in your first customer by the end of the week. That might be a dream. Instead, set the smaller step of meeting three potential new clients this week.
2. Community: Be around people who are doing what you

want to be doing. Social support and social competition foster change.

3. Important: To ensure change lasts, make sure it is *really* important to you.

4. Easy: Make it easy. People will do something if it's easier for them to do it than to not do it.

5. Neurohacks: Our minds play tricks on us. Use these tricks to your advantage. For example, follow Ben Franklin's advice to gain a new friend by getting someone to do something nice for you.

6. Captivating: People keep doing things if they're rewarded with things they need.

7. Engrained: Do things over and over. The brain rewards people for being repetitive and consistent.

The secret to changing behavior is to replace an old one with a new one. But new behaviors will stick only if you use the right forces. So that brings us back to our question from earlier: Which forces need to be used every time people want to create or change something? Is it enough to use just one of the seven forces?

My general answer is that, when in doubt, it's best to use as many as possible. But the more accurate answer: it depends on what type of behavior you're trying to change.

There are three types of behaviors, or what I call the A, B, and C's of behavior—automatic, burning, and common behaviors. Think of these three different behaviors as different types of problems, requiring different types of solutions. Changing A, B, and C behaviors requires different tools and processes.

The difference between A, B, and C behaviors lies in how much conscious control people have over them. In general, the more conscious thought goes into a behavior, the easier it is to change.

There are two steps to the process for creating lasting change. First, identify whether the behavior you're trying to change is what I call an A, B, or C behavior. Next, harness the forces needed to change that type of behavior.

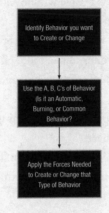

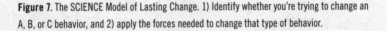

Figure 7. The SCIENCE Model of Lasting Change. 1) Identify whether you're trying to change an A, B, or C behavior, and 2) apply the forces needed to change that type of behavior.

THE A, B, AND C'S OF BEHAVIOR

Automatic Behaviors

Parents, here's a familiar example: My two-year-old daughter doesn't have the best motor skills. She often grabs valuable things, like the Brazilian guitar I got in the Amazon, and launches them into the wall or floor like they're pickaxes. After I race to grab it from her, I can't help but smile at her and laugh because she's still too young to know how to control herself. Now, I do explain to her why she shouldn't destroy things, because I believe it's good to teach kids to reason at an early age. But I don't expect she'll make a lasting change in her behavior just because I taught her why she should be more careful. That might work if she didn't know she should be more careful. But that's not the problem.

The problem is that she's too young to remember what I'm saying and too young to have the motor skills to prevent herself from doing it in the future. Even if she understands in that moment that she should be more careful with things, she usually doesn't have enough "situational awareness" to remember what she should and shouldn't smash against the floor in the future. It therefore wouldn't make much sense for me to solve the problem by having her gradually smash the guitar less and less each time (Stepladders), or by explaining why she should be more careful with it (Important), because she's not aware of what she's doing at that moment or capable of stopping it. Instead, the simple solution is to baby-proof the house—to keep my guitar out of her reach and give her something else she can destroy, like her stuffed pig or baby guitar (Easy), and to reward her for using it by giving her a treat or singing with her. (That should work for about two minutes until I have to find something else to give her.) This is the right solution to the problem. How do I know? Because the problem we want to change is an automatic behavior.

An automatic behavior is something that people do without conscious awareness. It is almost impossible for us to stop ourselves when we're doing automatic behaviors because we're not aware we're doing them. Automatic behaviors happen automatically, often under the same situations, or *conditions*. For that reason, one of the ways to change automatic behavior is to use *conditioning*. Unconsciously grabbing your phone while waiting at a light or holding a guitar and mindlessly starting to play a chord progression that you've played a thousand times are examples of "automatic behaviors." People aren't aware when they're doing it. It can be a reflex, like flinching when something is thrown at your face, or a repetitive unconscious behavior, like biting your nails or unconsciously eating half the bag of chips just because it was sitting on your lap. Automatic behaviors are heavily engrained in the brain and hard to change. They are the predominant behaviors for captive animals like dogs, monkeys, and rats, which typically react without thinking. But people also have automatic behaviors.

Because people aren't aware when they're doing something automatically, it won't work to use forces that require people to be conscious of what they're doing when they're trying to change. Just as Stepladders or Important won't prevent my daughter from destroying things in her path, because she's not aware of what she's doing, these forces won't work to change people's behaviors unless they're conscious when they're doing something they want to change. The forces won't hurt, but they won't really help. No matter how important it is for someone to stop unconsciously picking his nose in public, he won't be able to stop until he can be aware of himself *when* he's doing it. But other forces like Easy will work. If he puts on gloves, it doesn't matter whether he's aware of his nose picking; he won't be able to get the glove up inside the nostril to do it. Automatic behaviors are typically unconscious and therefore need to be "treated" with the science on how to create and change unconscious behaviors.

Just as animal trainers use food (Captivating) and objects like tennis rackets (Easy) to guide animals to automatically sit or jump, people need these forces to create and change automatic behaviors, too. Imagine you wanted to change the automatic behavior of unconscious nail biting and replace it with a different automatic behavior like chewing gum. You might first choose to make it easier to stop biting your nails. For example, you could wear gloves to make you aware of your nail biting and make it more difficult to get to your nails (Easy). You could also put a piece of gum in your mouth once you realized you were biting your nails.

In short, if you want to change automatic behaviors, use Easy and Engrained. If possible, also use Neurohacks and Captivating. It won't really help (or hurt) to use the other forces designed for changing behaviors that are more conscious.

Examples of Automatic Behaviors:

UNWANTED AUTOMATIC BEHAVIORS: Unconscious nail or lip biting, flinching, unconsciously picking your phone up at a stoplight, unconsciously getting stressed out, unconsciously eating food that is sitting in front of you, unconsciously sighing, forgetting that you're slouching

DESIRED AUTOMATIC BEHAVIORS: Instinctively jumping to block a ball coming over the net during a game of volleyball or block a ball being shot at the hoop in basketball; stepping in the middle of the street to grab and save your child who just ran into the street; playing a chord progression on a guitar you've played a thousand times; brushing your teeth with the same pattern you've done for years

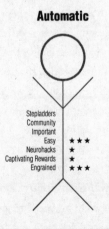

Automatic

Stepladders	
Community	
Important	
Easy	★ ★ ★
Neurohacks	★
Captivating Rewards	★
Engrained	★ ★ ★

Figure 8. Automatic Behaviors. Automatic behaviors are done without much thought. There are a specific set of forces needed to address automatic behaviors because they happen without awareness. The more stars, the more important that force is needed to change the behavior.

CASE STUDY: AUTOMATIC BEHAVIORS

This book offers people a prescription for achieving lasting change in life and work. But just as a doctor's prescription needs to be tailored to each patient, a prescription for lasting change needs to be tailored to each person's behavioral needs. A doctor might prescribe painkillers for a patient, but good doctors will tailor the prescription to factors like the patient's age, symptoms, and concerns about the drug.

We need to take the same approach here. In this book I give a high-level prescription for the seven forces for lasting change. The more of these forces that people can apply, the more likely people are to have lasting change. But just like with a doctor's prescription, these forces will be applied differently based on people's needs, and based on whether they are automatic, burning, or common behaviors.

How do you know how and when to use the seven forces? Starting below, and for each A, B, or C behavior, I try to answer that question by giving case studies of how different people could apply the seven forces into their lives and work. The case studies are based on real questions I have gotten from course lectures I've taught, emails I've received, and consulting work I've done on lasting change. I have integrated this material into common scenarios where people need help with lasting change.

Dear Dr. Sean,

I'm desperate! I'm a 51-year-old management consultant who loves sugary soft drinks. Unfortunately, my waistline recently realized that and punished me for it. I've tried diet plans and nutrition books to change the way I eat but haven't been able to stick to anything. The problem is, I don't even realize how much I'm drinking. I have a big bottle of Coke at my desk and by the end of the day it's empty.

How can I apply the seven forces to stop drinking so much sugar?

JP

Dear JP,

Avoiding junk food and sugary drinks can be tough. Who doesn't love a good chocolate truffle or cold soda on a warm day? But if you think you're consuming too much and want to slow down, here's what we're going to do . . .

I'm going to give you a prescription for lasting change. Like any prescription, we might need to adjust or tailor it for you, so try it out for a couple of days, let me know how it goes, and then we can adjust it to fit you and your needs.

Sean

1. Use the SCIENCE Model to decide whether you're trying to change an automatic, burning, or common behavior. It sounds like it's an automatic behavior because you said you're not aware when you're drinking soda. That actually makes the solution pretty easy. As you'll see in the chart, to change automatic behaviors, you'll need to use Easy, Neurohacks, Captivating, and Engrained.

2. Stop putting big bottles of Coke or sugary drinks at your desk! If they aren't there, you won't be able to unconsciously drink them (Easy).

3. Replace your soft drink habit with another one that satisfies you. If you're drinking it to keep your mouth from being dry, replace it with water. If you're drinking because you like the taste, experiment with other things like naturally flavored waters, or by adding your own fruits to the water. If the carbonation is what you like, use carbonated water instead (Captivating).

4. Make it routine. Put your replacement bottle of water or carbonated water there every day. Set an alarm or send yourself an email before you leave for work to remind yourself to bring your replacement bottle. This will help you get used to the routine and engrain it in your brain (Engrained).

5. Use tools to trick your brain into realizing you've changed. Keep a calendar of each day you bring the replacement water bottle instead of the soft drink bottle. As you reflect back on doing this a few days, you'll realize that you're changing (Neurohacks).

Burning Behaviors

Charlie Bracke's gaming addiction is what I call a "burning behavior." Charlie couldn't stop himself from gaming no matter what he tried. Depression medication didn't help. Neither did moving to a different state. Unlike unconscious automatic behaviors, Charlie was aware of what he was doing when he sat down to start gaming. He was so aware that he says he would convince himself that he was only going to play *one* game. He knew his behavior was unhealthy and needed to stop. He knew deep inside that one game would turn into hours of gaming, but he couldn't resist the burning urge to play.

Charlie ultimately found help. After his parents caught him at his lowest point, he moved to rural Washington State to a treatment facility called reSTART Life.[11] For forty-eight days, Charlie lived with other technology addicts—pornography addicts, chat room addicts, social media and Internet browsing addicts, and other gaming addicts. Together they were responsible for managing the house. They were taught to build a healthy routine of waking up on time, exercising, and cleaning. Knowing that it's almost impossible to live without technology in our world today, his program didn't focus on abstinence, but on creating a life plan for after treatment.

His plan was to ease into things with small steps and to make it more difficult to game by creating obstacles. When he left the treatment facility he used a flip phone instead of a smartphone to make it more difficult to game. He unfollowed people on Facebook and in his life who talked about gaming and he relies on a social support network of a therapist and his treatment partners to help him. Every Tuesday, he meets with them. When he got his job at Costco, he had to get permission to take off Tuesdays for what he calls "Treatment Tuesdays."

As Charlie looks back, he realizes he found a successful process for managing his gaming. He has a smartphone, is adhering to his medication, and hasn't gamed for a year. He relies on monitoring software that prevents him from spending too much time on apps he finds addicting, like Netflix. He has no gaming-related apps on his phone and stays away from places that have gaming apps, like the computer section in the library. Charlie's plan leveraged the forces of Easy, Stepladders, Neurohacks, and Community.

A burning behavior is a feeling of having an irresistible urge, or burning, to do something. Although automatic behaviors are the most firmly engrained behaviors because people *do* them automatically and typically without awareness, burning behaviors are the second most engrained behaviors because they are *thoughts* that feel impossible to not act on. People might *feel* like they can't stop themselves from following through with burning behaviors, but the ability to at least be aware of when they're engaging in them is what makes them different from automatic (no awareness) behaviors.

An addiction, craving, or obsession such as needing to have a cigarette or to check email is often an example of a burning behavior. Just as addictions can be rooted biologically in the brain, the repetitive and uncontrollable thoughts and urges from burning behaviors can be so strong that it is very tough to not act on them. Then why aren't they automatic behaviors? Because while the unconscious nature of automatic behaviors means that people can't stop themselves from doing them, people *can* stop themselves from doing burning behaviors.[†]

Burning behaviors are almost, but not quite, automatic, meaning that very similar forces are needed to change burning and automatic behaviors (Easy, Neurohacks, Captivating, and Engrained). But because people are also aware when they're doing something that's a burning behavior, other forces that require awareness are also helpful. For example, Charlie Bracke was aware enough when he felt the need to play video games that he could sometimes stop himself and call his therapist or friends from his support group (Community).

Examples of Burning Behaviors:

UNWANTED BURNING BEHAVIORS: Feeling like you need to check your phone when you wake up; feeling an intense need to immediately respond to an upsetting email.

DESIRED BURNING BEHAVIORS: Feeling the need to finish homework before going out to play; feeling the need to resolve a conflict in a relationship before going to bed; feeling the need to say a prayer or express gratitude each night.

[†] The same behavior might be automatic for one person and burning for another, depending on the cause of the problem. While a behavior like blinking in response to something that is thrown at your eye will be an automatic behavior for almost everyone, other behaviors, like checking email first thing in the morning, will be a burning behavior for some people and a common behavior for other people, depending on how conscious they are and their ability to control what they're doing in the moment.

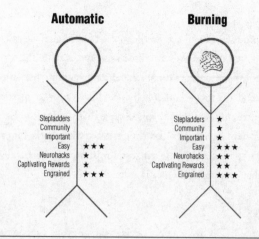

Figure 9. Automatic and Burning Behaviors. Compared to automatic behaviors, people are more aware of what they're doing during burning behaviors. I show this by putting part of a brain inside the person with a burning behavior while the person with an automatic behavior does not have a brain (this is for illustration purposes, as everyone has a brain!). Because of this difference in people's awareness during A and B behaviors, changing burning behaviors requires different forces than automatic behaviors. The more stars, the more important that force is to change the behavior.

CASE STUDY: BURNING BEHAVIORS

Dear Dr. Sean,

My husband and I have given birth to a zombie! Our 10-year-old daughter can't take her eyes off her iPad. Her only interest in life is using the iPad to watch cartoons and play video games. She yells, slams doors, and is rude to us when we take it away and won't spend time with us. Education is very important in our family but I'm worried that her addiction to the iPad will get in the way of her learning.

How can we get her to stop using the iPad so much?
Sarah M.

Dear Sarah,

Good products like iPads use the forces of lasting change to get people addicted. We have to use those same forces to do the opposite, to stop your daughter's digital addiction by pulling her away from the iPad and toward other activities. I have a few suggestions on what we can do, but as with any change that you want to last, we'll likely have to test out a few things to see what works for your daughter's situation. Try these suggestions below as a start and we'll check on her progress and tailor it as needed.

Sean

1. Use the SCIENCE Model to decide whether your daughter's use of the iPad is an automatic, burning, or common behavior. My thought is that it would be a burning or common behavior. Once you know what type of behavior it is, the chart will tell you which forces are the most important to use. I've listed all seven forces below so you can pick whichever ones are needed.

2. Start small. Introduce her to different activities to see what could get her to stop using the iPad for a few minutes (Stepladders).

3. Belong to a community. Get her to join a group of other kids her age who have fun without using iPads, like joining a sports team or arts and crafts group (Community).

4. Find something that is healthier and more important to her than an iPad, like earning allowance money for doing work, getting to see friends, or playing sports, and try to replace the iPad with that activity (Important).

5. Make it easy for her to do things besides using the iPad. Find other hobbies. Take her to places she likes but where iPads aren't allowed (Easy).

6. Use a neurohack. Get her to realize she doesn't need to use the iPad. The more she does other things without it, the more she'll

realize that she enjoys other things and doesn't need the iPad
(Neurohacks).

7. Make it fun. Tell her and show her that there are other activities that can be just as fun, like playing board games or dancing
together or going to a local park for a swim (Captivating).

8. Create a new routine. Find a replacement for the iPad like another activity that happens at the same time every day. This will
make the new activity become routine (Engrained).

Common Behaviors

The most common behaviors people try to change are called
common behaviors. When we're trying to motivate ourselves or
others to change something—such as to stick with a plan to retile
the bathroom this weekend, or to stop ordering unhealthy foods
when eating out—we are trying to change common behaviors.

Staying motivated to show up for work every day is an example of
a common behavior. People are aware they have to go to work, they
know they're capable of going, but after a bottle of wine the night
before, or a child or dog waking you up during the night, it can get
really difficult to be energized and ready to work the next day.

So how does the army get its recruiters to wake up at the crack of
dawn for work every day? How has Sergeant Morrison been able to
stick with being a recruiter for almost fourteen years? The answer is
that he uses every force in the book: "Every recruiter must complete
an eight-week training before reporting to recruiter duty . . . we are
trained from our first day to accept rejection in this job [Steplad-
ders]. . . . A typical army recruiter starts their day by conducting
an in-progress review (IPR) with his or her center leader. During
this IPR, the center leader discusses leads, prospects, and applicants
with the recruiter and provides guidance on each. Then, they dis-

cuss any prospecting activities that need to take place during the day. The recruiter then executes his/her plan of action for that day, ending with an after action review (AAR) with the center leader at the end of the day. This 360-degree communication is essential to any successful organization, as it prevents missed problems and provides valuable guidance to the recruiter." From their first day of basic training, recruiters are taught they are part of a united team.[12] Recruiters not only maintain this sense of camaraderie from boot camp, but another community bond is formed among recruiters and with their center leaders, making community a strong force designed to keep recruiters sticking with their jobs.

Sergeant Morrison said that 9/11 had a profound effect on him and continues to motivate him to serve his country (Important). "After graduating high school, I went almost immediately into the technology field, working as a programmer and computer technician for various companies in New England. On 9/11 I was working in the IRS building in Andover, Massachusetts, updating its systems to address the 2002 tax code change when the building was evacuated. We all thought it was a fire drill, until someone came to the parking lot to notify us that no one would be allowed back in the building. On the way back to the office, we heard on the radio what had happened. I was twenty-one years old at the time and decided that I needed to serve my country. I had only intended on serving my three- to four-year enlistment and getting out, but here I am, fourteen years later, still serving."

Sergeant Morrison also uses the force of Easy to keep working after getting rejected from phone calls or recruiting at a mall. He switches to do his recruiting from a digital device: "With the current generation, social media prospecting is highly effective, and the rejection percentage is fairly low; most won't respond at all if they're not interested. This is less stressful on the recruiter and the lead, so is proving to be a win-win scenario across the command.

Recruiters can reach more people in a shorter amount of time, and engage only with those who respond, which usually are the ones that are interested."

While bonus incentives are a common practice in most businesses, the army stopped giving recruiters financial rewards for enlisting new recruits. My guess is that it did this not only because it's unethical and could lead recruiters to coerce people to enlist, but also because it realized that while financial rewards work for a short time, they often are not a good approach for lasting change. Instead of giving bonuses to sign up new recruits, Sergeant Morrison's reward for productivity is to gain a promotion, a new patch on his uniform, and to be able to keep living at home in the United States (Captivating).

Sergeant Morrison's daily life, like that of any soldier in the army, is the definition of routine. Whether it's the time he wakes up in the morning, the daily meetings he has with center leadership, or the time that he goes to sleep at night, his life and work are routine (Engrained). For Morrison, putting on his uniform and "selling" potential recruits the idea of service in the U.S. Army without getting any financial reward is one of the best neurohacks. As he reflects on the challenges in his work every day, it's clear that his job is extremely important to him, or else he wouldn't keep doing it (Neurohacks).

Cyberbullying is another example of a common behavior. Students who bully others online are fully aware of what they're posting and have the ability to stop doing it. So, is knowing that people are aware and capable of stopping themselves from cyberbullying all we need to know in order to prevent cyberbullying? Yes, it's that simple.

One study in Finland invited 234 elementary and middle schools (28,000 students) to participate in a school-wide cyberbullying intervention over a two-year period.[13] The schools were randomly instructed to either keep doing things as usual (control condition) or to implement a cyberbullying intervention.

A program called KiVa was implemented in intervention schools. In addition to educating students, teachers, and parents about cyberbullying, KiVa was designed to foster an environment where students empathized with and supported cyberbullying victims and tried to prevent it. When bullying occurred, teachers met repeatedly with the victim and bully to address the situation. They also arranged meetings with two to four classmates there to support the victim and foster an empathetic community (Community). Students also received hands-on skills, like playing games and role-play exercises where they actively learned how to stop cyberbullying (Neurohacks). The program was based on research designed to make people less interested in cyberbullying: "positive changes in the behaviors of peers reduce the rewards gained by bullies and consequently their motivation to bully (Captivating)."[14]

The program was designed to be a routine part of kids' education (Engrained). Students in intervention elementary schools were given two one-hour sessions each month on cyberbullying. Students in intervention middle schools had lessons four times during the year. In between lessons, kids played computer games that reinforced what they had learned and allowed them to practice skills in a virtual environment. It's unclear whether at the beginning of the study students thought it was important to stop cyberbullying, but that didn't matter because results show that by the end it had become important to them. At the beginning of the study and six and twelve months later, students in all schools completed surveys on their experiences being cyberbullied.

The study found that students in intervention classrooms were less likely to be cyberbullied compared to students in schools that didn't get the intervention. Like many things in behavior change, the youngest people were easiest to change: the program had the strongest effects on the elementary school students, but also worked among middle school students, especially among classes with more male students. Like other success stories in changing common behaviors, the intervention used almost all of the seven forces, with a big focus on Community.

When people talk about habits—like saying they want to get rid of their habit of dating the wrong type of person, or want to adopt a new habit of going to sleep early or exercising more frequently—they're typically talking about changing common behaviors. Common behaviors can still be difficult to change, but they're not as engrained in the brain as automatic or burning behaviors. They also don't cause the obsessive thoughts that burning behaviors do.

Common behaviors are things that people do repeatedly and *consciously*, at least part of the time they're doing them. An example of a common behavior could be coming home from work and grabbing a handful of unhealthy snacks instead of waiting for dinner. A person might be aware that they're eating the snacks but that's not enough to get them to stop. They might wish they were patient enough to wait for dinner, or motivated enough to go for a run or swim instead. But they don't. They keep snacking because it's a common behavior that is tough to change.

Compared to automatic behaviors and burning behaviors, people are more conscious of what they're doing during common behaviors. Common behavioral problems feel like they're due to lack of motivation, such as being too tired to meet up with friends and instead falling back on the familiar routine of answering emails. Common behaviors don't occur unconsciously, so we need more than the forces that are used for automatic, unconscious behaviors.

Money is a captivating reward for most people but it's often not enough to change common behaviors. People could get paid a lot of money to go to the gym. That might even keep them going for a while. But if the gym is an hour away and they're only doing it for the money, they'll probably stop going.

Changing common behaviors requires using more forces designed for when people are aware of what they're doing. For example, if you're trying to stick with a gym routine you would want to go to a gym where friends also go (Community). If you're new to exercising you'd want to start a new exercise routine with a short walk rather than signing a yearlong gym contract (Stepladders).

Getting yourself to meditate is an example of a common behavior. How did army veteran David George get himself to stick to it? He used almost every force in the book. First, he started gradually, meditating for just a few minutes each day (Stepladders). He started meditating while participating in a research study to help vets, where he was guided by a researcher and belonged to a group (Community). He was suffering from severely debilitating PTSD and was highly motivated to get help (Important). After he had been on a streak of daily meditation he was able to look back and realize that he must be the "type of person who meditates"; otherwise he would've quit (Neurohacks). He made it a daily ritual (Engrained). Immediately after his first session, meditation acted as a Quick Fix and noticeably improved his symptoms (Captivating). But was it easy for him to meditate? I doubt it, but with six of the seven forces supporting him, David had enough support behind him to help him stick with it. The ultimate reward for David, and his reason for meditating, was that it calmed his mind and gave him peace.

In general, to create or change common behaviors, people should use as many of the seven forces as they can. I almost always use Community when changing routines in myself or others, as I find it's one of the strongest forces for changing common behaviors.

Examples of Common Behaviors:

UNWANTED COMMON BEHAVIORS: Wanting to eat junk food; consciously choosing to hit the snooze button on the alarm; sticking with the same sugar cereal instead of switching to a healthier alternative

DESIRED COMMON BEHAVIORS: Being able to consistently eat healthy, exercise, or study a new language

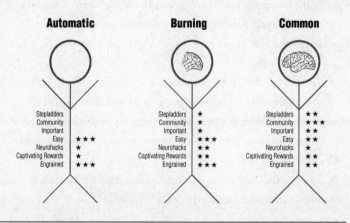

Figure 10. The Model of SCIENCE. This figure shows the A, B, and C's of behavior and the forces needed to change those types of behaviors. People are most aware of their behaviors during common behaviors (I show this by common behaviors having a full brain). There is a specific set of forces needed to change behaviors depending on whether it is an A, B, or C behavior. The more stars, the more important that force is to change the behavior.

CASE STUDY: COMMON BEHAVIOR

Dear Dr. Sean,

I live in Sunnyvale, California. Just like everyone else in Sunnyvale, I'm an engineer and built an app. My app helps people track their health behaviors. It's an amazing app. The only problem is, no one uses it. People download it but then they quit. I thought I was going to sell my app for billions of dollars. Good thing I still have my day job!

Can the seven forces help me get users engaged with my app?

Anita T

Dear Anita,

Here's a prescription to create lasting change among your users. Like any prescription, we'll need to slightly adjust it based on results, so reach out again once you try it so we can better tailor it to you.

Sean

1. Use the SCIENCE Model to decide whether getting people to use your app is an automatic, burning, or common behavior. My thought is that it would be a common behavior and that you can therefore use the list below and incorporate as many of the seven forces as you can.
2. Start small. Onboard users quickly. They don't need a complicated explanation or walk-through (Stepladders).
3. Create a community. Find out what your users want to share with others and let them share it (Community).
4. Make it important to people. Address an important need for your users (Important).
5. Keep it simple. They shouldn't have to think about how to use the app. It should have a clear purpose and navigation (Easy).
6. Trick their brain into staying engaged. Get buy-in from users

before you ask them questions or collect a lot of data from them. The gradual increase in commitment will get them more engaged and keep them using the app (Neurohacks).

7. Make it fun. Include rewards, gamification, or other incentives to make it fun (Captivating).

8. Engrain it in their brain. Use triggers and conditioning to build an easy habit (Engrained).

If you get nothing else out of this book, please remember this! There are two steps to the process for creating lasting change.

First, identify whether the behavior you're trying to change is an A, B, or C behavior. To determine whether something is an A, B, or C, you'll need to ask yourself what is stopping you (or someone else) from achieving the change. Finding the problem is often more difficult than it sounds, because people aren't always aware of what's stopping them from doing something. But if you sit and reflect on it, and use the case studies and chart, then with time you will be able to do this.

- Does the behavior happen without you realizing what you were doing at the time (you do it without being aware of yourself)? If yes, then it's probably an *automatic* behavior.
- Is it something you're aware of but feel powerless to stop? If yes, then it's probably a *burning* behavior.
- Is it something you're aware of and are just having a difficult time feeling motivated enough to change? Then it's probably a *common* behavior.

Second, once you know whether something is an A, B, or C, use the forces needed to change that type of behavior.

What if you're still not sure if something is an A, B, or C behavior? It's probably because you're not being specific enough about the behavior. Remember back to Stepladders, where one problem people have is that they think they are planning small steps but their steps are too big. A similar problem can happen with A, B, and C's, which can cause you to think you have a B problem when you really have an A or C. Different forces are needed for different behaviors, so it's important to get this right.

For example, people need to be more focused than just saying, "I want to get myself to be healthier." That could mean you want to change a lot of different behaviors. It might mean you want to stop snacking on cookies. It might mean you want to exercise more. It might mean you want to remember to keep good posture. It's hard to know whether something is an A, B, or C behavior only knowing that a person wants to be healthier. But, if you're more specific, like saying you want to stop your urges for late-night snacks, then you can know that it's a B behavior (because you're aware of what you're doing but it's hard to control not eating the snack).

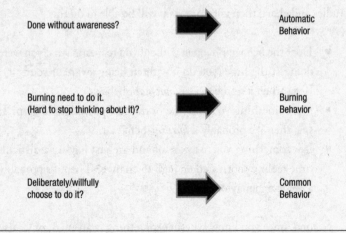

Figure 11. A, B, and C Behaviors. Use this figure to determine whether you're trying to create or change an A, B, or C behavior.

PUTTING IT ALL TOGETHER

As a general rule, ask yourself to be very specific in what you want to change. If the answer involves you using the word *unconsciously* or *automatically* doing something, it's probably an A behavior. If it involves you using words or phrases like *obsessed with*, *urge*, *compulsive*, or *burning desire*, it's probably a B behavior. If you're using words like *motivated*, *tired*, or *bored*, it's probably a C behavior.

WRAP-UP ASSIGNMENT

For this last chapter, your assignment is to incorporate the model of SCIENCE into your life so you can change—for good!

1. Now that you're familiar with each of the seven forces, think back on things you tried to change in life.
2. Use the SCIENCE Model in this chapter to help you realize why some changes stuck while others didn't.
3. Focus on the positive changes that you have been able to make in your life and work.
4. Write down what you were able to change, whether it was an automatic, burning, or common behavior, and the forces you used to change.

Congratulations! You now have the tools and the science to make lasting changes in your life and work. Reflect on the things you want to change and, like a researcher developing a behavior change intervention, use SCIENCE to create a plan for how you will use the seven forces. And there's no reason to wait to do this. Remember the Chinese proverb: The best time to plant a tree is twenty years ago. The second-best time is right now.

EPILOGUE

P icture a bright green leaf attached to a large sugar maple tree. As the seasons change, the leaf changes from green to gold, gold to red, and then red to brown. A gust of wind rips the leaf off the tree, and gravity pulls it down to the ground onto a patch of dirt. Over the next few days, a mixture of forces—wind, people's shoes, the hands of children—determine the path of the leaf as it winds up on a patch of grass. Then a dog walks by and pees on it.

People are similar to the leaf in a lot of ways. There are forces of nature that act on our lives and push us in certain directions. Who we spend time with affects whether we stick to hobbies, fitness routines, or learn new langauges. The places where we live and work affect how much we eat, drink, and smoke. Our ability to properly use reminders like calendars and alarms affects whether we keep jobs, adhere to medications, and have close friends. Many people feel that no matter what they try to do to change, they keep finding themselves unable to make a lasting change, unable to have control over their lives.

But, there's one major difference between people and objects like leaves. People have brains. People might not be able to change the forces of nature, but our brains allow us to choose the forces that create change. Leaves can't wait for a gust of wind and then jump in front of it if they want to move down a street. People can. People can use the SCIENCE model to help them get the right forces behind them. They can use stepladders to plan steps, goals, and dreams that are the right size so that they're *forced* to keep doing what they want to do. They can put themselves in communities that will encourage them to stick with things. They can remove obstacles by always keeping a water bottle with them or a pair of running shoes to make it easier for them to drink water or exercise.

Behavior change is difficult. Don't expect that it will happen automatically just because you read this book. But it is *doable*.

I went into psychology and medicine to help people, and I'm writing this book because I want to help *you*. I want to thank you for reading this book, and I hope that our relationship is just beginning. Please reach out to me at my website, seanyoungphd.com, where you can keep me posted on your progress and ask me questions.

The good news is, if you've gotten this far, you've already activated one of these forces, neurohacks. Just by finishing this book, you've proven that you're capable of sticking with something you want to do. Reflect back and congratulate yourself on your success of having finished this book. You're already on the path toward sticking with change. And you now have the tools to keep you going.

APPENDIX

Here are some other potential case examples where the seven forces can be applied.

1. People who have had trouble sticking to health and fitness routines
2. A human resources manager who wants to increase cooperation and respect among employees
3. A real-estate agent who is trying to retain her customers so she doesn't lose them to online sites
4. A corporate manager trying to get employees to complete tasks on time
5. A college student who has trouble getting up in time for class
6. A math teacher trying to increase student participation during class
7. A religious leader who wants to increase attendance during sermons
8. A single man or woman who dates a lot but has trouble committing to one person
9. A consultant who wants to improve his ability to build strong relationships
10. A manager trying to create lasting behavior change in the workplace
11. A financial (e.g. stock, options, futures) day trader who wants to stick to trading rules

12. A project manager who is trying to get employees to stick to deliverable deadlines
13. Artists or writers who are experiencing "writer's block"
14. A new mother who wants to start "sleep training" her child
15. Someone who wants to start training to run marathons
16. A restaurant owner who wants customers to keep coming back
17. A student who wants to get better grades
18. Parents who want their kids to study more frequently
19. Doctors, nurses, and health care professionals who want their patients to follow their health advice
20. Teachers who want their students to complete homework assignments on time
21. People who are shy but want to meet others to have larger social and business networks
22. Insurance agents who want to gain additional customers
23. Social workers and therapists who want to help their patients to be healthier
24. Politicians who want to organically grow a strong fan base
25. Financial and proprietary traders who want to consistently make money without risking a lot

ACKNOWLEDGMENTS

Thank you so much for reading this book! This is the first popular-style book I've ever written. It turned out to be just as difficult to write as my PhD dissertation. I planned to write this book over a summer, but it has taken two years! I kept getting feedback from people in order to improve the book and better connect with readers the way I like to do with my students. It has been an amazing learning experience for me, and I couldn't have done it without the guidance, support, and inspiration of so many of you. I believe that this book, like anything else I'm proud to have accomplished in my life, is the product of every person I've interacted with throughout my life. That's why I'm so appreciative toward everyone who has been a part of my life in some way. Here's a (somewhat) short list to personally thank the people who have had the greatest impact on this book.

Melody, Renee, and Ping-Wa, thanks for inspiring me and allowing me to be locked away for hours at a time. Mom and Dad, thank you for your feedback and unconditional support in anything and everything I do in life. Ian, you're the best brother ever. Grandma Billie and family, and Doris and Isador (Mom said you'd be proud as you've inspired our life and work so much, across music and medicine) and family above, thank you for the life and inspiration you've given me. Felner Family—Joel, Eric, and Kevin—you told me I should write a book and that's what started this journey. . . . Jim Levine (and your staff), thank you for the ride along through the ups and downs of this new process for me. Alice LaPlante, your questions, feedback, and edits have taught me so much and really helped. Thank you, Matt, Lisa, and Harper-Collins for your feedback and for publishing this work. Thank you to all of my friends who provided feedback or support. Oren Kaplan, Moshe Malkin, and Ken Garett, thank you for improving the writing; Elliot Berkman and Dara Ghahremani for your review of neuroscience; Olivier, thank you for giving me the story behind the "Stepladders" chapter, and to you and your dad for forcing me to keep climbing up the mountain.

My mentors in grad school at Stanford and undergrad at UCLA—Benoit Monin, Lee Ross, Jay Bhattacharya, Matt Lieberman, and Traci Mann, and all my other teachers throughout the years—thank you. My class at Stanford psychology in grad school—Asha Smith, Hal Hershfield, Evan Morrison, Fanny Eugene, Sapna Cheryan, Danny Oppenheimer, Chris Bryan, and the Celia's Happy Hour crew, thanks for teaching me about psychology and giving friendship. Dave Nussbaum, thanks for invading the dorms with me on the last day of our first year of grad school, and for giving me ideas that led to this research. This book could not have happened without you.

Thank you to my mentors and colleagues at UCLA. A special thanks to Bob Kaplan and Tom Coates who brought me to UCLA, and to my other colleagues and mentors, Drs. Steve Ellis (from NASA-Ames), Jeffrey Klausner, Chancellor Gene Block, Chris Colwell, Alex Hoffman, Steve Shoptaw, Keith Heinzerling, Lillian Gelberg, Doug Bell, Judy Gasson, Dean Jon Hiatt, Maureen Walton, Erin Bonar, Jose Baumeister, Patrick Sullivan, Hendricks Brown, and Bryan Mustanski. Thank you Gloria Varghese, Alison Orkin, Kip Kantelo, and the UCLA IRB for your support and feedback.

A big thank you to my Uncle Joel and cousins Eric and Kelvin Felner, as you were the ones who advised me to write a book. Thank

ACKNOWLEDGMENTS

you *Wall Street Journal*, *USA Today*, and all the editors at lists who made this a bestseller and a dream come true!

Thank you to the faculty, students, and research partners with the University of California Institute for Prediction Technology (UCIPT), especially to Professors Wei Wang, Mike Carey, Amarnath Gupta, Steffanie Strathdee, Christine Kirkpatrick, Vassilis Trotras, Chen Li, James Fowler, and Vagelis Hristidis. A very big thank you to David Bychkov, for your tremendous support and belief in our work, all the way from Virginia. Thank you to my research staff and students who have helped run studies or given feedback: Kiran Gill, Harkiran Gill, Justin Thomas, Sanam Shamtobi, and Claire Houlihan (and there are too many more to name and thank). The UCIPT Cloudberry group at UCI, including Mike and Chen, it's an honor to be working with you and having been part of a team to develop great visualization tools. (A quick plug for this group: Cloudberry is a freely available tool we've been working on that mines and visualizes social media data. We're working with public health and government departments so they can use it to do things like help hurricane victims, understand political sentiment, and prevent suicide. For more information and the ability to use it, you can check out http://predictiontechnology.ucla.edu/cloudberry-demo).

Thank you to our research partners and supporters. Keith Ferrazzi, thank you for giving me a chance to work with you and asking great questions that inspired ideas and theories behind this book. Thank you Chief Kevin Davis, Commander Jay Song and your team from the California Highway Patrol, along with Adam Fried and your team from Waze/Google, it's been a pleasure working with you on reducing car accident fatalities and getting first responders to the scene of accidents faster. We're excited about the upcoming opportunities in our work with you on the Marijuana laws in California. Thank you Karen Johnson and your team at Covered California for inspiring our work on helping people get health insurance coverage. Thank you to Detective Jeff Thompson (NYPD) and Alan Goodman for your police department work, efforts preventing and stopping suicide, and including me in it. Thank you to Major Jacob Gerstein, Lieutenant Colonel Sam Lightfoot, and your group at the Civil Air Patrol. We're excited for future work with your group.

I couldn't have done this work without my funders. Rosemary McKaig, Carlie Williams, Greg Greenwood, Susannah Allison, Chris Gordon, Andrew Forsyth, and so many of you at the National Institutes of Health. Johnathan Lee, Emma Zorensky, Vy Nguyen, Bridget Williams and Basis/Intel; Kelly Winters and Facebook; Mark McGrath and the AHF team; and Carina Wong and Emily Lockwood from the Gates Foundation. Meyer and Renee Luskin, thank you for inspiring me to write this and for supporting my work.

Last but certainly not least, I'd like to thank our research participants, especially the peer leaders from our HOPE online communities. You have truly been an inspiration and it is only through leveraging your social good that I've been able to make a difference in the world.

NOTES

Chapter 1: The SCIENCE of Lasting Change

1. "Nik Wallenda: About," http://nikwallenda.com/about-us/.

2. "Nik Wallenda," https://en.wikipedia.org/wiki/Nik_Wallenda.

3. "Diet Starts Today . . . and Ends on Friday: How We Quickly Slip Back into Bad Eating Habits within a Few Days," *Daily Mail*, September 16, 2013, http://www.dailymail.co.uk/news/article-2421737/Diet-starts-today-ends-Friday-How-quickly-slip-bad-eating-habits-days.html.

4. "Dieting Does Not Work, UCLA Researchers Report," University of California at Los Angeles, April 3, 2007, http://newsroom.ucla.edu/releases/Dieting-Does-Not-Work-UCLA-Researchers-7832.

5. Aurel O. Iuga, and Maura J. McGuire, "Adherence and Health Care Costs," *Risk Management and Healthcare Policy* 7 (2014): 35–44.

6. Bruce Jaspen, "U.S. Workforce Illness Costs $576B Annually from Sick Days to Workers' Compensation," *Forbes*, September 12, 2012, http://www.forbes.com/sites/brucejapsen/2012/09/12/u-s-workforce-illness-costs-576b-annually-from-sick-days-to-workers-compensation/#4cba1ad27256.

7. Personal communication with Josh Nava, Februrary 14, 2017.

8. Personal communication with Tom Sosnoff, February 8, 2016.

9. Lars Osterberg, and Terrence Blaschke, "Adherence to Medication," *New England Journal of Medicine* 353 (2005): 487–497.

10. *Ibid.*

11. People who participated in our interventions for lasting change were more than twice as likely to change than those who didn't participate in the interventions (44 percent of people compared to 20 percent of people in one study; 17 percent compared to 7 percent in another study). We followed these groups for more than fifteen months and found these results continued. See: Enrique Rivero, "Combo of Social Media, Behavior Psychology Leads to HIV Testing, Better Health Behaviors," last modified September 4, 2013, http://newsroom.ucla.edu/releases/behavioral-psychology-social-media-248056.

12. Daily Routines, "Ernest Hemingway," http://dailyroutines.typepad.com/daily_routines/2008/01/ernest-hemingwa.html.

13. Antonella Gasbarri, Assunta Pompili, Mark G. Packard, and Carlos Tomaz, "Habit Learning and Memory in Mammals: Behavioral and Neural Characteristics," *Neurobiology of Learning and Memory* 114 (October 2014): 198–208.

14. R.B. Zajonc, "Feeling and Thinking: Preferences need no Inferences," *American Psychologist* 35, no. 2 (1980): 151–175.

Chapter 2: Stepladders

1. "Brad Delson," https://en.wikipedia.org/wiki/Brad_Delson.

2. Karen E. Jacowitz and Daniel Kahneman, "Measures of Anchoring in Estimation Tasks," *Personality and Social Psychology Bulletin* 21 (1995): 1161–1166.

3. U.S. Government Printing Office. "Day Trading: An Overview," September 16, 1999, http://www.gpo.gov/fdsys/pkg/CHRG-106shrg61159/html/CHRG-106shrg61159.htm; "Do 95% of all traders lose?" HubPages, April 29, 2011, http://marketstudent.hubpages.com/hub/Do-95-percent-of-all-traders-lose.

4. Jack D. Schwager, *Market Wizards: Interview with Top Traders* (Hoboken, NJ: John Wiley & Sons, 2013).

5. Alexander M. Freud and Marie Hennecke, "Changing Eating Behaviour vs. Losing Weight: The Role of Goal Focus for Weight

Loss in Overweight Women," *Psychology & Health* 27, no. 2 (2012): 25–42.

6. Shelley E. Taylor, Lien B. Pham, Inna D. Rivkin, and David A. Armor, "Harnessing the Imagination: Mental Simulation, Self-Regulation, and Coping," *American Psychologist* 53, no. 4 (1998): 429–439. doi:10.1037/0003-066X.53.4.429.

7. Lien B. Pham and Shelley E. Taylor, "From Thought to Action: Effects of Process-Versus Outcome-Based Mental Simulations on Performance," *Personality and Social Psychology Bulletin* 25, no. 2 (1999): 250–260.

8. Gabriele Oettingen, "Positve Fantasy and Motivation," *The Psychology of Action: Linking Cognition and Motivation to Behavior*, ed. P. M. Gollwitzer and J. A. Bargh, (New York: Guilford, 1996) 236–259.

9. John R. Dyole, "Survey of Time Preference, Delay Discounting Models," *Judgment and Decision Making* 8, no. 2 (2013): 116–135.

10. Philippe N. Tobler, Christopher D. Fiorillo, and Wolfram Schultz, "Adaptive Coding of Reward Value by Dopamine Neurons," *Science (New York, N.Y.)* 307, no. 5715 (2005): 1642–45, doi:10.1126/science.1105370.

11. "Tabla," http://en.wikipedia.org/wiki/Tabla.

12. Lisa S. Blackwell, Kali H. Trzesniewski, and Carol Sorich Dweck, "Implicit Theories of Intelligence Predict Achievement Across an Adolescent Transition: A Longitudinal Study and an Intervention," *Child Development* 78, no. 1 (2007): 246–63, doi:10.1111/j.1467-8624.2007.00995.x.

13. Rebecca L. Shively, and Carey S. Ryan, "Longitudinal Changes in College Math Students' Implicit Theories of Intelligence," *Social Psychology of Education* 16, no. 2 (2013): 241–56, doi:10.1007/s11218-012-9208-0.

14. "Second Life," http://en.wikipedia.org/wiki/Second_Life.

15. Gustavo Saposnik, Mindy Levin, and for the Stroke Outcome Research Canada (SORCan) Working Group, "Virtual Reality in

Stroke Rehabilitation," *Stroke* 42, no. 5 (2011): 1380–86, doi:10.1161/STROKEAHA.110.605451.

16. Page L. Anderson, Matthew Price, Shannan M. Edwards, Mayowa A. Obasaju, Stefan K. Schmertz, Elana Zimand, and Martha R. Calamaras, "Virtual Reality Exposure Therapy for Social Anxiety Disorder: A Randomized Controlled Trial," *Journal of Consulting and Clinical Psychology* 81, no. 5 (2013): 751–60, doi:10.1037/a0033559.

17. "Creating Virtual Worlds to Train Your Salesforce," Direct Selling Education Foundation, May 16, 2012, http://www.dsef.org/2012/05/16/creating-virtual-worlds-to-train-your-salesforce/.

18. "Sexy Nude Beach," Second Life, http://maps.secondlife.com/secondlife/Sexy%20Nude%20Beach/220/150/23.

19. David R. Bassett, Holly R. Wyatt, Helen Thompson, John C. Peters, and James O. Hill, "Pedometer-Measured Physical Activity and Health Behaviors in U.S. Adults," *Medicine & Science in Sports & Exercise* 42, no. 10 (2010): 1819–25, doi:10.1249/MSS.0b013e3181dc2e54.

20. Albert Bandura, *Social Foundations of Thought and Action: A Social Cognitive Theory* (Englewood Cliffs, NJ: Prentice Hall 1986).

21. "Linkin Park," http://en.wikipedia.org/wiki/Linkin_Park.

22. Evan Polman, "Effects of Self—Other Decision Making on Regulatory Focus and Choice Overload," *Journal of Personality and Social Psychology* 102 no. 5 (2012): 980–93, doi:10.1037/a0026966.

23. "MyFitnessPal Acquires Rock Health-Backed Coaching Startup, Sessions," *Business Wire*, February 19, 2014, http://www.businesswire.com/news/home/20140219005652/en/MyFitnessPal-Acquires-Rock-Health-Backed-Coaching-Startup-Sessions#.VKISyf8CAJQ.

Chapter 3: Community

1. Devanie Angel, "The Power of Cults," August 12, 2004, https://www.newsreview.com/chico/power-of-cults/content?oid=31494.

2. "Democratic Workers Party," https://en.wikipedia.org/wiki/Demo cratic_Workers_Party.

3. Rebecca Schweier, Matthias Romppel, Cynthia Richter, Eike Hoberg, Harry Hahmann, Inge Scherwinski, Gregor Kosmützky, and Gesine Grande, "A Web-Based Peer-Modeling Intervention Aimed at Lifestyle Changes in Patients with Coronary Heart Disease and Chronic Back Pain: Sequential Controlled Trial," *Journal of Medical Internet Research* 16 no. 7 (2014): e177, doi:10.2196/jmir.3434.

4. Karen Foster and Dale Spencer, "It's Just a Social Thing: Drug Use, Friendship and Borderwork among Marginalized Young People," *The International Journal on Drug Policy* 24, no. 3 (2013): 223–30, doi:10.1016/j.drugpo.2012.12.005.

5. "Robert Downey, Jr.," http://en.wikipedia.org/wiki/Robert_Downey,_Jr.

6. Mim Udovitch, "The Sobering Life of Robert Downey, Jr.," *New York Times Magazine*, October 19, 2003, http://www.nytimes.com/2003/10/19/magazine/the-sobering-life-of-robert-downey-jr.html?pagewanted=2.

7. Sean D. Young, A. David Nussbaum, and Benoît Monin, "Potential Moral Stigma and Reactions to Sexually Transmitted Diseases: Evidence for a Disjunction Fallacy," *Personality and Social Psychology Bulletin* 33, no. 6 (2007): 789–99, doi:10.1177/0146167207301027.

8. Mark L. Hatzenbuehler, Jo C. Phelan, and Bruce G. Link, "Stigma as a Fundamental Cause of Population Health Inequalities," *American Journal of Public Health* 103, no. 5 (2013): 813–21, doi:10.2105/AJPH.2012.301069.

9. W. W. Darrow, J. E. Montanea, H. Gladwiw, "AIDS-related Stigma Among Black and Hispanic Young Adults," *AIDS and Behavior*, 13, no. 6, (2009), 1178–88.

10. Sean D. Young, William G. Cumberland, Sung-Jae Lee, Devan Jaganath, Greg Szekeres, and Thomas Coates, "Social Networking

Technologies as Emerging Tools for HIV Prevention: A Cluster Randomized Trial," *Annals of Internal Medicine* 159, no. 5 (2013): 318erna, doi:10.7326/0003–4819–159–5–201309030–00005.

11. *Ibid.*

12. Sean D. Young, "Social Media Technologies for HIV Prevention Study Retention among Minority Men Who Have Sex with Men (MSM)," *AIDS and Behavior* 18, no. 9 (2014): 1625–29, doi:10.1007/s10461–013–0604–z.

13. July 25, 2016, HOPE opioid community post.

14. *Ibid.*

15. Personal interview with Matei Zaharia on January 26, 2015.

16. "Samuel Adams," Facebook, https://www.facebook.com/Samuel Adams.

17. "Dos Equis," Facebook, https://www.facebook.com/DosEquis?ref=br_tf.

18. From January 1, 2013, to December 31, 2013, Dos Equis sold 7,910,841 cases of beer, totaling $236,406,800. Sam Adams sold 10,453,300 cases, totaling $329,422,200 in sales. "2014 U.S. Beer Category Report," http://www.bevindustry.com/2014beercategory report.

19. Personal communication with Marina Zdobnova, January 8, 2017.

20. Personal communication with Santa Monica New Tech member, Terence Lem, January 8, 2017.

Chapter 4: Important

1. Jeremy P. Jamieson, Wendy Berry Mendes, and Matthew K. Nock, "Improving Acute Stress Responses: The Power of Reappraisal," *Current Directions in Psychological Science* 22, no. 1 (2013): 51–56, doi:10.1177/0963721412461500.

2. Lindsey McDougle, Sara Konrath, Marlene Walk, and Femida Handy, "Religious and Secular Coping Strategies and Mortality Risk among Older Adults," *Social Indicators Research* 125, no. 2 (2016): 677–694, doi:10.1007/s11205–014–0852–y.

NOTES

3. United Nations Development Programme, "Poverty Reduction Scaling Up Local Innovations for Transformational Change," http://www.undp.org/content/dam/undp/library/Poverty%20Reduction/Participatory%20Local%20Development/Mexico_Progresa_web.pdf.

4. Peter Bate, "The Story Behind *Oportunidades*: How Two Visionary Social Scientists Forged a Program that Has Changed the Lives of Millions of Mexicans," Inter-American Development Bank, October 1, 2004, http://www.iadb.org/en/news/webstories/2004-10-01/the-story-behind-ioportunidadesi,5552.html.

5. "Oportunidades Mexico: A Brief Look at Its History," LACS 101, November 22, 2013, http://lacs101.academic.wlu.edu/2013/11/22/oportunidades-mexico-a-brief-loo/.

6. George E. Vaillant, *Triumphs of Experience: The Men of the Harvard Grant Study* (Cambridge, MA: Belknap Press 2012).

7. Tristen K. Inagaki, and Naomi I. Eisenberger, "Shared Neural Mechanisms Underlying Social Warmth and Physical Warmth," *Psychological Science* 24, no. 11 (2013): 2272–80, doi:10.1177/0956797613492773.

8. Naomi I. Eisenberger, Matthew Lieberman, and Kipling D. Williams, "Does Rejection Hurt? An fMRI Study of Social Exclusion," *Science*, 302: 290–292.

9. Nathan C. Dewall, Geoff Macdonald, Gregory D. Webster, Carrie L. Masten, Roy F. Baumeister, Caitlin Powell, David Combs, et al, "Acetaminophen Reduces Social Pain: Behavioral and Neural Evidence," *Psychological Science* 21, no. 7 (2010): 931–37, doi: 10.1177/0956797610374741.

10. "Don Francisco (television host)," https://en.wikipedia.org/wiki/Don_Francisco_(television_host).

11. "Zach's Story," http://zacharycrottystory.blogspot.com/p/a-mothers-journey.html and http://friendsdontletfriendsdie.com/smf/index.php?topic=385.0.

12. July 25, 2016, HOPE community post.

13. "William Addis (entrepreneur)," https://en.wikipedia.org/wiki/William_Addis_(entrepreneur).

14. Ying-Yao Cheng, Paichi Pat Shein, and Wen-Bin Chiou, "Escaping the Impulse to Immediate Gratification: The Prospect Concept Promotes a Future-Oriented Mindset, Prompting an Inclination towards Delayed Gratification," *British Journal of Psychology* 103, no. 1 (2012): 129–41, doi:10.1111/j.2044–8295.2011.02067.x.

15. CFED, "Assets and Opportunities Scorecard," http://assetsandopportunity.org/scorecard/about/main_findings/.

16. Personal interview with Tom Pugmire, January 6, 2017.

17. Hal Hershfield, "You Make Better Decisions if You 'See' Your Senior Self," *Harvard Business Review*, June 2013, https://hbr.org/2013/06/you-make-better-decisions-if-you-see-your-senior-self.

18. Nicholas A. Christakis and Paul D. Allison, "Mortality after the Hospitalization of a Spouse," *New England Journal of Medicine* 354, no. 7 (2006): 719–30, doi:10.1056/NEJMsa050196.

19. Chad Schultz, "Do People Really Fear Public Speaking More Than Death?" TM Vision, http://tmvision.org/speaking/people-fear-public-speaking-death/.

Chapter 5: Easy

1. "Joe Coulombe," https://en.wikipedia.org/wiki/Joe_Coulombe.

2. "7-Eleven," http://en.wikipedia.org/wiki/7-Eleven.

3. "Trader Joe's," http://en.wikipedia.org/wiki/Trader_Joe%27s.

4. Beth Kowitt, "Inside the Secret World of Trader Joe's," *Fortune*, August 20, 2010, http://archive.fortune.com/2010/08/20/news/companies/inside_trader_joes_full_version.fortune/index.htm.

5. Hein de Vries, Sander M. Eggers, and Catherine Bolman, "The Role of Action Planning and Plan Enactment for Smoking Cessation," *BMC Public Health* 13(April 2013): 393, doi:10.1186/1471–2458–13–393.

NOTES

6. Carla Alexia Campbell, Robert A. Hahn, Randy Elder, Robert Brewer, Sajal Chattopadhyay, Jonathan Fielding, Timothy S. Naimi, Traci Toomey, Briana Lawrence, and Jennifer Cook Middleton, "The Effectiveness of Limiting Alcohol Outlet Density As a Means of Reducing Excessive Alcohol Consumption and Alcohol-Related Harms," *American Journal of Preventive Medicine* 37, no. 6 (2009): 556–69, doi:10.1016/j.amepre.2009.09.028.

7. Bridget Freisthler and Paul J. Gruenewald, "Examining the Relationship between the Physical Availability of Medical Marijuana and Marijuana Use across Fifty California Cities," *Drug and Alcohol Dependence* 143(October 2014): 244–50, doi:10.1016/j.drugalcdep.2014.07.036.

8. Stanley Milgram, "Behavioral Study of Obedience," *The Journal of Abnormal and Social Psychology* 67, no. 4 (1963): 371–78, doi:10.1037/h0040525.

9. Stanley Milgram, "Some Conditions of Obedience and Disobedience to Authority," *Human Relations* 18, no. 1 (1965): 57–76, doi:10.1177/001872676501800105.

10. Nick Haslam, Steve Loughnan, and Gina Perry, "Meta-Milgram: An Empirical Synthesis of the Obedience Experiments," *PLoS ONE* 9, no. 4 (2014), doi:10.1371/journal.pone.0093927.

11. L. Festinger, S. Schachter, and K.W. Back, *Social Pressures in Informal Groups: A Study of Human Factors in Housing* (New York: Harper, 1950).

12. Chadwick Martin Bailey, "Match.com and Chadwick Martin Bailey 2009–2010 Studies: Recent Trends: Online Dating," http://cp.match.com/cppp/media/CMB_Study.pdf.

13. Jonathan D. D'Angelo and Catalina L. Toma, "There Are Plenty of Fish in the Sea: The Effects of Choice Overload and Reversibility on Online Daters' Satisfaction With Selected Partners," *Media Psychology* 20, no. 1 (2017): 1–27, doi:10.1080/15213269.2015.1121827.

14. S. S. Iyengar and M. R. Lepper, "When Choice Is Demotivating:

Can One Desire Too Much of a Good Thing?" *Journal of Personality and Social Psychology* 79, no. 6 (2000): 995–1006.

15. S. S. Iyengar, Wei Jiang, and Gur Huberman, "How Much Choice Is Too Much? Contributions to 401(k) Retirement Plans," Philadelphia, PA: Pension Research Council, http://www.nagdca.org/dnn/Portals/45/2015Annual/16.%20How%20much%20choice%20is%20too%20much%20choice.pdf.

16. H. Leventhal, R. Singer, and S. Jones, "Effects of Fear and Specificity of Recommendation Upon Attitudes and Behavior," *Journal of Personality and Social Psychology* 2(July 1965): 20–29.

17. "Women spend nearly one year deciding what to wear," *The Telegraph*, http://www.telegraph.co.uk/news/uknews/5783991/Women-spend-nearly-one-year-deciding-what-to-wear.html.

18. Jason Abbruzzese, "Why Zuck and other successful men wear the same thing every day," Mashable, last modified November 17, 2014, http://mashable.com/2014/11/17/mark-zuckerberg-and-other-insanely-successful-people-wear-the-same-thing-every-day-and-for-good-reason/#SAiv3lQTDuqR.

19. Matilda Kahl, "Why I Wear the Exact Same Thing to Work Every Day," *Harpers Bazaar*, last modified April 3, 2015, http://www.harpersbazaar.com/culture/features/a10441/why-i-wear-the-same-thing-to-work-everday/.

20. Christy Rutherford, "Matilda Kahl Negotiated with Zara for her Work Uniform," *Harpers Bazaar*, last modified April 9, 2015, http://www.harpersbazaar.com/culture/features/a10528/matilda-kahl-work-uniform-buying-in-bulk/.

21. L. Ross and A. Ward, "Naive Realism in Everyday Life: Implications for Social Conflict and Misunderstanding," *Values and Knowledge*, ed. T. Brown, E. S. Reed, and E. Turiel (Hillsdale, NJ: Erlbaum, 1996), 103–135.

22. J. Froyd and J. Layne, "Faculty Development Strategies for

Overcoming the 'Curse of Knowledge'," *2008 38th Annual Frontiers in Education Conference*, S4D–13–S4D–16, doi:10.1109/FIE.2008.4720529.

23. Ibid., "Do 95% of all Traders Lose?"

24. Gustaf Torngren and Henry Montgomery, "Worse Than Chance? Performance and Confidence Among Professionals and Laypeople in the Stock Market," *Journal of Behavioral Finance* 5, no. 3 (2004): 148–53, doi:10.1207/s15427579jpfm0503_3.

25. D. Dunning, D. W. Griffin, J. D. Milojkovic, and L. Ross, "The Overconfidence Effect in Social Prediction," *Journal of Personality and Social Psychology* 58, no. 4 (1990): 568–81.

26. Ulrike Malmendier and Geoffrey Tate, "CEO Overconfidence and Corporate Investment," *The Journal of Finance* 60, no. 6 (2005): 2661–2700, doi:10.1111/j.1540–6261.2005.00813.x.

27. Ioannis S. Salamouris, "How Overconfidence Influences Entrepreneurship," *Journal of Innovation and Entrepreneurship* 2, no. 1 (2013): 8, doi:10.1186/2192–5372–2–8.

28. Markus Glaser and Martin Weber, "Overconfidence and Trading Volume," SSRN Scholarly Paper ID 976374, Rochester, NY: Social Science Research Network, https://papers.ssrn.com/abstract=976374.

29. Todd R. Zenger, "Explaining Organizational Diseconomies of Scale in R&D: Agency Problems and the Allocation of Engineering Talent, Ideas, and Effort by Firm Size," *Management Science* 40, no. 6 (1994): 708–29.

30. Brian Wu and Anne Marie Knott, "Entrepreneurial Risk and Market Entry," *Management Science* 52, no. 9 (2006): 1315–1330.

31. Michael Hoerger, Benjamin P. Chapman, Ronald M. Epstein, and Paul R. Duberstein, "Emotional Intelligence: A Theoretical Framework for Individual Differences in Affective Forecasting," *Emotion* 12, no. 4 (2012): 716–25, doi:10.1037/a0026724.

32. Daniel Kahneman, "Evaluation By Moments: Past and Future,"

Choices, Values and Frames, eds. D. Kahneman and A. Tversky (New York: Cambridge University Press, 2000).

33. Timothy D. Wilson and Daniel T. Gilbert, "Affective Forecasting: Knowing What to Want," *Current Directions in Psychological Science* 14, no. 3 (2005): 131–34, doi:10.1111/j.0963–7214.2005.00355.x.

34. "Yo (app)," https://en.wikipedia.org/wiki/Yo_(app).

35. "The World's Most Innovative Companies: Amazon.com," *Forbes*, http://www.forbes.com/companies/amazon/.

36. Hayley Tsukayama, "What Amazon's Learned from a Decade of Prime," *Washington Post*, February 3, 2015, https://www.washington post.com/news/the-switch/wp/2015/02/03/what-amazons-learned -from-a-decade-of-prime/.

37. Sarah Perez, "Amazon Announces new Dash-powered Devices that can Auto-reorder Your Coffee, Air Filters, and More," *TechCrunch*, 2016, https://techcrunch.com/2016/11/22/amazon-announces-new-dash -powered-devices-that-can-auto-reorder-your-coffee-air-filters -and-more/?ncid=rss&utm_source=feedburner&utm_medium =feed&utm_campaign=Feed%3A+Techcrunch+%28Tech Crunch%29.

38. JuJu Chang and Mary Marsh, "The Google Diet: Search Giant Overhauled Its Eating Options to 'Nudge' Healthy Choices," *ABC News*, January 25 2013, http://abcnews.go.com/Health/ google-diet-search-giant-overhauled-eating-options-nudge/ story?id=18241908.

39. James Franklin, *The Science of Conjecture: Evidence and Probability before Pascal* (Baltimore, MD: Johns Hopkins University Press, 2001), 241.

40. "Occam's razor," https://en.wikipedia.org/wiki/Occam's_razor.

41. Lee Ross and Richard Nisbett, *The Person and the Situation: Perspectives of Social Psychology* (London: Pinter & Martin Ltd, 2012).

42. Kurt Lewin, *A Dynamic Theory of Personality* (New York and London: McGraw-Hill Book Company, Inc., 1935).

NOTES

Chapter 6: Neurohacks

1.   Mauricio Estrella, "How a Password Changed My Life," May 14, 2014, https://medium.com/the-lighthouse/how-a-password-changed -my-life-7af5d5f28038#.t1drsgv3s.

2.   Personal interview with Mauricio Estrella, Feburary 9, 2017.

3.   D. J. Bem, "Self-perception Theory," *Advances in Experimental Social Psychology*, ed. Leonard Berkowitz (New York: Academic, 1972).

4.   Psychologists debate whether this is due to cognitive dissonance or people's views about their past behaviors. For an argument supporting the former, see: Leon Festinger, *A Theory of Cognitive Dissonance* (Stanford, CA: Stanford University Press, 1957). For an argument supporting the latter, see: D. J. Bem, "Self-Perception: An Alternative Interpretation of Cognitive Dissonance Phenomena," *Psychological Review* 74 (1967): 183–200.

5.   Benjamin Franklin, *Autobiography of Benjamin Franklin [Edited from His Manuscript]*, ed. John Bigelow (Philadelphia: Lippincott, 1868).

6.   Rosanna E. Guadagno, Adam Lankford, Nicole Muscanell, Bradley Okdie, and Debra McCallum, "Social Influence in the Online Recruitment of Terrorists and Terrorist Sympathizers: Implications for Social Psychology Research," *Revue Internationale de Psychologie Sociale* 23 (2010): 25–56.

7.   F. M. Haemmerlie and R. L. Montgomery, "Purposefully Biased Interactions: Reducing Heterosocial Anxiety Through Self-Perception Theory," *Journal of Personality and Social Psychology* 47 (1984): 900–908.

8.   F. M. Haemmerlie and R. L. Montgomery, "Self-Perception Theory and Unobtrusively Biased Interactions: A Treatment for Heterosocial Anxiety," *Journal of Counseling, Psychology* 29 (1982): 362–370.

9.   Pablo Briñol and Richard E. Petty, "Overt Head Movements and Persuasion: A Self-Validation Analysis," *Journal of Personality and Social Psychology* 84, no. 6 (2003): 1123–39.

10. Stuart Valins, "Cognitive Effects of False Heart-Rate Feedback," *Journal of Personality and Social Psychology* 4, no. 4 (1966): 400–408, doi:10.1037/h0023791.

11. Stuart Valins, "Cognitive Effects of False Heart-Rate Feedback," In *Experimental Social Psychology*, eds. Chester A. Insko and John Schopler (New York and London: Academic Press, 2013).

12. John C. Barefoot and Ronald B. Straub, "Opportunity for Information Search and the Effect of False Heart Rate Feedback," *Integrative Physiological & Behavioral Science* 40, no. 3 (2005): 156–60, doi:10.1007/BF03159712.

13. Marcus A. Gray, Neil A. Harrison, Stefan Wiens, and Hugo D. Critchley, "Modulation of Emotional Appraisal by False Physiological Feedback during fMRI," *PLoS ONE* 2, no. 6 (2007), doi:10.1371/journal.pone.0000546.

14. J. D. Laird, "Self-Attribution of Emotion: The Effects of Expressive Behavior on the Quality of Emotional Experience," *Journal of Personality and Social Psychology* 29 (1974): 475–486.

15. Fritz Strack, Leonard L. Martin, and Sabine Stepper, "Inhibiting and Facilitating Conditions of the Human Smile: A Nonobtrusive Test of the Facial Feedback Hypothesis," *Journal of Personality and Social Psychology* 54 (1988): 768–777.

16. R. B. Zajonc, Sheila T. Murphy, and Marita Inglehart, "Feeling and Facial Efference: Implications of the Vascular Theory of Emotion," *Psychological Review* 96, no. 3 (1989): 395–416, doi:10.1037/0033-295X.96.3.395.

17. M. Axel Wollmer, Claas de Boer, Nadeem Kalak, Johannes Beck, Thomas Götz, Tina Schmidt, Muris Hodzic, et al, "Facing Depression with Botulinum Toxin: A Randomized Controlled Trial," *Journal of Psychiatric Research* 46, no. 5 (2012): 574–81, doi:10.1016/j.jpsychires.2012.01.027.

18. Michael B. Lewis and Patrick J Bowler, "Botulinum Toxin Cosmetic Therapy Correlates with a More Positive Mood," *Journal of*

Cosmetic Dermatology 8, no. 1 (2009): 24–26, doi:10.1111/j.1473 –2165.2009.00419.x.

19. Tiffany A. Ito, Krystal W. Chiao, Patricia G. Devine, Tyler S. Lorig, and John T. Cacioppo, "The Influence of Facial Feedback on Race Bias," *Psychological Science* 17, no. 3 (2006): 256–261, doi:10.1111/ j.1467–9280.2006.01694.x.

20. Christopher J. Bryan, Gregory M. Walton, Todd Rogers, and Carol S. Dweck, "Motivating Voter Turnout by Invoking the Self," *Proceedings of the National Academy of Sciences* 108, no. 31 (2011): 12653 –56, doi:10.1073/pnas.1103343108.

21. Christopher J. Bryan, Gabrielle S. Adams, and Benoît Monin, "When Cheating Would Make You a Cheater: Implicating the Self Prevents Unethical Behavior," *Journal of Experimental Psychology: General* 142, no. 4 (2013): 1001–5, doi:10.1037/a0030655.

22. C. R. Critcher and T. Gilovich, "Inferring Attitudes from Mindwandering," *Personality and Social Psychology Bulletin* 36 (2010): 1255–1266.

23. J. P. Brunelle, "The Impact of Community Service on Adolescent Volunteers' Empathy, Social Responsibility, and Concern for Others," *The Sciences and Engineering* 62 (2001): 2514.

24. "Improvisational Acting Rules," https://en.wikibooks.org/wiki/ Improvisational_Acting/Rules.

25. Nancy L. Collins and Lynn Carol Miller, "Self-Disclosure and Liking: A Meta-Analytic Review," *Psychological Bulletin* 116, no. 3 (1994): 457–75, doi:10.1037/0033–2909.116.3.457.

26. C. K. Waterman, "The Facilitating and Interfering Effects of Cognitive Dissonance on Simple and Complex Paired Associates Learning Tasks," *Journal of Experimental Social Psychology* 5 (1969): 31–42.

Chapter 7: Captivating

1. Brad Tuttle, "Former 'Extreme Couponer' Admits: It's a Waste of Time," *Time*, last modified November 5, 2012, http://business.time.

com/2012/11/05/former-extreme-couponer-admits-its-a-waste-of
-time/.

2. "Why One Extreme Couponer Gave Up Clipping," National Public
Radio, last modified October 30, 2012, http://www.nprorg/2012/
10/30/163950605/why-one-extreme-couponer-gave-upclipping.

3. "We Are a Coupon Nation," RetailMeNot, Inc., last modified Sep
tember 8, 2014, http://retailmenot.mediaroom.com/2014–09–08
-We-Are-a-Coupon-Nation.

4. "CPG Digital Coupon Circulation Grows By 23.4% in 1H16,
Reaching 3.7 Billion," Kantar Media, August 15, 2016, http://www
.kantarmedia.com/us/newsroom/press-releases/cpg-digital-coupon
-circulation-grows-by-23–4-in-1h16.

5. "Improving Economy, Increasing Shopper Demand for Digital Offers Impacting Coupon Use," Inmar, February 1, 2016, http://www
.inmar.com/press-release/improving-economy-increasing-shopper
-demand-for-digital-offers-impacting-coupon-use/.

6. *Ibid.*

7. Sherri Kuhn, "The Wealthy Are More Likely to Use Coupons,
Ironically," SheKnows, February 10, 2014, http://www.sheknows
.com/living/articles/1029861/the-wealthy-are-more-likely-to-use
-coupons-ironically.

8. "Is Metal Detecting Worth It?" Metal Detecting Forum, last modified January 5, 2011, http://metaldetectingforum.com/showthread
.php?t=62457.

9. Lulu Chang, "Americans spend an alarming amount of time checking social media on their phones," Digital Trends, June 13, 2015,
http://www.digitaltrends.com/mobile/informate-report-social
-media-smartphone-use/.

10. Edward Lee Thorndike, "Animal Intelligence: An Experimental
Study of the Associative Processes in Animals," *Psychological Review
Monograph Supplement* 2 (1901): 1–109.

11. Daniel Schacter, *Psychology* (2nd ed.) (New York: Worth, 2011), 17.

12. "Top Secret WWII Bat and Bird Bomber Program," HistoryNet, last modified June 12, 2006, http://www.historynet.com/top-secret -wwii-bat-and-bird-bomber-program.htm.

13. Bruce K. Alexander, Robert B. Coambs, and Patricia F. Hadaway, "The Effect of Housing and Gender on Morphine Self-Administration in Rats," *Psychopharmacology* 58, no. 2 (1978): 175–79, doi:10.1007/BF00426903.

14. Eryn Paul, "Why Germans Work Fewer Hours But Produce More: A Study in Culture," KNote, http://knote.com/2014/11/10/why -germans-work-fewer-hours-but-produce-more-a-study-in-culture/.

15. Kim Witte and Mike Allen, "A Meta-Analysis of Fear Appeals: Implications for Effective Public Health Campaigns," *Health Education & Behavior* 27, no. 5 (2000): 591–615, doi:10.1177/1090198 10002700506.

16. Allison Earl and Dolores Albarracín, "Nature, Decay, and Spiraling of the Effects of Fear-Inducing Arguments and HIV Counseling and Testing: A Meta-Analysis of the Short- and Long-Term Outcomes of HIV-Prevention Interventions," *Health Psychology* 26, no. 4 (2007): 496–506, doi:10.1037/0278–6133.26.4.496.

17. Kirk Mitchell, "Limon prison incentive programs keep inmates in check," *The Denver Post*, November 14, 2010, http://www.denver post.com/2010/11/14/limon-prison-incentive-programs-keep -inmates-in-check/.

18. Daniel Kahneman and Angus Deaton, "High Income Improves Evaluation of Life but Not Emotional Well-Being," *Proceedings of the National Academy of Sciences* 107, no. 38 (2010): 16489–93, doi:10.1073/pnas.1011492107.

19. *Ibid.*

20. Mark R. Lepper, David Greene, and Richard E. Nisbett, "Undermining Children's Intrinsic Interest with Extrinsic Reward: A Test of The 'overjustification' hypothesis," *Journal of Personality and Social Psychology* 28, no. 1 (1973): 129–37, doi:10.1037/h0035519.

21. Mark R. Lepper and David Greene, *The Hidden Costs of Reward* (London and New York: Psychology Press, 1978).

22. E. L. Deci, R. Koestner, and R. M. Ryan, "A Meta-Analytic Review of Experiments Examining the Effects of Extrinsic Rewards on Intrinsic Motivation," *Psychological Bulletin* 125, no. 6 (1999): 627–668–700.

23. Jesse Singal, "Awareness is Overrated," Science of Us, July 17, 2014, http://nymag.com/scienceofus/2014/07/awareness-is-overrated.html.

24. National Institute on Drug Abuse, "Evaluation of the Office on National Drug Control Policy (ONDCP) National Youth Anti-Drug Media Campaign," 2006, http://archives.drugabuse.gov/initiatives/westat/.

25. Carlos D. Sánchez, L. Kristin Newby, Darren K. McGuire, Vic Hasselblad, Mark N. Feinglos, and E. Magnus Ohman, "Diabetes-Related Knowledge, Atherosclerotic Risk Factor Control, and Outcomes in Acute Coronary Syndromes," *The American Journal of Cardiology* 95, no. 11 (2005): 1290–1294, doi:10.1016/j.amjcard.2005.01.070.

26. Alfie Kohn, "Why Incentive Plans Cannot Work," *Harvard Business Review*, 1993, https://hbr.org/1993/09/why-incentive-plans-cannot-work.

27. Richard A. Guzzo, Richard D. Jette, and Raymond A. Katzell, "The Effects of Psychologically Based Intervention Programs on Worker Productivity: A Meta-Analysis," *Personnel Psychology* 38, no. 2 (1985): 275–291, doi:10.1111/j.1744–6570.1985.tb00547.x.

28. *Op cit.*, Kohn.

29. Amy Adkins, "U.S. Employee Engagement Holds Steady at 31.7%," Gallup, May 7, 2015, http://www.gallup.com/poll/183041/employee-engagement-holds-steady.aspx?utm_source=EMPLOYEE_ENGAGEMENT&utm_medium=topic&utm_campaign=tiles.

30. "Gamification: Engagement Strategies for Business and IT," Gartner, http://www.gartner.com/technology/research/gamification/.

31. "Gartner Predicts Over 70 Percent of Global 2000 Organisations Will Have at Least One Gamified Application by 2014," Gartner, November 9, 2011, http://www.gartner.com/newsroom/id/1844115.

32. "Gartner Says by 2014, 80 Percent of Current Gamified Applications Will Fail to Meet Business Objectives Primarily Due to Poor Design," Gartner, November 27, 2012, http://www.gartner.com/newsroom/id/2251015.

33. "Wupperman Steel," Enterprise Steel Consultancy, last modified February 7, 2015, http://enterprise-gamification.com/mediawiki/index.php?title=Wuppermann_Steel.

34. Steve Lopez, "Disneyland workers answer to 'electronic whip,'" *Los Angeles Times*, October 19, 2011, http://articles.latimes.com/2011/oct/19/local/la-me-1019-lopez-disney-20111018.

35. Damien Brevers and Xavier Noël, "Pathological Gambling and the Loss of Willpower: A Neurocognitive Perspective," *Socioaffective Neuroscience & Psychology* 3 (September 2013), doi:10.3402/snp.v3i0.21592.

36. David Skorton and Glenn Altschuler, "America's Foreign Language Deficit," *Forbes*, August 27, 2012, https://www.forbes.com/sites/collegeprose/2012/08/27/americas-foreign-language-deficit/#5796b5ac4ddc.

37. Suzie Lechtenberg, "Is Learning a Foreign Language Really Worth It?" Freakonomics, March 6, 2014, http://freakonomics.com/podcast/is-learning-a-foreign-language-really-worth-it-a-new-freakonomics-radio-podcast/.

38. Bryan Caplan, "The Numbers Speak: Foreign Language Requirements Are a Waste of Time and Money," Library of Economics and Liberty, August 10, 2012, http://econlog.econlib.org/archives/2012/08/the_marginal_pr.html.

39. John Cassidy, "The Next Crusade: Paul Wolfowitz at the World Bank," *New Yorker*, April 9, 2007, http://www.newyorker.com/magazine/2007/04/09/the-next-crusade.

40. Theo Merz, "Russian commuters win free Metro travel if they can prove physical prowess," *The Telegraph*, November 8, 2013, http://www.telegraph.co.uk/news/worldnews/europe/russia/10437306/Russian-commuters-win-free-Metro-travel-if-they-can-prove-physical-prowess.html.

41. Chris Clackum, "Frequent Flyer Miles Going Unclaimed," NECN/NBC, January 26, 2014, http://www.necn.com/news/new-england/_NECN__Frequent_Flyer_Miles_Going_Unclaimed_NECN-247767111.html.

42. Blake Fleetwood, "Frequent-Flyer Programs Are Convoluted, Mysterious, and a Maddening Fraud," *Huffington Post*, May 4, 2011, http://www.huffingtonpost.com/blake-fleetwood/frequentflier-programs-ar_b_856623.html.

43. *Ibid*.

44. Jed Williams and John Swanciger, "Why Small Businesses Should Be Utilizing Customer-Loyalty Programs," *Entrepreneur*, April 25, 2014, https://www.entrepreneur.com/article/233362.

45. "Best Buy Increases Loyalty Rewards in Move to Spur Sales." 4-traders, April 3, 2014, http://www.4-traders.com/BEST-BUY-CO-INC-11778/news/Best-Buy-Increases-Loyalty-Rewards-in-Move-to-Spur-Sales-16603892/.

46. Meredith Derby Berg, "Turnaround Tales from JC Penney, Best Buy," *AdvertisingAge*, February 24, 2014, http://adage.com/article/cmo-strategy/turnaround-tales-jc-penney-buy/291813/.

47. Fida Chaaban, "Social Entrepreneurship Is on the Rise: Soushiant Zanganehpour's Advice for 'Treps Acting as Agents of Change'," *Entrepreneur Middle East*, October 22, 2015, https://www.entrepreneur.com/article/251981.

48. Blake Mycoskie, "The Founder of TOMS on Reimagining the

Company's Mission," *Harvard Business Review*, 2016, https://hbr
.org/2016/01/the-founder-of-toms-on-reimagining-the-companys
-mission.

49. Jeff Chu, "Toms Sets Out To Sell A Lifestyle, Not Just Shoes," *Fast
Company*, June 17, 2013, https://www.fastcompany.com/3012568/
blake-mycoskie-toms.

50. Laura L. Carstensen, "The Influence of a Sense of Time on Human
Development," *Science* 312, no. 5782 (2006): 1913–15, doi:10.1126/
science.1127488.

Chapter 8: Engrained

1. Anna Rose Childress, Ronald N. Ehrman, Ze Wang, Yin Li, Na-
than Sciortino, Jonathan Hakun, William Jens, et al, "Prelude to
Passion: Limbic Activation By 'unseen' drug and Sexual Cues," *PloS
One* 3, no. 1 (2008): e1506, doi:10.1371/journal.pone.0001506.

2. Kimberly A. Young, Teresa R. Franklin, David C. S. Roberts,
Kanchana Jagannathan, Jesse J. Suh, Reagan R. Wetherill, Ze
Wang, Kyle M. Kampman, Charles P. O'Brien, and Anna Rose
Childress, "Nipping Cue Reactivity in the Bud: Baclofen Prevents
Limbic Activation Elicited by Subliminal Drug Cues," *Journal of
Neuroscience* 34, no. 14 (2014): 5038–43, doi:10.1523/JNEUROSCI
.4977–13.2014.

3. "Gabrielle   Giffords,"   https://en.wikipedia.org/wiki/Gabrielle
_Giffords.

4. Todd Ackerman, "Meet Therapy Team Helping Giffords," *Houston
Chronicle*, November 20, 2011, http://www.chron.com/news/houston
-texas/article/Meet-therapy-team-helping-Giffords-2279624
.php.

5. Bogdan Draganski, Christian Gaser, Volker Busch, Gerhard Schu-
ierer, Ulrich Bogdahn, and Arne May, "Neuroplasticity: Changes
in Grey Matter Induced by Training," *Nature* 427, no. 6972 (2004):
311–12, doi:10.1038/427311a.

NOTES

6. Antonella Gasbarri, Assunta Pompili, Mark G. Packard, and Carlos Tomaz, "Habit Learning and Memory in Mammals: Behavioral and Neural Characteristics," *Neurobiology of Learning and Memory* 114 (October 2014): 198–208, doi:10.1016/j.nlm.2014.06.010.

7. R. B. Zajonc, "Feeling and Thinking: Preferences Need No Inferences," *American Psychologist* 35, no. 2 (1980): 151–175.

8. Henry H. Yin and Barbara J. Knowlton, "The Role of the Basal Ganglia in Habit Formation," *Nature Reviews Neuroscience* 7, no. 6 (2006): 464–476, doi:10.1038/nrn1919.

9. G. F. Koob and M. Le Moal, "Drug Abuse: Hedonic Homeostatic Dysregulation," *Science (New York, N.Y.)* 278, no. 5335 (1997): 52–58.

10. G. F. Koob and M. Le Moal, "Drug Addiction, Dysregulation of Reward, and Allostasis," *Neuropsychopharmacology* 24, no. 2 (2001): 97–129, doi:10.1016/S0893-133X(00)00195-0.

11. George F. Koob, "Alcoholism: Allostasis and Beyond," *Alcoholism, Clinical and Experimental Research* 27, no. 2 (2003): 232–243, doi:10.1097/01.ALC.0000057122.36127.C2.

12. *Op cit.,* Zajonc, p. 160.

13. A. J. DeCasper and W. P. Fifer, "Of Human Bonding: Newborns Prefer Their Mothers' Voices," *Science* 208, no. 4448 (1980): 1174–76, doi:10.1126/science.7375928.

14. R. B. Zajonc, "Mere Exposure: A Gateway to the Subliminal," *Current Directions in Psychological Science* 10, no. 10 (2000): 224–28.

15. Jennifer L. Monahan, Sheila T. Murphy, and R.B. Zajonc, "Subliminal Mere Exposure: Specific, General, and Diffuse Effects," *Psychological Science* 11, no. 6 (2000): 462–66, doi:10.1111/1467-9280.00289.

16. David J. Kelly, Paul C. Quinn, Alan M. Slater, Kang Lee, Alan Gibson, Michael Smith, Liezhong Ge, and Olivier Pascalis, "Three-Month-Olds, but Not Newborns, Prefer Own-Race Faces," *Developmental Science* 8, no. 6 (2005): F31–36, doi:10.1111/j.1467-7687.2005.0434a.x.

17. Leslie A. Zebrowitz, Benjamin White, and Kristin Wieneke, "Mere Exposure and Racial Prejudice: Exposure to Other-Race Faces Increases Liking for Strangers of That Race," *Social Cognition* 26, no. 3 (2008): 259–75, doi:10.1521/soco.2008.26.3.259.

18. Lara Salahi, "Meditation Heals Military Vets with PTSD," ABC News, June 6, 2011, http://abcnews.go.com/Health/Depression/meditation-heals-military-vets-ptsd/story?id=13756395.

19. Michael Christopher, "A Broader View of Trauma: A Biopsychosocial-Evolutionary View of the Role of the Traumatic Stress Response in the Emergence of Pathology And/Or Growth," *Clinical Psychology Review* 24, no. 1 (2004): 75–98, doi:10.1016/j.cpr.2003.12.003.

20. Emily A. Holmes, Ella L. James, Thomas Coode-Bate, and Catherine Deeprose, "Can Playing the Computer Game 'Tetris' Reduce the Build-Up of Flashbacks for Trauma? A Proposal from Cognitive Science," *PLOS ONE* 4, no. 1 (2009): e4153, doi:10.1371/journal.pone.0004153.

21. Sara W. Lazar, Catherine E. Kerr, Rachel H. Wasserman, Jeremy R. Gray, Douglas N. Greve, Michael T. Treadway, Metta McGarvey, et al, "Meditation Experience Is Associated with Increased Cortical Thickness," *Neuroreport* 16, no. 17 (2005): 1893–97.

22. Rochard J. Davidson, Jon Kabat-Zinn, Jessica Schumacher, Melissa Rosenkranz, Daniel Muller, Saki F. Santorelli, Ferris Urbanowski, Anne Harrington, Katherine Bonus, and John F. Sheridan, "Alterations in Brain and Immune Function Produced by Mindfulness Meditation," *Psychosomatic Medicine* 65, no. 4 (2003): 564–70, doi:10.1097/01.PSY.0000077505.67574.E3.

23. Emma M. Seppälä, "20 Scientific Reasons to Start Meditating Today," *Psychology Today*, September 11, 2013, https://www.psychologytoday.com/blog/feeling-it/201309/20-scientific-reasons-start-meditating-today.

24. Eileen Luders, Arthur W. Toga, Natasha Lepore, and Christian Gaser, "The Underlying Anatomical Correlates of Long-Term

Meditation: Larger Hippocampal and Frontal Volumes of Gray Matter," *NeuroImage* 45, no. 3 (2009): 672–78, doi:10.1016/j.neuro image.2008.12.061.

25. July 25, 2016, HOPE online community.
26. Eric Vilas-Boas, "What the Hell is Michael Phelps' Arm-Swinging Warmup About?" Thrillist, August 10, 2016, https://www.thrillist .com/news/nation/rio-olympics-2016-michael-phelps-arm-stretch -swimming.
27. "What the Greatest Olympic Athlete Ever Can Teach You about Becoming a Champion," Competitive Advantage, https://www .competitivedge.com/what-greatest-olympic-athlete-ever-can-teach -you-about-becoming-champion.
28. Joseph D. Lyons, "Michael Phelps' Pre-Race Playlist Is Highly Sought After for a Very Good Reason," Bustle, August 8, 2016, http://www.bustle.com/articles/177333-michael-phelps-pre-race -playlist-is-highly-sought-after-for-a-very-good-reason.

Chapter 9: Putting It All Together

1. Personal interview with Charlie Bracke, February 2, 2017.
2. Sarah Klein, "I Went To Rehab For My Technology Addiction," *Prevention*, October 19, 2016, http://www.prevention.com/mind -body/i-went-to-rehab-for-my-technology-addiction.
3. Yu-Kang Lee, Chun-Tuan Chang, You Lin, and Zhao-Hong Cheng, "The Dark Side of Smartphone Usage: Psychological Traits, Compulsive Behavior and Technostress," *Computers in Human Behavior* 31(February 2014): 373–83, doi:10.1016/j.chb.2013.10.047.
4. Richard Emanuel, Rodney Bell, Cedric Cotton, Jamon Craig, Danielle Drummond, Samuel Gibson, Ashley Harris, et al, "The Truth About Smartphone Addiction," *College Student Journal* 49, no. 2 (2015): 291–99.
5. Sean D. Young, "Explaining Pokémon Go through the 'Science of

Social,'" July 22, 2016, http://seanyoungphd.com/blog/2016/7/22/explaining-pokmon-go-through-the-science-of-social.

6. Jenny S. Radesky, Jayna Schumacher, and Barry Zuckerman, "Mobile and Interactive Media Use by Young Children: The Good, the Bad, and the Unknown," *Pediatrics* 135, no. 1 (2015): 1–3, doi:10.1542/peds.2014–2251.

7. Nick Bilton, "Steve Jobs Was a Low-Tech Parent," *The New York Times*, September 10, 2014, http://www.nytimes.com/2014/09/11/fashion/steve-jobs-apple-was-a-low-tech-parent.html?_r=0.

8. Personal interview with Sergeant Morrison, January 8, 2017.

9. "Operant conditioning," https://en.wikipedia.org/wiki/Operant_conditioning.

10. Henry L. Roediger III, "What Happened to Behaviorism," Association for Psychological Science, 2004, http://www.psychologicalscience.org/observer/what-happened-to-behaviorism#.WG1ue33JLaU.

11. *Op cit.*, Klein.

12. "Recruit training," https://en.wikipedia.org/wiki/Recruit_training.

13. Christina Salmivalli and Elisa Poskiparta, "Making Bullying Prevention a Priority in Finnish Schools: The KiVa Antibullying Program," *New Directions for Youth Development* 133 (2012): 41–53, doi:10.1002/yd.20006.

14. Anne L. Williford, Christian Elledge, Aaron J. Boulton, Kathryn J. DePaolis, Todd D. Little, and Christina Salmivalli, "Effects of the KiVa Antibullying Program on Cyberbullying and Cybervictimization Frequency Among Finnish Youth," Journal of Clinical Child & Adolescent Psychology 42, no. 6 (2013): 820–33, doi:10.1080/15374416.2013.787623.

INDEX

A

ABCs of Behavior. *See* Automatic
    Behavior(s); Burning
    Behavior(s); Common
    Behavior(s)

Acquired immune deficiency
    syndrome (AIDS). *See* HIV/
    AIDS

Addiction
    creating HOPE (community),
        65–66
    digital (gaming/video games),
        203–204, 210–211, 220–225
    drug research/treatment, 185–187
    forming community through,
        55–56
    gambling, 176
    overcoming engrained patterns,
        185–187
    prescription drug abuse, 93–94

reaching an "epiphany moment,"
    133–134

shopping/couponing, 157–160

Addis, William, 95–96

Advertising, changing customer
    behavior, 9, 74–76, 139, 182.
    See also Marketing

Agoraphobia, 38

Alcoholics Anonymous (AA), 56

Alcoholism. *See* Addiction

Ames Research Center, 9

Anchoring, 25–26

Animal behavior
    applying neurohacks, 146–147
    comparison to humans, 208, 216
    conditioning, 160–162,
        207–208
    engrained behaviors, 192

Animal conditioning, 192

Anxiety, 38, 93, 154, 197. *See also*
    Depression

INDEX

INDEX

Biofeedback, 199

Body movement, as neurohacks, 139–141

Bracke, Charlie, 203–206, 210–211, 220–222

Brain. *See also* Neurohacks

about choosing the forces to create change, 237–238

arriving at homeostasis, 191

automatic behaviors, 215–216, 220

burning behaviors, 221–223

common behaviors, 229–233

creating engrained patterns, 14–15, 185–187, 190–194, 213

dopamine and reaction to rewards, 32–33

engrained addiction behaviors, 185–187

magnetic behaviors, 200–201

meditation effects, 198–200

physiological and emotional responses, 141–144

plasticity, 190

rehabilitation from traumatic injury, 187–190

repetition and engrained behaviors, 194–195

response to psychological trauma, 195–198

response to social connections, 90–91

using stepladders (chain links), 153

Brand(s)/branding

changing behaviors, 107–109

creating customer loyalty, 74–77

Brown, Susan, 37

Burke, Brian, 171–172

Burning Behavior(s)

about making lasting change, 10–11

as SCIENCE model of lasting change, 15

compared to automatic behaviors, 223

compared to common behaviors, 231

defined/described, 220–222

examples/case study, 222–225

learning to create or change, 233–235

Buy one-Give one (TOMS Shoes "One for One" giveaway), 181–182

C

Captivating

a part of the SCIENCE framework, 14, 213

about extreme couponing/ shopping, 157–160

applied to your personal life, 163–164

behind the science of, 160–162

273

INDEX

INDEX

INDEX

Neurohacks, applying, 154–155

Captivating, making rewards, 182–183

Engrained, establishing routine to become, 202

wrap-up assignment, 235

F

Facebook

behavioral research, support of, x, 9

building social communities, 74–77

Failure

achieving change often ends in, ix, 3–5, 201–202

an "epiphany moment" can overcome, 134

community overcomes a sense of, 51, 65, 78–79

importance overcomes, 104

incorrect information creates, 11–12

motivation as factor in, 172

psychology behind easy as factor, 109–111

science behind lasting change, 206–214

self-identifying as a, 131–132

stepladders help to overcome, 12, 31, 47

Fearmongering, 170–171

Fear(s)

agoraphobia, 38

conventional wisdom for overcoming, 130, 146n

as motivation, 165–168

sharing with a group, 60–61

stigma of seeking help, 57

training and engrained behaviors can overcome, 195

using neurohacks to overcome, 135–136, 138

virtual-world therapies, 38–39

Feedback, 173, 197–199

Felner, Doris Levine ("Grandma Doris"), 81–85, 102–103

Felner, Meryl, 82, 84

Financial planning, 96–101

Fitness goals/routine

behavior has to have importance, 13, 83, 86, 210

bringing about change, ix, 237

creating a plan or map for, 115–117

"keep it simple, stupid" (KISS), 125–126

SCIENCE application to, 239

"there's an app for that," 45–46, 152

using social communities, 56–57, 79

wearable digital technologies, 39–40

INDEX

INDEX

INDEX

INDEX

Motivation
    achieving personal goals, 3–4
    behavior has to have importance,
      85–87
    books, speakers, and dreams are
      not enough, 10, 23–24, 85,
      207
    changing common behaviors,
      225–235
    community helps maintain,
      53–54, 63, 71, 77–79, 86
    conditioning does not create,
      208–210
    exercise, health and lifestyle, 7–8,
      45, 88–89, 92, 211
    fear as, 165–168
    gamification and competition as,
      171–175
    goals are more useful than
      dreams, 27–31
    importance creates, 94, 100, 104
    magnetic behaviors as, 200–201
    money as, 87–90
    rewards and punishment as,
      160–162, 168–171, 181
    social connections as, 90–92
    stepladders help to maintain,
      31–33
    the "trick fix," 176–178
    willpower is not enough, 12
MSM (men who have sex with other
    men), 58–61

Mycoskie, Blake, 181
MyFitnessPal (app), 45–46, 152

N

Napolitano, Janet, 9
National Aeronautics and Space
    Administration (NASA), 9
National Institutes of Health (NIH), x
Nava, Josh, x–xi, 4–6
Near-death experiences, 195
Negative self-talk, 130, 132
Neurohacks. *See also* Brain
    a part of the SCIENCE
      framework, 13–14, 213
    application to your own life,
      146–151
    behavior change begins in the
      mind, 129–131
    changing behaviors in others,
      137–139, 151
    conventional wisdom comparison
      to, 146n, 154
    defined/described, 131–137
    exercises, 154–155
    getting choice buy-in, 151–153
    medications/medical treatments
      as, 133
    physiology and emotions behind,
      141–143
    speech and cognitive, 144–146
    use for social good, 12n, 132n, 151

INDEX

INDEX

INDEX

Westgate studies (MIT, 1950), 113–114

Whole Foods (grocery store), 109

William of Occam (philosopher), 126

Wisdom Toothbrushes, 96

Wolfowitz, Paul, 176–178

Wuppermann AG (steel company), 172–173

X

Xero (band), 19–20, 42–44

Y

Young, Beatrice ("Grandma Billie"), 81–85, 102–103

Z

Zaharia, Matei, 71–73

Zajonc, Bob, 144

Zamolodchikova, Elena, 179

Zedillo, Ernesto, 87

Zhukov, Alexander, 179

Zuckerberg, Mark, 14, 117

ABOUT THE AUTHOR

SEAN D. YOUNG is a UCLA medical school professor and the founder and executive director of the UCLA Center for Digital Behavior (CDB) and the UC Institute for Prediction Technology (UCIPT), which have been featured in the *New York Times*, the *Washington Post*, the *Huffington Post*, and *Science*, and on NPR, Yahoo Finance, TechCrunch, Mashable, CNN, CBS News, and other major media outlets. He has a PhD in psychology and a master's in health services research from Stanford University. He lives in Southern California.